Intimate Communion

Awakening Your Sexual Essence

DAVID DEIDA

Health Communications, Inc.
Deerfield Beach, Florida

www.hcibooks.com

Library of Congress Cataloging-in-Publication Data

Deida, David.
   Intimate communion : awakening your sexual essence / David Deida.
      p. cm.
   ISBN-13: 978-1-55874-374-8
   ISBN-10: 1-55874-374-X
   1. Man-woman relationships.   2. Intimacy (Psychology)   3. Sex.   I. Title.
   HQ801.D4497 1995
   306.7—dc20   95-25372
                                                                         CIP

Publisher: Health Communications, Inc.
            3201 S.W. 15th Street
            Deerfield Beach, Florida 33442-8190

R-09-07

Cover art by Lorrie Bortner.
Cover and book design by Paul Volk.
Author photo by Thomas J. Johnson.

TABLE OF CONTENTS

1

What Is Intimate Communion?

INTRODUCTION

Nipples, lips, warmth and caress: it starts with two bodies entwined as one, moving like a sensitive snake of tongue and fire, shivering up the spine and down the belly. Then, mind gives way to flesh, and flesh gives way to love. The very surfaces of touch open out into the light of love. Mouth opens, body opens, mind opens, so wide and bright that you are gone in love, your partner is gone in love, and love is all that remains.

As a woman, you have become the all of his desire. As a man, you have become the spine of her surrender.

Grateful for your demise in light, the Divine is alive in every lover's smile.

This book is for men and women who are turned on by sex, love and true spiritual ecstasy. It is for people who enjoy tangled bodies, open hearts and enlightened minds. If you are not delighted by a style of intimacy involving deep passion, deep devotion *and* deep under-standing—all three—then this book is not for you.

When a man and woman embrace one another without guarding themselves, without protecting themselves or holding back, then they naturally transmit to one another an ecstatic force of sexual energy, love and oneness. At the beginning of many intimacies, this transmission is often body-blissing, heart-rending and mind-blowing. But after several years, many intimacies become, at best, loving friendships between two people who, in truth, desire something much deeper—deeper sexual union, deeper devotion, deeper understanding.

Many of us have experienced "old-style" intimacies based on roles of male control and female giving, and have found such relationships to result in unhealthy dependence and pain. Many have then grown into "modern-style" intimacies based on independence and fairness. What has been the result?

Have our well-intentioned efforts toward internal balance and self-responsibility inadvertently eroded the attractive power in our intimate relationships? Is there actually another step to take, beyond even per-sonal independence and healthy self-esteem, by which we can finally let down our guard in intimate love and relax deeply into our natural sexual core? How do we take this next step toward heartfelt passion and spiritual vitality in modern intimacy—beyond male domination, beyond idealistic feminism, and beyond safe but lukewarm "50/50 partnerships"—without losing the ground we have gained?

After years of counseling and conducting relationship workshops across the United States, it seems obvious to me that it is time for men and women to take the next step in their style of intimate relationship. This new style of intimacy would extend beyond old sex roles for men and women. It would also extend beyond the guarded sense of in-dependence that often holds passionate sexual surrender at arm's length and prevents deep and vulnerable emotional opening in many modern relationships. This book describes how to make the transition to this next stage of relationship, which I call "Intimate Communion."

All intimate relationships grow, stage by stage, through three major cycles of glorious passion and frustrating failure. Up to now, our culture has only been aware of the first two of these stages, so we haven't known what to do when we have grown beyond an imbalance of power in our intimacy and have achieved a more balanced 50/50 Relationship—often at the expense of deep sexual passion and spiritual aliveness, or so it seems.

As we begin to take the next step in intimacy, it's important that we know what to do when our relationship feels like it has come to a standstill. Knowing when to leave a relationship—and when to "lean into" the sometimes difficult process of intimate growth—is a key to practicing Intimate Communion. Learning how to navigate through each crisis, and knowing where you are going, allows you to consciously progress through each stage of intimacy, into a deeper and deeper giving and receiving of sex, love and spirit.

BEYOND 50/50

Many people today believe in a myth that says intimate happiness is attained through a 50/50 ideal of equality based on a notion of "sameness" between men and women. Belief in this myth of the 50/50 partnership is one of the major reasons that men and women have been unable to cultivate and deepen sexual, emotional and spiritual union in intimacy. As many of us have discovered, when we focus on dividing the pie equally, our intimate embrace often becomes more like a business handshake than a delicious swoon that dissolves two lovers into a single heart of desire.

Culturally, the modern "50/50 Relationship" was born of dissatisfaction with the old style of suppressive relationships between the sexes, wherein men and women were confined to rigidly defined sex roles that dictated how they were supposed to behave—or what they could achieve—just because they happened to be men or women.

Men were not supposed to express their emotions and were confined to the role of "breadwinner." Women were confined to the role of "housewife," with little political or economic power and few opportunities to move beyond their household lives.

Because neither men nor women in this old, or "first-stage," style of relationship were allowed to develop their full capacities, they became dependent on one another for what they lacked by themselves. Men became dependent on women for sex, nurturing, and care of the home and children. Women became dependent on men for money, affection and status.

Eventually, many men and women found that they wanted to be free. They no longer wanted to depend on, or be depended on by someone else. As individuals and as a culture, we began to embrace the ideals of wholeness and of individual completion, by accepting the Feminine and Masculine energies that lie within each of us. Men began to accept their "internal goddess" by learning to express their emotions and nurture themselves, while reconnecting with their vulnerability in relationships. Women began to accept their "internal warrior" by developing their careers and strengthening their political clout, thereby freeing themselves from economic dependence on men.

Intimate relationships between men and women evolved from first-stage "Dependence Relationships" to second-stage relationships based on the modern ideal of two independent people, whole unto themselves, coming together as equals and evenly splitting the responsibilities of the household, finances and childrearing. I call this second-stage style of intimacy the "50/50 Relationship."

Nobody would disagree that the 50/50 Relationship is a positive step toward liberation from the dependence-inducing gender roles of the first stage. The trouble is, many modern women have had to cloak their unique and natural expression of "Feminine radiance" in order to succeed in today's more Masculine-oriented economy. And many modern men, stuck in a vague transition point between old models of the masculine and new identities, have become ambiguous at their core, unable to be fully present and confident in relationships and in their lives.

Although efforts toward social and economic equality between men and women have obviously been necessary and enormously beneficial, it appears we have also suffered an unplanned side-effect to this well-intentioned movement: Men and women have inadvertently become more and more sexually neutralized, unable to give each other what they really want in intimacy. We are restraining the fullness of the Masculine and Feminine forces that lie within each of us.

Rather than celebrating the attractive differences between the Masculine and the Feminine qualities in each of us (which often bring intimates together in the first place), some people have begun to deny that there even *is* a difference. Some people seem to believe that, in terms of inherent Masculine and Feminine energy, all people are actually the same.

Of course, there is at least *some* difference that we could feel; otherwise, we wouldn't have a sexual preference. On the contrary, most of us know the kind of lover we want. Regardless of whether we are heterosexual, homosexual or bisexual, most of us have a preference for either a more Masculine lover or a more Feminine lover.

While fully supporting social, financial and political equality between men and women, as a personal consultant and educator I also want to acknowledge some of the major complaints men and women have about each other in *intimacy*.

Women are complaining that men are becoming weaker, less committed in intimacy, and seemingly lost in their lives. In short, women often ask me why men are such "wimps" these days.

Men are complaining that women are becoming hardened, more resistive and sharply independent, to the point that they are no longer very attractive to the men. In short, men often ask me why women are becoming such "ballbusters" these days.

Modern men and women have discovered that equality, by itself, does not make for a passionate and growing relationship. So where do we go from here? Surely we don't want to return to the painful, regressive Dependence Relationships of the first stage. But if we are dissatisfied with the safe but lukewarm independence typical of second-stage 50/50 Relationships, and we are also dissatisfied with first-stage relationships based on inequality and sex roles, where else can we go?

Intimate Communion, the style of relationship described in this book, is an entirely different style of relationship from either Dependence or 50/50 Relationships. Intimate Communion is not about the old style of sex roles, nor is it about the modern ideal of "fairness," wherein the essential strengths of the Masculine and Feminine forces are often denied along with the attractive differences between them. Intimate Communion is about opening our hearts and giving the unique gifts that lie deep in our sexual, emotional and spiritual core.

However, in the name of economic security and emotional safety, many of us have developed a shell of protection that hides our native gifts. For fear of becoming too vulnerable or dependent, many of us have lost trust in our natural Feminine style of gifting, preferring a more aggressive or independent stance in the world. For fear of becoming too macho and insensitive, many of us have lost trust in our natural

Masculine style of gifting, and in doing so we have lost touch with our real direction in life and are afraid to take a strong stand in our intimacies and in the world.

After interviewing thousands of men and women about their true desires in an intimate relationship, I must report that when most men and women achieve a 50/50 Relationship, they find they want a partner who expresses more Feminine radiance or Masculine presence in intimacy. These interviews reveal that men and women are filled with wild and beautiful Masculine and Feminine gifts they are afraid to share, and they are also reluctant to fully express their own real desires in intimacy: sexual, emotional and spiritual desires.

To grow through the three stages of intimacy, we must come to terms with our deepest desires to give and receive our sexual, emotional and spiritual gifts. We may find that we are hiding some of our real desires, thinking they are unfair or taboo. Before we can learn to give and receive our deepest gifts, whether gently or wildly, we must understand why we often confine our loving, and how we can liberate the mysterious force of love that lies yearning in our hearts.

INTIMATE COMMUNION

What is the ultimate pleasure in intimacy that men and women seek? Where is it to be found, once and for all? As many of us have already discovered, it is not finally to be found in any specific person we can "own," acquire or on whom we can depend. Neither is it to be found in a carefully arranged 50/50 Relationship with a "safe" man or woman. Rather, it is to be found in the process of open-hearted surrender, of being overwhelmed in love.

This is the secret that all passionate lovers know: In the moment of true ecstasy, we die to ourselves in love, and this surrender itself is our sweetest pleasure. Surrender of self into love is the basis for Intimate Communion.

To admit this pleasure of sweet surrender is taboo in our culture. For instance, our culture expects us to be strong and independent; "surrendering" to love is considered an act of weakness by many people. Likewise, we are always supposed to be in control of ourselves. Yet, when two lovers surrender their boundaries and melt into a single body of passion, they are anything but "in control." In the heat of love and desire, we are liable to ravish our partner or submit ourselves in a way that we would be hesitant to talk about in public.

Most of us have blissfully let go of our boundaries to some degree during orgasm or in the delicious ecstasy of emotional surrender in love. In order to explore the fullness of Intimate Communion, we must be willing to embrace the taboos of extreme pleasure, which our society would rather not discuss. Even though most of us have a line that we don't want anyone to cross, we must be willing to explore the deepest hidden Masculine and Feminine desires for surrender in our heart.

If you are willing to give your true gift and express your true desires, you can create perfect intimacy, moment by moment. This kind of intimacy is something you *do*, not something you *have*. It is an ongoing practice of sexual union, emotional openness and spiritual trust. It is a practice of love.

This is one way Intimate Communion differs from the psychological techniques offered by most relationship books that deal with our "inner child" or with finally getting the love we always wanted from our parents. Rather than looking at how our past has resulted in the present state of our intimacy, the practice of Intimate Communion involves consciously practicing a new style of intimacy in this present moment, thus making the past obsolete.

There is no reason to remain mediocre in our intimate relationships. Step by step, in Intimate Communion, we can breathe new light into our bodies, minds and hearts, even to the point of unbounded joy. We can understand the stages of intimacy we have already grown through and those through which we have yet to grow. We can honor and find humor in the attractive and potentially frustrating differences between the Masculine and Feminine ways of loving. And we can embrace the taboos of love that we secretly desire, so that the depth of our ecstasy in union is no longer limited by the *shoulds* and *shouldn'ts* of our time.

This practice of Intimate Communion is not based on the sex roles of yesterday, nor on the 50/50 idealism of today. Rather, this new style of intimacy is a next step for men and women who are ready to yield their protected sense of separate self to the blissful force of unrestrained love—a step that liberates men and women from past and present confines by requiring them to surrender the fearful boundaries that guard their heart. By understanding the natural flow of sexual energy, and by trusting the inevitable stages in which love grows, men and women can relax into Intimate Communion, the next step in intimacy beyond the 50/50 Relationship.

2

Untangling Love

THE THREE WAYS OF "LOVE"

"I *love* you, son."

"Look at that young couple, they are so in *love*."

"My God, how badly I want to make *love* with you."

In our culture, we have a tendency to use the word "love" for three very different feelings. We can begin to understand some of the complexities of our intimate life when we untangle these three different threads of our loving. The practice of Intimate Communion depends on a clear understanding of these three separate elements in an intimate relationship: love, romance and polarity.

Love

Of the three—love, romance and polarity—love is the simplest to understand and the most difficult to practice. Love is simply what *is* when your heart is open.

You could love your husband, your dog, your mother, your car, a book, your child, a painting or the seashore—or all of them at once. Love is simply the opening of your heart. When your heart is open, you love whomever, or whatever, is in your life. Love is the union of you and the one you are with.

Love is what *is* when your heart is open. To *do* love is to open your heart. If you are waiting to feel love, as if love will come to you, you may be waiting for a long time. Love happens whenever your heart opens, whether 10 years from now or right now, in this very moment.

Love has nothing to do, necessarily, with sex. You can love someone and not have sexual desire for them. You can want to have sex with someone you don't even know, or someone you are not loving. You exist as love when your heart is unguarded and opened, and you close yourself off to love when you guard your heart.

You can actually learn to love. You can learn how to open your heart, even when circumstances are difficult. Even when your relationship is painful, even when you feel hurt, you can practice opening your heart. You can practice love. This is the foundation of Intimate Communion: to practice opening your heart in every moment, including when you feel hurt. Rather than turn away or close down, you can practice loving. This practice of love extends far beyond conventional therapy.

There are many good books about how our intimate relationships often replicate our relationships with our parents. There are many good therapists who know how to work with childhood issues that come up in our intimacies. And when we work with a therapist, we often begin by examining our past, our parents, our childhood.

Our childhood stuff seems endless, once we begin to dig. A little digging is good, in order that we understand the roots of our search for love and *its resulting frustration.* But after a little digging, it is time to release the past and practice intimacy *right now*, in the present. Rather than concerning ourselves with the past cause of our present unhappiness, we can instead practice opening our hearts, right now. And through this moment to moment practice of open-hearted intimacy, this practice of *being* love, the power of the past weakens.

When you fall and wound your knee, it hurts. It's good to take a few moments, inspect the wound, clean it and put a bandage on it. Without doing much else, it will heal. Unless, of course, you keep falling on your knee and re-wounding it.

In the same way, your childhood wounds will heal on their own, as long as you don't repeat the old pattern of wounding yourself over and over again. It is much better to practice true intimacy *now* than it is to continually focus on the past, just as it is much better to learn how to walk without falling rather than it is to focus on your wounded knee.

Eventually, through this practice of loving, our old childhood patterns of turning away or closing down when we feel hurt, or punishing our partner for hurting us, dissolve. We may still feel hurt when our partner acts unlovingly, but our hurt does not become closure. Our pain does not create distance in our relationship. Likewise, when we act unlovingly toward our partner, he or she can practice love, rather than striking back, closing down or becoming distant.

Romance

Imagine that you are at a party and you meet a person of the opposite sex. The two of you begin a conversation and the rapport is instant. The talk seems effortless. You really enjoy being with this person and you feel really comfortable. In fact, the familiarity is startling. You look at this person and say, "It's hard to believe that we just met a few minutes ago. I feel like I've known you for a long time. Maybe we knew each other in a past life or something!"

Have you finally met "the one," the mate you have always been hoping to find? You leave the party thinking about this person. You feel happy, maybe even a bit giddy inside. The two of you begin seeing each other, spending more and more time together. You feel the specialness of the relationship. There is a sense of uniqueness and destiny; you feel that it was meant to be.

This is romantic attraction, infatuation, "falling in love."

Romantic attraction begins with a strong feeling of oneness and of bonding, a feeling that you have "always known each other." You have probably felt this way about some person at some point in your life. If you have, you know that the feeling doesn't last. After several months, or, if you are lucky, several years, the feeling of romantic attraction wears off.

And when it does, it always seems to turn into something very specific. This person who was once so magical to you, this one who seemed to be *the one* who was going to give you everything you ever wanted, who was going to bring unending love into your life once and for all, seems to turn into precisely the person who does not give you what you want.

Eventually, relationships based on romantic attraction *always* result in not getting the love you want. Why? Because romantic attraction is based on an imprint in our psyche that formed during our childhood. As many of us have already discovered through therapy or personal reflection, those people to whom we are romantically attracted are exactly those people who embody the qualities, good and bad, of our parents. Whatever our parents didn't give us enough of (love, attention, praise, freedom, etc.), is exactly the thing we will not get from our romantically chosen partner.

It seems like we "always knew" our romantic partner because we *did* know him or her: in the familiar texture of our parents, imprinted in our

childhood psyche! Our new partner seems so special because we unconsciously hope to continue the relationship we had with our parents
and finally get the love we always wanted, the acceptance we always
desired, the fulfillment of our heart that we always craved. And,
because we have unconsciously chosen our parents in our partner, we
have chosen someone who will *not* give us what we always wanted, in
exactly the same way that our parents didn't. (Even if our romantic
partner does give us what we want, we often cannot receive it,
because our childhood imprint doesn't believe it is real.)

As the thrill of being "in love" wears off, your romantically-chosen
partner seems to be perfectly suited to cause you pain. He or she seems
to have an uncanny ability to poke at your weak spots and hurt you,
though not necessarily on purpose; the person who used to bring out
the best in you now seems to bring out the worst, just by being himself
or herself. And you do the same for your partner. Because romantic
attraction is based on qualities in your partner that you unconsciously
recognize from your childhood experiences, you will be as fulfilled and
as unfulfilled by your partner's love as you were by your parents'.

Sexual Polarity

The subtle power of sexual polarity pervades all our lives. It draws
us toward our lover. It makes us uncomfortable with our spouse's best
friend. It keeps a marriage full of life, and when it is gone, it takes the
life with it. What is sexual polarity?

You are standing in the supermarket choosing tomatoes. You look up,
straight into a very attractive stranger's eyes, a stranger of the opposite
sex. A jolt of electricity runs through you. Your eyes remain engaged
a little longer, and then you look down at the tomatoes. Your body is
flush with energy and aliveness.

Sexual polarity—the magnetic pull or repulsion between the

Masculine and Feminine—affects all our lives. A few moments of sexual polarity can cause the memory of your trip to the supermarket to linger in your mind for hours or even days. Total strangers can raise your body temperature, cause your face to blush and make your heart pound. On the other hand, when sexual polarity is weak in our intimate relationships, we begin to feel that something is missing, and we often blame our partners or ourselves.

Sexual polarity either is or isn't happening—or so it seems at first. Before we understand that sexual polarity can be consciously turned on or off, we call it "chemistry." It seems that either your intimate relationship has it or it doesn't. In today's modern ideal of a relationship based on friendship, we sometimes act as if sexual polarity is not as important as, say, good communication. So, over time, our intimate relationships tend to become more talk and less action.

However, whether we like to admit it or not, talk is not enough for many of us. We also want to share the energetic juice of sexual polarity with our intimate partner.

So, in the practice of Intimate Communion, we learn to consciously practice the art of cultivating and sharing sexual polarity. We face the fact that for most of us, the force of polarity is at the core of our sexual attraction in intimacy. This mysterious force affects all our lives, yet remains mostly at an unconscious level.

We begin to master sexual polarity by becoming sensitive to its flow in everyday life. Imagine you are in a room talking with your good friends who are the same sex as you. The conversation is flowing effortlessly. You are laughing together and listening together. The mood is free and easy.

Suddenly, an extremely attractive person of the opposite sex walks into the room. The energy shifts. The conversation halts for a moment and then begins again, a bit more choppy, a bit contrived. You feel slightly self-conscious. And you are aware of *him* or *her*, the attractive one whose mere presence in the room has shifted the energy. This is the force of sexual polarity.

We are affected by sexual polarity from head to toe. Our minds become simple in the midst of a loving embrace and our thoughts are triggered to race by the inviting eyes of a stranger. Our heartbeat, skin temperature and posture are also affected by sexual polarity. Notice the shifts in your body the next time you are standing face to face with a highly interesting other. Merely imagining his or her eyes lingering on your body causes a shift in blood flow, breathing and muscle tone.

INTIMATE COMMUNION IS NOT ABOUT ROMANCE

To prepare for the practice of Intimate Communion, we must understand that love, romance and sexual polarity are not the same. You can love anyone. You can love everyone. You can love a mountain or a flower, a painting or a stuffed animal. Love is simply when you open your heart. In love, you allow yourself to relax your sense of separation, so that you become one with whomever or whatever you are contemplating, whether a child, a lover or the Grand Canyon. Love is unity, openness to the point of oneness, ultimately. And there is no limit to the number of people, things or places you can love.

Romance is an exclusive feeling. The main feeling in romantic infatuation is, "Finally, here is the person I have been waiting for all my life." You feel a deep sense of familiarity with this special person. Most people only feel this way with one person, or maybe several people throughout their lives. Whereas love is the action of opening your heart, romance is the less-common feeling of familiarity and "at-homeness" you feel with the special person in your life. And, inevitably, while loving only increases loving, romance often ends in disappointment when your special partner begins to irritate you or frustrate your desire for love more than anyone else in your life.

Sexual polarity is an arc of energy that flows between two people. It could happen in the grocery store with a person you don't even know, let alone love. It is a flow of energy that runs through your body, mind and emotions, and you might experience it many times a day—at work, on the street or at home.

There are two main threads to the practice of Intimate Communion. The most important one is the practice of love itself: the conscious practice of opening our hearts and feeling through our obstructions to loving in every moment. The secondary practice is the conscious and artful use of the force of sexual polarity in the transmission of love. In the practice of Intimate Communion, the sex act itself can become a spiritual union, a communication of the force of life and love, a passionate transmission of openness and ecstasy. Whether sexual polarity is practiced or not, Intimate Communion is about relaxing more and more into perfect coincidence with love, surrendering our fears and resistances. To be freely open even in the midst of fear involves a moment-to-moment discipline of loving. To be free and loving is the ultimate discipline—and this is the practice of Intimate Communion.

3

Creating
Sexual Polarity

HOW POLARITY WORKS

To master sexual polarity in Intimate Communion, you must become sensitive to the flow of sexual polarity itself. You must learn to feel the very moment when polarity diminishes or increases. For instance, your partner barks something mean at you and your body shuts down, becoming numb and weak. You may even become disgusted. On the other hand, there are times when your partner's beauty and presence awe your heart and love magnifies to the point of bliss.

We do not have to remain slaves to sexual polarity, obeying its unreasonable desires and despairing over its inevitable departure. With practice, sexuality can become an exploration of unseen healing energies as well as a way of contacting and expressing our deepest love. Eventually, by surrendering to the wisdom inherent in sexual polarity, lovemaking becomes an exquisite, whole-body prayer, or contemplation of the eternal mystery of man and woman.

To understand our shifts from passion to disgust and back again, we must understand how sexual polarity works. Like electricity and magnetism, sexual polarity is a natural energy that requires two poles. For electrical energy to flow, you need a positive pole and a negative pole. For magnetic energy to flow, you need a north pole and a south pole. For sexual energy to flow, you need two poles, too. These two poles are not called positive and negative, or north and south. Rather, based on our intuitive sense of what we find sexually attractive, we can call these two poles "Masculine" and "Feminine."

A natural energetic force flows between the Masculine and Feminine poles, and this is why a conversation with your friends is disrupted when an attractive person of the opposite sex walks into the room—a force automatically flows between the Masculine and Feminine poles, and your body-mind is re-oriented just like a compass needle.

When two magnets are oriented so that their opposite north and south poles come close together, then these poles are attracted to each other. But when two magnets are oriented so that their like poles come together—for instance, two north poles touching—then the magnets repel each other. Magnetic energy can either be attractive or repulsive, depending on which poles are brought together.

Just so with sexual polarity. In intimacy, when one partner's Masculine energy is brought near the other partner's Feminine energy, an attractive force of sexual polarity pulls them together. But when both of their Masculine energies are brought together, for instance, their attractive passion is neutralized or they may even feel repelled by an unseen force, pushed away like two north poles of a magnet.

MASCULINE AND FEMININE ARE NOT GENDER-BASED

Masculine and Feminine do not mean "man" and "woman," but are universal sexual forces. Some people only experience an arc of polarity with members of the opposite sex, but most people experience polarity with all kinds of people and even places. For instance, Hawaii is an extremely feminine place. When you walk outside in Hawaii you see double rainbows and colorful birds overhead. You are surrounded by lush tropical foliage and the smell of ripe papayas and guavas. You feel as though you've just walked into a huge woman. Your whole body may experience a deeply enjoyable flow of sexual polarity with the island itself, which is very enlivening.

When people go to Hawaii, they usually go to be enlivened, to be filled with energy, to let go of their mental concerns and tension, and to relax. The island is so Feminine—you feel so open and stress-free—that a vacation there is similar to having great sex for two weeks. You feel so opened and relaxed.

Most people who go to Hawaii for a vacation spend their usual working day in the Masculine mode which is the exact opposite of the life force of Hawaii. New York, for instance, is a city that is very Masculine compared with Hawaii.

The feeling of New York is very vertical, very one-pointed, very focused. When you're in New York, you're often in your "do-mode" and you're just doing one thing after another, step by step, trying to achieve some goal. That driven, goal-oriented, focused energy is Masculine energy, whether it's emanating from a man or a woman. Your own Masculine energy, as well as the Masculine energy of a place like New York, is goal-oriented, scheduled, directed, focused, self-disciplined energy. Your Feminine energy, as well as the Feminine energy of a place like Hawaii, is flowing, open, wild, radiant, life force—it's the energy of nature.

If you want more Feminine energy in your life, then you go to a place like Hawaii. Your body relaxes, you feel a flow of energy and you're healed by it. The healing force of life-energy is a Feminine quality, whether it is given by a man, woman or place.

If you want to get a lot done, you might not want to go to Hawaii. It's very difficult to be disciplined and focused in Hawaii. But if you go to New York, you can't help but get a lot done. Even if you just want to relax on the streets, the crowd pushes or carries you along. You're moved by the Masculine, this forward thrust of energy.

These qualities also exist in people. Again, it's not a matter of man and woman; it's not gender-determined. Masculine energy and Feminine energy are universal forces. As a person, man or woman, you have both Masculine and Feminine energy. When you finish with your Masculine workday of focus, focus, focus, then it's nice to go home and relax in your Feminine energy, the life flow in your body. It feels great to get a massage. It's wonderful to eat a delicious meal, enjoying the sensations of taste and smell. It's fantastic to take a walk in nature, with or without your lover. In these kinds of moments, when you're connected to your senses, when you're in the flow of the natural elements, when you're really aware of your physical surroundings and your body is in rhythm with the unseen forces of nature, then you are in your Feminine energy.

On the other hand, on your way to a business meeting, you may be thinking, "Okay, where's my checklist? Do I have this? Did I remember that? What are the main points? Will I be successful? Okay, let's go." Then you get to the meeting, where everything is structured and organized. During this time, you are in your Masculine energy. When you are directed and focused, if someone was to walk up to you and say, "Hi, let's chat," you might say, "Not now—can't you see I'm busy?"

When you're in your Masculine energy, you're very modal, you're focused into one mode. For instance, have you ever tried to interrupt a man while he was watching a football game? Waxing his car? Balancing the checkbook? Reading the newspaper? It's as if his mood was, "Not now, can't you see I'm busy?" Of course, this type of mood happens for women, too, when they're in their Masculine energy. Anyone in his or her Masculine energy is very focused and doesn't like to be interrupted.

For anyone who is in Feminine energy, however, interruption doesn't really exist. Maybe the phone rings while you're working on a project and watching TV, so you answer it and talk until a friend comes to the door. "I'll call you back in a few minutes," you say, before hanging up the phone and greeting your friend properly. Then you re-member that you put something on the stove before the phone rang so you take care of that, talking to your friend the whole time, continuing to keep an eye on the TV. When you are in your Feminine energy you can more easily flow from one thing to another. The Feminine is a genius at flow, whereas the Masculine is a genius at getting a single thing done. And they are both useful at different times.

You probably know people, both men and women, who seem to have more Masculine energy than Feminine. They are more like New York than Hawaii, always working, always focused on a project, always fol-lowing a list or a schedule. And other people are more like Hawaii than New York. They animate more Feminine energy than Masculine. They are flowing, radiant people who often don't stay focused on long-term projects because of their quality of flowing from one thing to another, but they're happy. And then there are some other kinds of people who are in between the extreme of Masculine and Feminine, New York and Hawaii. These people are relatively more balanced or neutral in their energy. They don't have the emotional hurricanes of Hawaii, nor are they as lush and radiant. They don't have the depersonalized drive of New York, nor are they as focused and organized. They have some of Hawaii and some of New York, but are not too extreme.

There are all kinds of people and if you look at yourself, you'll see that you are more like one of these kinds: Masculine, Feminine or Neutral. Usually you can't see yourself all that clearly, so it's best to ask someone else who knows you, "Which kind am I?" and they'll say something like, "Are you kidding? You're Hawaii!"

Whenever someone who is animating Masculine energy comes into the vicinity of someone who is animating Feminine energy in the moment, an arc of polarity flows between them. That's the feeling of sexual polarity. It happens when one person is in Masculine and another person is in Feminine.

It is very important to understand that the flow of sexual polarity does not imply either romantic attraction or love. Sexual polarity can happen in the absence of the sense of "this is the special person I've always been looking for," which signals romantic attraction. And sexual polarity can flow between two people who don't even know each other and have never spoken a word to each other, much less love each other. It is a natural force that flows between any Masculine and Feminine pole.

If a college professor is putting out strong Masculine energy—confidence, transcendental vision, guidance—then it is not unusual for his women students to develop a "crush" on him. An arc of sexual polarity naturally occurs between them, as it also does between a therapist who offers steady guidance (Masculine) to a client who opens herself or himself to the therapist in trust (Feminine). Sexual polarity is virtually inevitable in such a case, though it certainly need not be acted upon.

Likewise, if a close woman friend offers a man her care and affection—or a businesswoman gives her male colleague her attentive support—then it is not unusual for him to begin to desire her. Again, sexual polarity naturally occurs whenever a strong Masculine pole comes close to a strong Feminine pole. Sexual polarity is a magnetic force, a natural force, not necessarily a sign of love.

You can feel an arc of sexual polarity flow between you and anyone who is in the opposite sexual pole. It is natural. It is not intentional. It is innocent. It is powerful. But it is not love. And it is not romantic attraction. Just because you feel a flow of sexual polarity with your boss does not mean you should get into a relationship with him or her. It doesn't mean anything—other than the fact that you were full of Masculine or Feminine energy and your boss was full of the opposite. Hence, you felt a flow of sexual polarity; so did your boss.

Our culture has lost the wisdom of the laws of sexual polarity, and we tend not to be very conscious of the type of energy—either more Masculine or more Feminine—that we are putting out in any given moment. This lack of awareness frequently leads to conflicts with our intimate partners and misunderstandings with our friends and business associates.

To consciously work with the flow of sexual polarity in our intimacies and in the workplace, we must become sensitive to the type of energy that we are putting out: Masculine, Neutral or Feminine. By cultivating this sensitivity we can choose to increase polarity, thereby magnifying passion and sexual attraction in our intimate relationships, or decrease sexual polarity, thereby minimizing the flow of sexual energies with our friends and co-workers. The choice of how to use the powerful force of sexual polarity is in our hands, once we understand the principles of its flow.

A RELATIONSHIP FEELS OVER
WHEN POLARITY IS GONE

Love and sexual polarity are not the same. We can love our children, our friends and our pets, but that doesn't mean we want to share sexual polarity with them. The opposite is also true: We may feel strong sexual polarity with a perfect stranger, someone whom we don't know very well—we might not even know his or her name!

Although a Masculine pole and a Feminine pole are necessary for full and passionate sexual polarity, such poles are not necessary for the flow of real love. Very frequently, in fact, long-term relationships lose their sexual polarity over time, yet the partners still love each other very much.

Some of this decrease in sexual polarity is quite natural. For many of us, especially as we grow older, sexual polarity becomes less and less important, although we still want love to flow in our relationship. However, some of us have experienced a less desirable situation. We may love our partner, though are no longer sexually attracted to him or her. Yet, we still want passion and sexual polarity in our lives. There is no real conflict involved. It just feels like the sexual part of our relationship is "over."

We should understand that unless we consciously practice the art of cultivating sexual polarity, the passion in our intimacy will always tend to decrease over time because we are inadvertently neutralizing the polarity through our behaviors and misunderstandings. This does not mean that we should leave the relationship, but that we should learn what we are doing to cause this decrease in passion and how we can "re-polarize" our relationship. To practice Intimate Communion we must understand how we consciously or unconsciously magnify, neutralize or reverse the flow of sexual polarity with our partner.

MAGNIFICATION OF POLARITY

Most often in our culture, the play of sexual polarity occurs between a man and a woman. However, it is quite possible, of course, for two men or two women to practice sexual polarity in Intimate

Communion, as long as one of them is playing the Masculine pole and the other is playing the Feminine pole during intimate moments. It is also possible for a Feminine-pole man and a Masculine-pole woman to practice sexual polarity together in Intimate Communion.

The most common situation, however, is when the woman is playing the Feminine pole and the man the Masculine pole. As we shall see, if these poles are suddenly shifted or made ambiguous, then attraction between intimate partners decreases and conflict increases. But first, let's look at how polar attraction can be magnified.

Imagine you are a man sitting on the couch with your lover, watching TV. She gets up, fixes your favorite snack and brings it to you, sitting down close to you on the couch. As she sits her skirt reveals the smooth flesh of her bare thighs. She feeds you from her own fingers, letting her hand trace a line from your lips down to your chest. You look into her eyes and she is completely open to you, loving you. You embrace her, feeling her body yield against you. She gives herself to you. You desire her in every way, with your whole body and heart. Such is the magnification of polarity.

Although this scene may be familiar to many of us, what are the mechanics behind it? Why is polarity magnified in this case?

The woman is feeding the man with her personal energy. She is *attracting* him from the abstract glow of television to the living radiance of her flesh. She relaxes his head, energizes his body and awakens his heart, just like the tropical beaches of Hawaii. She is drawing him into herself, into the garden of life, by opening, attracting him in by love. She is radiating Feminine energy, and thus she is magnetizing his Masculine energy in the full arc of sexual polarity.

NEUTRALIZATION OF POLARITY

Imagine you are a woman lying in bed with your lover. You have worked all day and you are tired. When you returned home from work, your lover kissed you on the cheek and went back to reading his book. While he continued reading, you made a quick dinner for yourself, showered and got into bed. Finally he finished reading and got into bed, setting his alarm clock and arranging his night stand as he does every night. You think he probably now wants sex with you. You could have sex if he really wants to, but you aren't feeling too excited yourself. Such is the neutralization of polarity.

Let's look closely at this case of neutralization. The woman comes home from work and gets a cursory kiss on the cheek. Where is the Masculine force? He is neither opening her with love nor penetrating her with desire—his Masculine presence is completely absent. Or, rather, it is absent from playing in polarity with her and is instead absorbed in a book. She continues doing what she needs to do, making dinner for herself and then taking a shower. Because she is tired, she doesn't have the energy to rev up her own Feminine force. Neither of them is active as the Feminine or Masculine pole, and thus sexual polarity is neutralized.

REVERSAL OF POLARITY

You are a man with an exciting plan about how to make money. You are telling your wife about it and she interrupts you to tell you how silly you are. She gives you several reasons why she thinks your plan is foolish and won't work. Then, she continues to do her work around the house as she proceeds to tell you about her own strategy for making money.

"And what about our plans tonight to go out with the Smiths?" she says. She continues to busy herself around the house. Then she asks, "Have you made up your mind yet? We have to leave soon, you know. Well, what are we going to do?"

You couldn't care less. You have no desire to do anything tonight, especially with your wife. She tells you her shoulders ache and she wants you to rub them. You don't even want to touch her. Such is the reversal of polarization.

What is happening here? The man is telling his wife his idea for making money. He is trying to share his direction, guidance and transcendental vision, playing the Masculine pole of universal energy, like the energy of New York. Suddenly, his wife interrupts him. She ceases being open to his vision, saying that he is wrong, his directionality is lousy and she could do it better. Perhaps this is true. But at the level of polar energy, this is equivalent to telling her husband that he's a lousy lover and that she would make a better man. Polarity is immediately neutralized.

But she doesn't stop there. She continues with her purposes around the house. She tells him her vision of how things should be done. That is, she animates the Masculine force of guidance, purpose and transcendental vision. She has reversed her polar energy from Feminine to Masculine. This would be fine if her husband was in his more Feminine energy, open to receiving her advice. But he, too, is in the midst of a Masculine moment, in the midst of telling her about his great idea. Just like similar poles of two magnets repelling one another, her sudden reversal of sexual polarity causes a repulsion and distancing between her own Masculine energy and that of her man.

THE TEXTURES OF
MASCULINE AND FEMININE

What are some of the Masculine and Feminine qualities as they appear in people? For simplicity's sake, let's anthropomorphize these universal qualities and call the Masculine force (in men and women) "He," and the Feminine force (in men and women) "She."

Like the directional energy of New York, the Masculine always seems involved in a mission, a search or a project, be it fixing a car, furthering a career or finding a path in God. Also, He sees things from a transcendental position. That is, like a concrete skyscraper, He likes to stand above things, outside of His emotions: in thoughts, in knowledge or perhaps in so-called "mystical purity."

From His transcendental perspective, everything fixed in life — everything concrete — may seem like a limitation or a trap. For instance, an open-ended relationship is one thing, but marriage is quite another. For anyone with a lot of Masculine energy, marriage seems like a potential trap, a constraint, a loss of freedom. A commitment to marriage is a decision to leave the transcendental realm of endless possibility and to enter the earthbound realm of endless responsibility.

For the Feminine, marriage is not a constraint, but a liberation of loving. The Feminine force, in man or woman, is about opening to love and giving love. The Feminine force is the goddess-force of energy that is sometimes wild and unpredictable and sometimes nurturing and life-giving, like Hawaii. Unlike the Masculine, the Feminine is at home in life, in sensuality, in the natural elements. Anyone with a lot of Feminine energy abhors a vacuum, filling empty shelves with seashells, flowers or other objects of beauty.

Whereas the Masculine pole is directed toward the sky, like the buildings of New York, the Feminine pole is grounded in the earth, flowing with the force of life. The Feminine is a radiant ocean of sudden storms and rejuvenative healing, a garden of bountiful love and wild energy.

The Feminine's radiance and beauty attract the Masculine into the garden of life and Her heart tempers His relentless search. The Feminine force embraces the Masculine's arid directionality and couples it with feeling, sensitivity and the inherent wisdom of the body. Without the Feminine force, the Masculine force is mere directionality, mere purpose, mere goal orientation without feeling. In the negative extreme it is exploitation for profit, rape and fascism.

On the other hand, without the directionality of the Masculine force, the movement of the Feminine force alone is one of opening or closing. For instance, consider a person with a lot of Feminine energy and very little Masculine energy. Eating chocolates, this person may feel either open and happy or closed and miserable about it, but often has difficulty choosing a different direction, like moving away from chocolate for good.

More seriously, if the Feminine couples with an abusive partner, she often has difficulty directing Herself out and away, but instead opens and suffers, closes down and then opens again. Without being balanced by the Masculine force of guidance and directionality, the extreme Feminine force cycles through good times and bad, hoping it will work out, alternately loving and suffering, being hurt and then giving it one more chance.

Another way of looking at the Masculine and Feminine forces in men and women is to look at sexuality itself. For a man, sexual union happens outside of his body, whereas for a woman, sexual union occurs inside of her. During sexual loving a man's sexual flesh becomes rigid, directed, pointed and seeks release. A woman's sexual flesh opens, becoming more and more vulnerable to penetration, her whole body and emotional state opening in love, wanting to give love by opening, wanting to receive her man's love deeply.

The Masculine force is a directional force and it is one-pointed, as is a man's polarized sexual flesh. In a larger sense, it is the force of discipline (one-pointedness) and guidance (directionality) and tends to move in a transcendental (upward) direction.

Just as a man's sexual flesh reveals his one-pointed directionality and his up-up-and-away orientation, a woman's sexual flesh reveals her desire to draw a good man in, open herself in union with him and be filled with unending love. The Feminine opens in love and closes when hurt. The Masculine moves into relationship in love and pulls out of relationship when hurt. Both the Masculine and the Feminine forces exist to some extent in every man and woman, although some people animate more Masculine energy like New York, some animate more Feminine energy like Hawaii, and some are more Neutral or balanced in their expression.

As a general characterization, then, the Masculine pole in each of us points upward, away from the body and life. The Masculine force is a force of conscious directionality and intent, which sometimes gets stuck in the head. The Feminine pole in each of us is at home in the body and in life. The Feminine force is a force of radiance and opening, which sometimes gets stuck in the emotions.

MASCULINE AND FEMININE PARTNERS BALANCING EACH OTHER

When a more Masculine person comes together in love with a more Feminine person, they can enjoy the enlivening force of passionate sexual polarity that naturally flows between them. Those with a more Neutral person would probably prefer to balance his or her internal energies through more solitary or non-sexual means.

For those more sexually inclined, however, there is an option. In Intimate Communion, partners can serve to naturally balance and heal each other through the dynamic force of sexual polarity that flows between their native Masculine and Feminine poles.

For instance, when a Masculine man is polarized by a Feminine woman, he is attracted out of his head, out of his fantasy realm of possibilities, and is moved to engage a living actuality: her. He begins to act from his feelings rather than live in his thoughts. Love draws him into the body, his and hers.

The Feminine force attracts the Masculine into the dance of life, of love, of intimate partnership. Therefore, if his woman becomes like New York, bossy or sharp, or withdraws her Feminine energy in any way, a man suddenly feels trapped—he has left his realm of possibility and has committed to an actual relationship, something that limits his possibilities.

If his partner's Feminine force of attraction becomes non-active, if he does not feel enlivened by her Hawaii-like energy, then he feels the relationship as a constraint. The relationship seems like a weight of obligations rather than a source of energy and delight. His Masculine force is no longer magnetically polarized by the Feminine force, and he naturally begins to move up, up and away, back into his tower of possibility, where he hopes to avoid unnecessary constraints and maybe eventually find another source of Feminine energy.

"I want out of here!" This is the Masculine voice when the Feminine no longer polarizes Him.

The essential form of the Masculine bad mood is feeling tired, burdened, constrained by obligations. For instance, no amount of talking with his woman will relieve a man of his sense of being duty-bound and trapped. However, if she doesn't collapse, feeling rejected by his mood, but rather stays in relationship as the force of Hawaii, active in her loving, then the Feminine force can transform the moment into a garden of delight. She can enliven his burdened heart as only his cherished source of Feminine energy can do.

What happens to the Feminine partner—a woman, for instance—when her man loses his Masculine presence and becomes weak and ambiguous in his loving? She feels empty and she yearns to be filled. Where she once felt the Masculine presence of love, she now feels a void.

"I want love in here!"

The essential form of the Feminine bad mood is the hurt of being unloved and the anger that results from feeling rejected or abandoned.

When a man (or anyone in a Masculine moment) is in a bad mood, he wants to understand why. He tries to figure it all out. So when his woman is in a bad mood, he tries to do for her what he tries to do for himself—figure it out. He tries to use his head to solve her emotional problems.

However, a man's mental analysis is useless and frustrating to a woman (or anyone in a Feminine moment) who is in a bad mood. The Feminine's bad mood is only Her desire for perfect love—why shouldn't the Masculine just give His love most directly? The Feminine receives love most directly in Her native language, which is not a language of analysis but of body and emotion. It is a language of touch, of presence, of feeling. A Feminine woman's mood is not subject to mental analysis, but she is opened into the present moment by a man's encompassing embrace, his caring humor and his strong, loving Masculine presence.

In the practice of Intimate Communion, we learn to transmit love through the force of sexual polarity. And to enjoy sexual polarity, we must be clear about what we want from our partner and where we fall on the spectrum of Masculine and Feminine. Are we more like New York or are we more like Hawaii? Do we have a balance? Or, are we confused and divided inside?

UNIFYING INTERNAL DIVISIONS

If you are comfortable with your natural sexual energy—Masculine, Feminine or Neutral—then the flush of sexual polarity is enlivening. If you are at home in your body and mind, as man or woman, then you are at ease with the feeling of sexual desire. Furthermore, your body is unified with your mind as one gift—with your heart at its center—and you know, spontaneously, how to love without hesitation. You are not internally divided or confused.

However, if you *are* internally divided, your body and mind are not one with your heart: You want to attract a mate, but you find it difficult to let down your guard. You want to relax during sex, but you feel so self-conscious. Your husband tells you he loves you, but you just don't feel it. Your best friend's girlfriend is obviously taken, but she seems so available. Your heart is always ambiguous and divided.

As a necessary preliminary to cultivating sexual polarity in Intimate Communion, we learn to allow ourselves to be whole and undivided. With love, we embrace our darkest and lightest thoughts. With love, we embrace our most savage and holy desires.

By healing our internal divisions and fully accepting ourselves as we are, we learn to accept and empower our sexual core, and we learn to honor our unique expression of Masculine and Feminine gifts. We fully incarnate in our bodies, at home and at ease in a man's body or a woman's body. And we learn to love with complete abandon, as free men and women, without rules or roles or guarded hearts.

We freely enchant one another, love one another, with no inhibitions.

Sometimes our fingers gently trail down the inside of our lover's wrist. At other times our passion growls and claws like a wild tiger. There are long hours of silence together, simply touching, loving, breathing. There are sudden moments of inspired desire, in the kitchen, in the car, in the shower—our juices flow, our hearts pound and we gasp with pleasure. There may be days, months or years of happy celibacy, since sexuality is only one form of human loving.

Fully incarnated as Masculine and Feminine forces in the practice of Intimate Communion, partners are free to play the full spectrum of loving, from bucking sweat-dogs to motionless archetypes, radiant with divine love.

Most people have experienced glimpses of truly ecstatic Intimate Communion: moments of loving so expansive that you lose awareness of your body—and so profound that your heart opens wider than it seems possible. Simple gazes, single hugs and genital conjunctions can be of such magnitude that the universe is rendered beyond form, if only for a few moments.

In the practice of Intimate Communion, we can learn to master sexual polarity so that ecstatic loving is the rule, not the exception. Intimate Communion, sexually and in daily life, is a sacred art that can be practiced.

4

Understanding
Your Sexual Essence

WHAT IS A SEXUAL ESSENCE?

Suppose you are wearing sexy clothes that complement the shape of your body. If your business colleague looks you up and down and squeezes your ass, it would probably be a case of sexual harassment. Yet, if your lover did the same thing, you would probably welcome it. When it comes to emotional and sexual expectations, your business colleague and your lover are probably not equal in your eyes.

What do you really desire from your intimate partner? Are you clear about your emotional and sexual expectations? We often expect our partner to be everyone for us: our business colleague, our lover, the parent of our children, even our friendly therapist. It doesn't work. The spark disappears. The passion peters out. Little things about our partner begin to really annoy us.

In our hopes to achieve a 50/50 Relationship, a relationship based on meeting each other halfway and sharing responsibilities equally, we usually forget what drew us together to begin with: our unique and special gifts as embodiments of Masculine and Feminine. Not just the gift of a business colleague, with whom we can share our financial strategies. Not just the gift of a therapist, whom we can visit when we want to talk about our problems. Not just the gift of a childcare professional, whom we can hire by the day or by the month. But the unique gift that we share *only* with our intimate partner—the gift of our uninhibited sexual essence. When we have forgotten this unique gift, our intimacies become flat.

What exactly is your sexual essence?

Imagine that you live in the future, at a time when intimate partners are built from scratch. You look through a catalog, picking and choosing exactly what you want in an intimate partner. First you look at the "Anatomy" section. One page in the catalog displays pictures of arms to select. Do you want a partner with hairy arms or smooth arms? Do you want a partner whose arms are stronger than yours or more lithe? You make a selection and continue flipping through the catalog, looking at pictures of eyes, legs, mouths, genitals and torsos. There are even scratch-and-sniff pages. You take your pick, creating the intimate partner of your choice.

Then you turn to the "Emotional Character" section of the catalog. On each page is a whole spectrum of emotional qualities, ranging from joyous to angry, silly to serious, expressive to reserved.

For instance, one page is dedicated to "Control-Yielding Spectrum." Do you want a partner who enjoys taking control of a situation, or a partner who enjoys following your lead? Do you want a partner who likes to make the decisions half the time, leaving you to make the decisions the other half of the time? Or would you prefer one who lets you make most of the decisions? Perhaps you would like a partner who is very dominant in bed, but less so when it comes to daily decisions. You can create the exact partner you want, so why not get specific?

Finally, you turn to the "Sexual Essence Spectrum" section of the catalog. Each page offers a full range of sexual essences, described as "expressions of the heart": the way your intimate partner will express his or her love, affection and desire for union. Just as your partner's potential arms were displayed in a spectrum of hairy to smooth or massive to frail, the sexual essences are also arranged in a spectrum. The range of sexual essences spans the spectrum from the extreme Masculine at one end, to the more balanced or Neutral types in the middle, to the extreme Feminine at the other end.

By choosing a sexual essence, you are choosing the texture of your partner's love. For example, what do you want to feel when your partner embraces you? You can choose from selections like "Visionary Hero," "Gallant Prince" or "Big and Dangerous," which are different types located toward the extreme Masculine end of the spectrum. Or you could choose from "Innocent Waif," "Wild Goddess" or "Radiant Dancer," types located toward the extreme Feminine end.

Or you might choose your partner's sexual essence from the "Good Friend" part of the spectrum, somewhere near the middle. This type of partner has a more balanced or Neutral type of sexual essence, which allows him or her to be able to listen to you and really understand your thoughts and feelings. An extremely Masculine or Feminine partner, on the other hand, may lead all discussions toward deadly serious debate, flowing emotional roundabouts or delicious sexual embrace. Since the extreme Masculine and the extreme Feminine speak such different languages, they often find it more communicative to passionately embrace each other or turn away in silence, rather than to speak in rational words, which often seem to get in the way of what they really want to "say." People with more Neutral sexual essences, however, find it quite easy and fulfilling to speak honestly and clearly with each other, without getting into fights or tense silences.

At any given time in our lives, each of us has a preference: We either want a partner who loves us in a more Feminine way, a more Masculine way or a more Neutral way. And likewise, your own sexual essence is, itself, more Feminine, Masculine or Neutral. It doesn't matter whether you are a woman or a man; your sexual essence may still be Masculine, Feminine or Neutral.

How can you figure out what your sexual essence is right now?

SEXUAL ESSENCE QUIZ

This is a simple quiz to help give you a feeling for your sexual essence. Try to answer each question as honestly as possible. As you are answering each question, imagine that you are in bed with a sensitive and sexy intimate partner whom you trust completely. Following the quiz is a key to help you determine your sexual essence from the answers you have chosen.

1. I would more often prefer that my sexual partner was
  A. physically stronger than I am
  B. physically less strong than I am
  C. my exact same strength

2. I would more often prefer that my sexual partner was
  A. physically larger than me
  B. physically smaller than me
  C. the exact same size as me

3. Although I may like variety in the bedroom, I would prefer this situation more often:
  A. I surrender to my partner, who sexually ravishes me in love
  B. I sexually ravish my partner, who surrenders to me
  C. nobody surrenders and nobody gets ravished

4. It would hurt me most if my partner were to say to me:
    A. "You are looking really old and wrinkled lately."
    B. "You are really losing your edge—you seem lost."
    C. "You really treat men differently from women."

5. I am more often turned on when
    A. I give up control and let my partner be in charge sexually
    B. my partner gives up control and I am in charge sexually
    C. nobody gives up control and nobody is in charge

6. If I had to choose from one alternative, I would rather
    A. have a sequence of unfulfilling vocations but a perfectly fulfilling intimacy
    B. have a sequence of unfulfilling intimacies but a perfectly fulfilling vocation
    C. have a sequence of partially fulfilling intimacies and partially fulfilling vocations

7. When my partner does something that really hurts me, I most often
    A. close down emotionally
    B. have an impulse to leave the relationship, just for an evening or for a long time
    C. discuss things rationally with my partner without closing down or wanting to leave

8. Which sentence most accurately describes the majority of the intimate partners you have had in your life?
    A. My partners have tended to get upset when I gave them directions while they were driving.
    B. My partners have tended to change their minds about our plans, based on the emotion of the moment.
    C. My partners have tended to be like good friends, with great communication and very little misunderstanding between us.

9. *Which statement is most true?*

A. My partners often seem to assume they are right about everything.

B. My partners seem to like to tell me that I think I'm right about everything and that I am inflexible.

C. My partners and I have rarely had a discussion about who is right, because it has rarely been an issue.

10. *I find that my partners have been the kind of people who*

A. focus while working or watching TV to the extent that they hardly notice me

B. flow from one task to another, even while conversing, very easily—although often they don't completely finish one task before moving on to another

C. can easily talk to me while watching TV and also finish most every task that they begin

Scoring Key

If you answered mostly A's, your sexual essence is more Feminine. If you answered mostly B's, your sexual essence is more Masculine. If you answered mostly C's, your sexual essence is more Neutral. Don't be confused if your answers were not clear cut. As we will see later, most of us have layers of false Masculine and Feminine energy surrounding our true sexual essence.

WHAT DO MEN AND WOMEN REALLY WANT? A SURVEY

It doesn't matter whether you are a woman or a man. Your sexual essence could still be more Masculine, more Feminine or more Neutral.

You may not be fully aware of your true sexual essence, though. It may be covered over by layers of mistrust, fear or denial. You may have developed your "opposite" energy for positive reasons, too. You may have developed your Masculine energy in order to succeed at a career, even though deep down you have a more Feminine sexual essence. Or, you may have developed your Feminine energy in order to deepen your intuition or healing ability, though deep down you have a more Masculine sexual essence.

You may feel that you are somewhere toward the middle of the spectrum, a more balanced or Neutral person. If this were true, then you would prefer a more Neutral intimate partner, since you are always attracted to your opposite. However, the vast majority of people are not Neutral, but strongly prefer a partner who gives them a particularly Masculine or Feminine gift of love. In fact, in surveys I have given throughout the United States, the qualities that most men want in their women are quite different from the qualities most women want in their men. No wonder the attempts of women and men to meet halfway in their relationships often lead to such tepid results. Most women and men don't want a sexually "halfway" partner. They want an enlivening Feminine or Masculine gift.

In workshops I have led across the United States, from Hawaii to New York, I separate the participants, putting all the men in one room and all the women in another. Then I ask each group, "List the six most important qualities you want in an ideal intimate partner." This list is only of those qualities desired specifically from their intimate partners or lovers—not those gifts they would also want from their friends, parents or co-workers. For instance, a woman may want her intimate partner to be loving, but she also wants her friends, her children and her cat to be loving, so "loving" is not included on this list.

I remind them that although their ideal partner will have many more qualities than these six, these are the six qualities they would insist on in the creation of their ideal intimate partner. Finally, and this is critical, the whole group must agree on the same qualities. Any qualities that only a few people want are not included. All the women must come to a unanimously determined list in their room, and all the men must do the same in their room.

After asking hundreds of educated and successful women and men to make these lists at workshops across the United States, I have found that the results are amazingly consistent from city to city. What emerges are lists of qualities that describe the ideal man or woman, the intimate partner of our fantasies.

These lists of qualities have very little overlap. Women and men want distinctly different qualities in their intimate partners. This is to be expected. After all, most (but not all) of us have a preference: we want to be sexually intimate with a person who is more Masculine or more Feminine.

What exactly were the qualities that people most wanted in their intimate partners?

Virtually every woman agreed that foremost among the qualities they wanted in their man were:

1. Presence
2. Intelligence
3. Strength
4. Passion
5. Direction
6. Humor

Did the men want the same qualities in their women?

No. In fact, in two different cities, the men made lists that began like this:

1. Great in bed

2. Great in bed

3. Great in bed

After I reminded them that they had to choose six *different* qualities, they laughed and rewrote their list.

The qualities that men across the country wanted most in their women were:

1. Beauty
2. Sexual openness
3. Trust of their (man's) direction
4. Support for their (man's) vision
5. Intelligence
6. Healthy radiance

Notice that except for "intelligence," the idealized qualities for men and women are entirely different. (The mutual desire for "intelligence" may result in part from the background of the workshop participants; most were highly educated.) For instance, these women wanted their "ideal man" to have a strong sense of direction. Although this may also be a quality that men want in their women, it never showed up on any group's list as one of the top six qualities that men want in their ideal intimate partner. The reciprocal was also true; these men wanted their "ideal woman" to trust their direction, but it apparently wasn't as important to the women that their ideal man trusted theirs. More important to the women was that their ideal man be full of presence, strength, passion and humor. Yet these qualities never showed up on the men's wish list. In their ideal woman, men want beauty, sexual openness, healthy radiance and support of their man's vision. The idealized qualities for men and women are not equal.

As these lists show, many of us definitely desire some qualities of the extreme Masculine or Feminine in our partners. Many of us definitely desire sexual polarity, or a highly charged attraction, in our intimacies. We may want a man, full of presence, to desire us and come forward in confident love. Or, we may want a radiant woman to desire us and respond to us by trusting, opening and inviting us deeper.

Some of us may want the qualities of the Masculine on one day and of the Feminine on the next. But the fact is, if we have any sexual desire at all, it is a desire for polarity. We can go to our friends and family to get non-sexual love. But this kind of love is not enough for most of us. Most of us want sexual polarity. We want to feel love transmitted in Masculine or Feminine ways.

Some of us might, if we had that catalog in the future, choose a partner with interchangeable sexual anatomy, but very few of us would be turned on by a neutralized blob of pink flesh, indeterminate of sexual origin. Some of us might prefer an intimate partner with unchanging anatomy, male or female, but with interchangeable sexual essences: We sometimes want a strong Masculine tiger to pounce on us and at other times we want a coy Feminine pussycat to lick our fingers.

The point is, whatever our sexual preference, heterosexual, homosexual or bisexual, very few of us would choose neutralized anatomy and a Neutral sexual essence in a partner with whom we want to share passionate sexual loving. It is the uniqueness, the non-equivalence, of the Masculine and Feminine form and essence that creates and sustains attraction and sexual polarity in our intimacies. When we deny the differences between the Masculine and Feminine sexual essences, we deny what most men and women really want in their intimate partners. We end up being dissatisfied with our partner's way of loving us. We end up neutralizing the very passion that drew us together to begin with.

My guess based on surveys at workshops around the country is that roughly 80 percent of women have a Feminine sexual essence and 80 percent of men have a Masculine sexual essence. About 10 percent of men and women have a Neutral sexual essence. And about 10 percent of men have a Feminine sexual essence and 10 percent of women, a Masculine sexual essence.

Therefore, I will frequently use men in my examples of people with Masculine sexual essences and women in examples of the Feminine sexual essence. This will apply to roughly 80 percent of you reading this. If you feel that you are a man with a Feminine sexual essence or a woman with a Masculine sexual essence, simply reverse the genders in the examples. Keep in mind that your sexual essence is most easily discovered in your secret desires for an intimate partner. For instance, you might be a very successful businesswoman, a woman who is a real corporate warrior, and yet also want to be with a Masculine man. That is, you may have successfully developed your Masculine energy to be successful in the competitive world of Masculine business, yet still feel like a goddess deep in your heart and want to be cherished and honored as a Feminine woman.

SOCIAL EQUALITY AND SEXUAL PASSION

One problem in our intimacies today is that many of us have confused social gender equality with the neutralization of our native Masculine and Feminine sexual essences. We must differentiate what we want in bed from what we want at the workplace. We want passion in our intimacies but neutrality in the employment office. We want our intimate partner to cherish and appreciate our sexual essence and anatomy, and yet we want our sexual essence and anatomy ignored when we are conferring in the boardroom. If we confuse functional roles in the workplace with the naturally different sexual desires of most men and women, everybody suffers.

The Feminine sexual essence must be honored in its own right if intimacy is to flower, as must the Masculine sexual essence. However, the workplace often places a higher value on the Masculine way of operating and often demands that both women and men act more "business-like." Because of this, women often hide their radiance and take on a competitive edge in order to be taken seriously. Men often suppress their language, behavior and even sexual urges in order to work alongside women. Just because men and women can both wear gray suits doesn't negate the fact that each of us is a unique sexual being.

As individual men and women in the economic and political world, we should all be given the same opportunities and treated with the same respect and "equal eye." In an effort to achieve this, men and women are learning to treat each other as equals and, to some extent, even treat each other as non-sexual beings. Unfortunately, we have confused the equality of the workplace with sexual neutralization in our intimate relationships. In our intimate relationships, we have inadvertently negotiated the neutering of our sexual essence in order to be treated as equals.

We need to make a distinction between what we want in the workplace and what we want in our intimate lives together.

Sexual fulfillment in intimacy is not based on neutrality, but on the attractive differences, playful opposition and pleasurable non-equivalence of the Masculine and Feminine gifts, anatomical, emotional and spiritual. This is a key to why the modern ideal of an intimate relationship can be so dissatisfying. In a modern relationship, in which equivalence between men and women is often emphasized, we may never receive the *full* gifts of Masculine or Feminine loving that we truly desire.

In order to freely express our loving in Intimate Communion, we must be free to express our native sexual essence, whether it be Neutral, Masculine or Feminine.

BLOCKED-UP AND COVERED-OVER SEXUAL ESSENCES

Suppose you are a woman whose sexual essence is naturally more Feminine. You will lose trust in your partner if you find that he is always ambivalent and undirected, waiting for you to take the lead most of the time. In this case, your partner is waiting to follow your direction, to trust and follow your Masculine sense of "mission."

"What do you want to do tonight?" you ask.
"I don't care, what do *you* want to do?" he answers.

If your sexual essence is actually more Feminine, you will find yourself wishing that your partner would take you into account and just make a decision. Your Feminine essence wants to feel his Masculine energy, direction, presence and passion. You want to feel him take a stronger lead in your lives together, rather than being ambiguous and unclear.

"What do you want to do tonight?"
"How about if we go out to dinner and then go for a walk in the park?"

However, if your natural Feminine sexual essence is covered over by your own Masculine energy, then you will attract a partner who is polarized by your Masculine energy. Masculine and Feminine energies always attract your reciprocal. If you are putting out Masculine energy, you will attract a man who puts out Feminine energy. You will attract a partner who lacks strong directionality, presence and confidence. He may be radiant and intuitive, but his life will be ambiguous and undirected, and therefore he will be attracted to *your* Masculine energy.

If you find that you are repeatedly disappointed that the men (or women) you attract are somewhat weak or lost, unable to completely follow through with what they start, wishy-washy or threatened by your success, then you are probably animating more Masculine energy than is true of your natural sexual essence. Your Feminine sexual essence may be looking for a really good source of Masculine love, but the Masculine energy you are putting out is attracting men who *need* more Masculine in their lives, and who are therefore attracted to yours. But they don't fulfill the deepest desires of your Feminine sexual essence.

Suppose that you are a man with a naturally Masculine sexual essence. Time after time you are disappointed by your intimate partners. You seem to attract women, again and again, who don't trust your direction, who are more directed in their lives than you are, or who insist that you follow their direction—even though you want to follow your own direction.

If this is the case, you have attracted partners who are animating more Masculine energy than Feminine. If your sexual essence is Masculine, the only way you could be attracting such women is if your Masculine expression is blocked. Thus, your potential partners feel your more Feminine energy. They feel that they have "space" in the relationship to fill with their Masculine directionality, even though, deep inside, you are not turned on by a partner who usually wants to take the lead.

If you have had a series of intimate partnerships that ended because you no longer found your partner was "woman enough" or "man enough," then you probably are animating a false sexual character yourself. Probably, you are putting out less Masculine or Feminine energy than would be natural for you if you were free. Therefore, you attract a partner who is polarized by your diminished sexual essence—that is, a partner who also expresses relatively less Masculine or Feminine energy than is his or her true essence. If you are falsely neutralized, you will attract partners who are also falsely neutralized: indecisive men and pushy women.

If your sexual essence is *actually* Neutral, you will prefer your partner to be more Neutral or balanced between Masculine and Feminine. For instance, you will enjoy following your partner's strong lead half the time, and you will equally enjoy providing a strong lead for your partner to follow half the time. If you have a Neutral sexual essence, this is the kind of relationship that you most want, that will turn you on sexually the most, that will inspire love, passion and gratitude in your intimate life.

But if you have a more Feminine or Masculine sexual essence, you will find yourself yearning to be ravished by, and to be the ravisher of, your intimate partner. Safe and neutral discussions by themselves just won't do.

ATTRACTING AN APPROPRIATE PARTNER

Regardless of your native sexual essence, you may have spent time developing your Masculine energy to accomplish goals or your Feminine energy to contact your hidden emotions. This is a positive step: to become whole by developing both Masculine and Feminine energies. However, if you want to attract a partner who will complement your native sexual essence, you must learn to let go of your more superficial Masculine or Feminine skills and relax into your deep core, the heart of your true intimate desires. If you always put out more Masculine or Feminine energy than is true of you, you will attract partners who need you to be more Masculine or Feminine than is true of you. You can always attract the kind of partner you really want if the energy you put out in intimacy is true to your native sexual essence.

We should keep the success and sensitivity we may have developed as we mature in our lives, but we should also learn to relax into and offer gifts from our natural sexual essence if we want to attract partners who appreciate our *native* gifts, rather than our more superficially acquired gifts. Otherwise, if we don't allow our true sexual essence to shine, our partners will tend to complain that what we give them is not enough—that we are not Masculine enough or Feminine enough—or we will feel this way about our partners.

In your intimacy, you will always evoke in your partner the reciprocal of your own energy. If you begin to animate more Masculine energy—for instance, by concentrating on your career—your partner will feel the need to "carry" more of the Feminine energy of the relationship. If you begin to animate more Feminine energy—for instance, by taking a retreat from your worldly challenges in order to re-connect with nature, your body or your emotions—your partner will begin to carry more of the Masculine energy of the relationship.

That is, if you are a woman with a Feminine sexual essence and over time become more and more directed in your life, then you can expect that your man will become less and less Masculine—weaker, less certain and less willing to take the lead—in his loving of you. Or he may try butting his Masculine head against yours, since challenge and competition are natural forms of Masculine-Masculine communication. If you express more Masculine energy, you can also expect that your man may begin looking elsewhere for a source of Feminine energy: perhaps a more radiantly Feminine lover, frequent massages, or trips into the Feminine energy of nature via surfing, snow skiing, golfing or fishing.

If you are a man with a Masculine sexual essence and over time you become ambiguous in your outward life, so that your "mission" becomes weakened or unclear, then you can expect that your partner will become less and less Feminine—less radiant, less vibrant, and more insistent on taking the lead—in her loving of you. She may feel that she needs to take charge in the relationship, since your Masculine energy has been diminished.

You can also expect that your woman will begin looking elsewhere for a source of Masculine energy: another lover perhaps, even just a Masculine "friend," or perhaps the Masculine energy of a successful career or worldly "cause."

As a culture, we have grown from the "old days." Men and women are no longer as stuck in old roles of sexual stereotypes as they used to be. Men and women are more free to act in whatever style they choose. Naturally, the first thing men did was to balance their outdated "macho" energy with the more emotional and relational energy of their internal Feminine.

Likewise, the first thing women did was to balance their outdated "submissive housewife" energy with the more competitive and assertive energy of their internal Masculine.

Men and women are no longer dependent on each other for wholeness as they were in the old days. Men have developed their Feminine energy and women have developed their Masculine energy. This is a step in the right direction. But there is another step to take if we are to end the epidemic of so-called wimps, ballbusters and lukewarm relationships.

50/50 SQUELCHES OUR SEXUAL ESSENCE

I am suggesting that, as we have grown in wholeness, many of us have lost touch with our own true sexual essence as well as our partner's, so we aren't getting what we really want in a relationship. Instead of enjoying the uniqueness of each person's sexual essence, we often settle for a fair, relatively healthy, yet mediocre sense of equality.

For instance, we may think we want to share "old-style" Masculine and Feminine responsibilities equally with our intimate partner. So, we agree to a fair, 50/50 split right down the middle—but we really don't enjoy cooking half the time or changing the oil in the car half the time. It just doesn't feel authentic to our core. It doesn't feel like our true gift. Our sexual essence ends up feeling squelched. It's not completely fulfilling, but at least it's fair.

We also end up unfulfilled when we disregard the sexual essence of our intimate partner. For example, we want our partners to be receptive and listen to us as if they were our therapists, but we also want them to ravish us as if they were gods or goddesses of love. Our partners may become so used to "giving us space" and listening to our problems, however, that they no longer feel free to spontaneously ravish us with the wild force of their love.

When we lose touch with the unique expressions of our sexual essence or our partner's, we get confused, our partner gets confused and both of our true desires remain starved. Our obligation in intimacy is to give and receive the deepest gifts of love—gifts that are unique to each person and that cannot be predetermined by some outdated cultural ideal of the proper roles for men and women, or by a modern cultural ideal that men and women should be more alike, capable of and interested in the same careers, emotions and life-goals. Ongoing passion and growth in intimacy requires us to let go of our ideas of what we "should" be doing and instead trust the wisdom inherent in our unguarded heart and uninhibited body.

By becoming conscious of our native sexual essence, we are no longer confused about what we want to receive in intimacy and from whom we want it. We are empowered to give our unique gifts as sexual beings and also to attract a partner who will give us the special gifts that we want from our chosen source of intimate emotional and sexual loving—not from our friends, business partners and therapists, but from our lover, our consort, our spouse. When we are ready to grow beyond the fair but flat confines of a 50/50 Relationship, we learn to reconnect with the great gifts of our unique sexual essence. We learn how to trust it, how to give it and how to receive it from our partner. We can stop treating each other as generic people and begin savoring the refreshing delicacy of uninhibited sexual essence.

5

The Three Stages
of Intimacy

FOR WHAT STAGE ARE YOU READY?

How do you respond to the extreme expressions of Masculine and Feminine energy? Your response to the exaggerated play of sexual polarity can give you a clue to the stage of relationship for which you are most ready.

Imagine you happen to discover a videotape beneath a tree while taking a walk through the woods. Curious about it, you bring it home and pop it into your VCR. There on the screen are a naked man and woman having sex beneath the very tree under which you found the videotape. You feel strange about watching it. The woman makes a high-pitched screaming sound. The man pulls back her head by her hair, exposing her neck, which he licks and kisses. The woman seems to be struggling—or is she writhing in ecstasy? Just then, your child walks into the room, so you quickly turn off the TV and remove the videotape.

You think about what you have just witnessed for the rest of the day.

Were you watching a videotaped rape? Or was it a passionate couple at the peak of sexual rapture? That night, as you are lying in bed trying to sleep, images of the videotaped sex scene dance through your head.

Part of you may want to make love in such an abandoned and passionate fashion. Another part of you may be queasy, wondering if the "passion" was actually forced against the woman's will. Or was it just the couple's ravishing sexual play with one another? You decide to watch the rest of the tape in the morning and then either show it to your intimate partner, in the hopes that it will evoke deeply passionate love-making between you, or show it to the police, so they can get started on the case.

You wake up in the morning and as soon as you are alone in the house, you pop the videotape back into the VCR and turn on the TV.

The woman seems to be resisting, but it's hard to tell. Suddenly her back arches and a long moan slides from her throat. She begins to claw the man's back, her fingernails digging deeply into his skin and muscles, dragging and scratching their way down to his buttocks. He kisses her neck, her breasts and her nipples, at first gently nipping and then biting. The videotape ends.

How you respond to this videotape depends on the stage of intimacy for which you are ready.

THE THREE STYLES OF INTIMACY

By understanding your current style of intimate relationship, you can understand the next step you need to take. Which of the three styles is most like your current or recent relationship: Dependence, 50/50 or Intimate Communion? Each of these three styles is also a stage that you can grow through, if you are willing to be lovingly humorous about your own patterns in intimacy.

1. Dependence Relationship

"Men are men and women are women."

In the imaginary video, were you viewing a man and a woman in the abandoned throes of sexual ecstasy or was the man subjugating, biting and penetrating the woman against her will? In a Dependence Relationship, sex and power are often painfully mixed up; partners often confuse some version of the master/slave relationship with real love. They are engaged in some kind of power play. In a Dependence Relationship, one partner often needs to feel in control, while the other partner often gives up his or her authentic power in order to feel loved and accepted.

A Dependence Relationship involves partners who become dependent on each other for money, emotional support, parenting or sex. Although the sex is sometimes good in this style of relationship (especially during the making-up period after a fight), partners often end up feeling limited by old-style gender roles or by an imbalance of financial or physical power. Therefore, they attempt to transition to the next style of relationship. To do so they learn to build personal boundaries and take care of themselves, rather than always catering to the needs of their partners.

2. 50/50 Relationship

"Safe boundaries and equal expectations for men and women."

Partners in a 50/50 Relationship want to feel safe, so the videotape might seem harsh and violent to them. On the surface, they might seem completely turned off and react as if any form of forceful and passionate sexual ravishment is an act of rape. Deep down, however, they might be wistfully turned on, reminded of the depth of sexual loving that may be missing from their safe but lukewarm love life.

The 50/50 Relationship is the "modern" style of relationship that is based on two independent people coming together and working out an equitable partnership. Each partner is expected to shoulder half the responsibilities, more or less, right down the middle. Both often have their own source of income and together, they negotiate a 50/50 plan to divide household duties, parenting and financial obligations. To accomplish this, they attempt to strike their own inner balance between Masculine and Feminine qualities, both at home and in the workplace.

However, as many of us have discovered, there is a potential problem with this ideal of a 50/50 Relationship. We begin to lose our aliveness. Sexuality loses its passion. Our inner fire begins to fade. And we feel an incompleteness at our center. Why? Because many of us have a sexual essence that is naturally more Masculine or Feminine than it is equally balanced or Neutral. *Thus, a side-effect of this effort toward 50/50 is the suppression or starvation of our naturally more Masculine or Feminine sexual essence.*

For some of us, a cooperative partnership that emphasizes communication and shared responsibilities is sufficient. Others in this situation eventually suffer a feeling of incompleteness and develop a yearning to touch and be touched far more deeply and more passionately—both sexually and spiritually—than a 50/50 Relationship often allows.

3. Intimate Communion

"I relax into oneness and spontaneously give my deepest gift."

If we have grown beyond a 50/50 Relationship, we are no longer cautious about giving our love to our intimate partner. At certain moments we might beg and whimper; at other moments we might aggressively ravish our partner in love. Still at other times our loving is serene and sweet. But whether shouting, screaming, pleading, pushing, pulling, biting or hugging, we are gifting our partner with our uninhibited and free love, flowing directly from our sexual essence without fear or doubt.

If we have grown into the practice of Intimate Communion, the imaginary videotape does not pose a dilemma since we understand that the fundamental difference between rape and ravishment is simple: Love. Is love the motive of every squeeze, shriek and nibble, regardless of how forceful, aggressive or passionate? Or is it a motive of need— the need for sex, the need for power, the need for control?

Most important, in the practice of Intimate Communion we learn that love is something you *do*, not something you "fall into" or "out of." Love is something that you practice, like playing tennis or the violin, not something you happen to feel or not. If you are waiting to feel love, in passionate sex or safe conversation, you are making a mistake. Love is an action that you do—and when you do it, you feel it. When you are loving, others find you lovable. Love is an action you can practice.

Therefore, in Intimate Communion we learn to practice loving even when we feel hurt, rejected or resistant. First we practice love, and then our native sexual essence blooms, naturally, inevitably, because we are learning to give from our core, which includes the root of our sexuality.

THE STORY OF PAUL AND LEAH

Paul and Leah represent the thousands of couples I have worked with who have, in their unique ways, grown through the three stages of intimate relationship. This process is universal, though the details are never exactly the same.

Paul and Leah are good examples of two people who were once dependent upon each other and therefore trapped in the conventional roles of "good husband" and "good wife." Over time, they learned to grow beyond these roles of dependence into the healthy wholeness and independence of a 50/50 Relationship, but their journey did not end there.

Stage One: Dependence Relationship

Most of us are very familiar with this kind of relationship, either in our own lives or the lives of our friends or parents. What does a Dependence Relationship look like for Paul and Leah?

Still single, Paul wants to make money, have a family and be with a woman who looks up to him. Leah wants to find a man she could depend on, a man she could have a family with, someone who would give her affection and take care of her. Paul and Leah meet and get married. Sometimes it's great. Sometimes they fight. Sex starts off fresh and spontaneous, and eventually tapers down to a routine.

Leah is afraid of losing Paul because she is emotionally and financially dependent on him. Paul is afraid of losing Leah because he is emotionally dependent on her and also depends on her to take care of their children and their home. Over time, Paul feels more and more burdened and trapped. Leah feels more and more unloved and unfulfilled in her life. For the sake of the children, they wait as long as they can but eventually divorce.

Stage Two: 50/50 Relationship

It takes awhile to start life over after the divorce, but finally Leah feels her independence growing. She begins to discover her undeveloped talents, and then becomes established in a career. She feels stronger and stronger. Her circle of friends grows, both men and women. She knows she will never be in a Dependence Relationship with a man again. She develops financially as well as intellectually, reading the newest books on psychology, the arts and the "new partnership." She is her own woman.

Paul feels the loss at first, but eventually recovers. He resounds in his new freedom. He dates younger women, buys the things he always wanted to but never could before and begins to look after himself in new ways. He goes to the spa and works out regularly. He finds himself enjoying long walks on the beach by himself. He even takes a men's workshop, singing, banging drums and freely expressing his grief with other men as he has never done before. He has never felt so whole and balanced.

Leah and Paul each try several short- and medium-term relationships. They have a good time with their new partners, sharing interesting conversations and philosophical outlooks. But nothing really clicks for either of them. They both have many "just friends" of the opposite sex.

Once they have enough money and friends, they switch from "getting more" to "getting better." Since the children are somewhat older and able to take care of themselves, Leah joins a women's group, attends weekly Yoga and dance classes, and even takes out the oil paints she had put away when the kids were younger and demanded all her attention. Paul becomes an environmental activist, joins a Tai chi class and works toward writing the novel he always wanted to write but couldn't because of his family obligations.

In the past, when Paul and Leah were in a Dependence Relationship together, Paul's "certainty" expressed itself as always needing to be right about everything. Leah could never express any disagreement without Paul becoming outraged. He didn't want to listen to her ideas. In fact, if she came up with a good idea, he would somehow make it his own.

After they were divorced, Paul began to realize how he was unfairly rigid and suppressive of Leah. He began to soften. He learned to listen. As a man ready for a 50/50 Relationship, Paul learned to give and take with the new women he met in his life. He became truly committed to achieving a 50/50 Relationship. By spending time in nature and learning to contact his previously hidden emotions, Paul cultivated his underdeveloped Feminine energy.

Paul and Leah each eventually find new intimate partners. In the new relationships, they retain their own bank accounts and create a joint account to share with their new partners, who are also financially stable, more or less. They trade off cooking, every other day. Even their vacations are based on equality: one vacation chosen by one partner, the next by the other. They have each achieved a 50/50 Relationship with their new partners.

However, as we have seen, only people with Neutral sexual essences will be fully satisfied when they achieve a 50/50 Relationship. For instance, no man with a strong Masculine sexual essence will be fulfilled by committing himself to the form of a 50/50 Relationship, once and for all. This is so because in emotional and sexual intimacy, the core of the *Masculine* sexual essence is completed and fulfilled only by a partner who gives gifts of *Feminine* love — not the more sexually Neutral love of a 50/50 Relationship.

So, even though Paul says he is committed to his 50/50 Relationship, his partner can feel his inner uncertainty. Paul seems not only cautious about dominating his new partner's life, but also unwilling to enter her life very deeply at all, with full commitment. His uncertainty prevents her from relaxing fully in the trustable pervasiveness of stable and passionate Masculine loving. She never feels fully satisfied. Stuck in the behavioral ideals of 50/50, Paul is safe but he is also relationally weak, unwilling to plant the staff of his commitment and stand the ground of his love.

Paul is willing to split the "power" of the relationship in a 50/50 fashion, but his passion is likewise split. He has become indecisive and unclear about the whole of his life and his direction, as have many of today's men. His energy for relationship seems to be somewhat contained within his inner conflicts. His ability to give love is weakened by his own unclarity. He has lost touch with his sexual essence and therefore is unsure about anything, including his love for his new partner. And she can feel it.

With her new partner, Leah is experiencing her own version of a 50/50 Relationship. In her old Dependence Relationship with Paul, Leah had found herself surrendering to his needs. Over time, she lost touch with her own real desires, and instead catered to Paul's choices and wants, hoping to feel his love. Leah lost her healthy boundaries, her independent sense of self, and became Paul's woman instead of her own woman.

After they were divorced, Leah decided that she would not lose herself again. She would no longer be weak, unable or unwilling to stand up for what she really wanted. So Leah practiced strengthening her boundaries. She learned to say "No" when necessary. She learned to speak what was on her mind, no longer afraid of her man's reactions. She learned how to stand up for herself. She became whole unto herself, no longer a "pushover," and her new men friends seemed to appreciate her strength and independence. Her new intimate partner appears to like the fact that she is so committed to a true 50/50 Relationship, rather than being a needy or dependent woman.

Leah has made it quite clear that she doesn't *need* a man, but she is certainly interested in a loving relationship between two whole and independent people. But her new partner doesn't really seem to be the "right" man, and, in fact, none of the men she meets do. No man really seems willing and strong enough to match her. Her deep core, her

Feminine sexual essence, remains unsatisfied by her new partner and by the men she dated before him. If she had a more Neutral sexual essence, then she would be satisfied by a more "50/50 man," a man who wanted her to make half the money and mow the lawn half the time, a man who wanted to calmly discuss everything as good friends, rather than express his passionate Masculine desire for her as a woman.

Because she has emphasized building her personal boundaries, she attracts men who likewise are more interested in establishing clear boundaries than in dissolving in the ecstasy of boundary-less Intimate Communion. Because she wants the space to animate her well developed Masculine energy, she attracts men who want to give her space rather than enter her and deeply touch her core heart-desires. That is, she tends to attract "safe" men.

Just as Paul has temporarily lost touch with the native desires of his Masculine sexual essence, becoming indecisive and non-committal in the process, Leah has lost touch with the native desires of her Feminine sexual essence. She feels like the core of her womanhood is withering from lack of deep loving.

In a well-intentioned effort to grow beyond the rigid sex roles of a Dependence Relationship, Paul and Leah each temporarily emphasize developing the energy *opposite* of their native sexual essence.

Paul temporarily neglects the inherent needs for the strong life-direction and vision that his Masculine sexual essence would naturally demand, and instead he develops his Feminine energy of sensitive listening and cooperative sharing. Thus, he attracts women who unconsciously want to be with a man who has a relatively weak sense of direction. These women have plenty of their own direction and are attracted to the "space" that Paul gives them.

Leah temporarily neglects the inherent needs for deeply and pas-sionately shared love that her Feminine essence would naturally demand, and instead she develops her Masculine energy of life direction and vision. Thus, she attracts men who unconsciously want to be with a woman who has a relatively weak desire for profound and passionate union. These men seem to be in union with themselves, and are attracted to the direction in Leah's life since they lack their own.

Paul and Leah each have fun with their new partners, but deep inside they both wonder, "Is this it?" They feel pretty good for the most part, but are beginning to experience a sense of emotional and sexual unfulfillment.

Paul is happy that his new partner has her own direction and doesn't depend on him. But sometimes he wants to feel her soften, relax her independent stance, open to him and really surrender into love. Paul begins to feel that his partner is more concerned with being right and "equal to him" than in playing together in the depths of passion and trust. Paul wants to dance with a goddess but feels he spends more time jousting with a warrior. He starts to be attracted to women who are more unabashedly Feminine than his partner, and their relationship finally breaks apart.

Leah is quite happy that her new partner gives her emotional support and safe, nurturing affection. But sometimes she wants to feel him take a strong stand, to express his Masculine side, to move in the world with confidence and success, and to playfully ravish her with full presence and undividedly passionate loving. Leah expresses her needs to her new partner, but he feels criticized and hurt, and responds by becoming even weaker in his presence, commitment and surety of love. Both partners are unsatisfied but they hang on, hoping something will change.

Stage Three: Intimate Communion

One night, Leah gets a little drunk and really lets go. She has the best sex she's ever had. She totally abandons herself into the lovemaking and feels her boundaries expand to infinity as her heart and body dissolve in wave after wave of intense loving. She later wonders why she doesn't always feel this way during lovemaking.

During a Yoga class one day, Leah feels currents of energy moving through her body, filling her with a delicious flow of grace, love and openness that reminds her of her recent sexual ecstasy. Overwhelmed by a new sense of body and surrender, she wants to explore these new feelings of deep energy and profoundly passionate and sacred sexuality.

Leah can no longer settle for the sensitive but lackluster man whom she is with currently. She wants to open the depths of her heart with a man who is willing to be fully present and committed in his intention, a man who is trustworthy and also strong enough to sweep her off her feet. Leah realizes that she wants a man who is not afraid to persist in his loving, to enter deeply into her heart and to embrace her gift of radiant and vulnerable goddesshood as well as her equality and personhood. Leah enters a new period in her life, wherein she is continually opened and moved by the immense power of love that flows in her heart and body.

Around the same time, Paul's older brother, whom Paul had always looked to for advice, dies. Paul feels like the carpet has been pulled out from under him. He "wakes up" and realizes that he doesn't like his job, doesn't have any really close friends and is getting older. He feels like he hasn't given his gift to the world. And he isn't even so sure what that gift would be, since he has spent so much time absorbed in his job and relationships.

Paul goes through a period of intense self-investigation involving private therapy, group work and contemplative solitude. He seeks out knowledgeable teachers and cultivates friendships with other men who are discovering their deep truth. After a lot of hard work, he starts to understand himself. He begins to face himself directly without flinching. He dives deep into his unprotected heart, discovering his essential desires. And he commits himself to living on the basis of his deepest truths. He begins a whole new way of life. Every day becomes a day of purpose, clarity and humor for Paul—after all, once you see *all* of yourself it's hard to take yourself overly seriously.

Paul no longer settles for a woman who is satisfied if he does the dishes on Monday, Wednesday and Friday. He wants to be free to live at the edge, and he wants to find a partner who is willing to risk comfort for infinity.

One day, Paul and Leah happen to run into each other. Before they exchange any words at all, she can feel his change. Like most women, Leah is extremely sensitive to the relative fullness of a man's Masculine sexual essence. Paul's energy is strong and his presence is full. He looks directly into her eyes and she can feel that he is at peace with himself, relaxed and confident—not divided inside. His mere presence feels like a blessing to Leah, like a breath of fresh, clean air. His smile is unencumbered by unfinished business and loose ends. He is not elsewhere, inside his head or dwelling in the past. He is present with her. And through his presence she can feel the fullness of his heart.

The way he moves, the tone of his voice, the way he touches her shoulder—they are all pervaded by confident love. His presence and love are like keys that unlock Leah's heart and she naturally opens to him, without fear, because she trusts him as a full man. Leah and Paul begin seeing each other once again.

Over time, Leah continues to witness Paul's steady loving, his persistent care and his unwavering integrity. Certainly there are moments when Paul does something stupid. But he is the first to laugh at himself, correct his ways and continue with a life that is guided by a tangible sense of strong purpose, humor and compassion. Paul has reclaimed his sexual essence; he can now love Leah with an undivided heart.

In a Dependence Relationship, Paul's love was limited by his need to be right. In a 50/50 Relationship, he was crippled by his compromised sexual essence, leading to self-doubt and an inability to commit in love. He sought an intimacy in which he could "get away with" being weak—he would rather give a woman her own space than stand his ground in love, sensitively entering her life with his love, melting through the resistances that might guard her heart.

Now, in Intimate Communion, his love is not encumbered by unresolved inner dilemmas, but is strongly demonstrated in his humorous, confident and passionate presence. Leah trusts his love implicitly and knows that he will not turn away in moments of difficulty. She can feel his integrity and commitment to the practice of love, moment by moment. Leah can feel Paul's trust in her and his reverence for the Feminine gifts that she offers.

In a Dependence Relationship, Leah's love was limited by her need to please her partner in the hope of getting more love from him. In a 50/50 Relationship, she was crippled by the protective gesture of guarding her heart for fear that she might be hurt again. She sought an intimacy that would not really test her capacity for trust—she attracted "safe" men who did not elicit or require her deep Feminine essence.

Now, her expression of love is not limited by past resistance to incarnating her naturally radiant and flowing Feminine sexual essence in every inch of her body. She is still successful in the world—she hasn't lost her ability to animate her Masculine warrior energy when she needs to—but she is also able to relax as a goddess. Her gifts shine brightly, full of the mysterious Feminine force. Leah's emotional and bodily expressions are free, spontaneous, sometimes wild, sometimes graceful, but always a blessing of love, beauty and healing. Paul can feel Leah's total commitment to the practice of love even when she suffers a moment of hurt. He can feel her trust in him and her reverence for the Masculine gifts that he offers.

Leah and Paul have now joined together not as co-dependents or as co-independents, but as co-practitioners. As practitioners of Intimate Communion, they practice opening to love rather than closing in pain or punishment when hurt. Leah and Paul practice the art of direct relationship, rather than the game of avoiding each other when wounded and withdrawing into private worlds of emotion and thought.

In the practice of Intimate Communion, Paul and Leah are willing to awaken beyond the childish dream of a parent-like partner whom they could always depend on for support and attention. That is, they are willing to grow beyond a Dependence Relationship. Likewise, they are willing to awaken beyond the adolescent dream of an equitable partner who will leave them alone in their private world of self-involvement, demanding neither deep commitment nor deep surrender. That is, they are willing to grow beyond the independent stance of a 50/50 Relationship.

Through an intimate life of trial and error, Paul and Leah have come to understand that love is a discipline requiring the moment-to-moment practice of commitment and surrender. They are adults choosing to practice Intimate Communion with one another, rather than denying their fullest gifts in co-dependent roles or guarded independence.

Paul and Leah have tasted delicious moments of seamless love, of sexual union in unguarded oneness and of emotional communion in perfect trust. They are unwilling to turn back and seek the safe boundaries and business-like "equality" promised by a 50/50 Relationship because they know that such a relationship often denies the fullest expression of their Masculine and Feminine sexual essences.

Leah is unafraid of gifting Paul by attracting him out of his rigid mind and body with the relaxed radiance of her uniquely Feminine happiness, beauty and love. Paul is unafraid of entering through Leah's resistances and blooming her heart with the humor and fully present strength of his Masculine love. Because Paul and Leah are no longer afraid of expressing their unique and very different sexual essences, they are free to be spontaneous and unguarded in their expressions of love in Intimate Communion. As man and woman, they are free to be the gift of love: bodily, emotionally and spiritually.

ACHIEVING 50/50 AND THEN MOVING BEYOND IT

Spurred on by a variety of reasons—dissatisfaction with seeing our parents' relationships, living with earlier models of uncomfortable and unacceptable sex roles, women's claim to their equality or just our own hard-earned lessons from past relationships—we have evolved the modern 50/50 Relationship as a genuine improvement. For most people, 50/50 is preferable to the traditional situation where men's needs are paramount and women are overpowered or disregarded. A 50/50 Relationship is preferable to one in which both partners are either indirectly manipulating or overtly controlling one another.

Naturally, we would want to evolve to the type of relationship where each person is equally important, where sharing partnership, internal balance and self-reliance allow the relationship to be one of mutuality rather than dependency.

This 50/50 Relationship is a definite improvement over a relationship based on sex roles and dependence. It is a necessary step in the progression toward a truly intimate and fulfilling relationship. Indeed, for some people the 50/50 Relationship may be the perfect form in which to enjoy intimacy. This may be all they have ever wanted from their relationship and they may be quite content to be loving—but relatively independent and less sexually passionate—friends.

However, there is another step for those who want it. The next step in intimacy for modern men and women who have a more Masculine or Feminine sexual essence goes beyond both co-dependence and 50/50-style co-independence. This next step goes beyond limiting a person's power because of his or her gender. It also goes beyond subtly negating the different desires of the Masculine and Feminine sexual essences so that partners can function like identical cogs in a "working" relationship: paying the bills, picking up the kids, keeping the wheel turning one more day.

The next step is about reclaiming your sexually-alive core, your naturally Masculine or Feminine sexual essence, which may have been neglected in order to further your career or to reach a working compromise in a 50/50 Relationship.

The 50/50 Relationship is a necessary basis for taking this next step in intimacy. In order to go beyond 50/50, you must have already developed the capacity to creatively manage your parenting and your finances. You must be already capable of standing free and whole: autonomous.

For those who are ready for Intimate Communion, becoming a fully functional person is just the starting point. After becoming a "whole person," you can also learn to relax in your body and spirit as a woman or a man, pleasurably cultivate your sexual essence and offer your spontaneous love as a gift to a partner who is doing the same.

In the old-style Dependence Relationship, "men are men and women are women," however narrowly that was defined. To achieve the modern 50/50 Relationship, we learned to see past our sexual differences and establish relationships based on friendship and mutual respect—essential qualities for any lasting partnership, be it a business partnership or a love relationship. In the meantime, many of us have become bored by the lack of energy, passion and consummate union in our intimate relationships.

The next step is to reclaim our sexual essence and realize that it is a gift to be given—not something to be suppressed, ignored or withheld, but something to be appreciated and honored. Re-owning our uniquely Masculine or Feminine sexual essence is a key to re-establishing the fullness of sexual polarity and moving beyond the stalemate of a typical 50/50 Relationship, without letting go of the equality and mutual respect we have gained.

One difference between the old style of relationship and the relationship beyond 50/50 is this: In an old-style Dependence Relationship, you are obliged to act like "a man" or "a woman," however this may be defined by cultural standards. But beyond 50/50 you feel deep into your heart and *practice* giving the *unique* gift of your own sexual essence as a gift of love. That is, you are free to play your natural Masculine or Feminine pole in the dance of sexual loving, in your own unique way, instead of following a culturally pre-defined role. And you are free to *be* love altogether—to surrender your resistance to love and to relax completely in the native happiness of your heart—practicing love with your chosen partner in Intimate Communion.

If you were completely free, how would you live? How would you express your love? Beyond 50/50, you commit yourself to giving your gift in freedom, rather than holding back out of fear. You give the gift that is your unique bloom, the flower of your unique heart, the essence of your sexual being, as well as the expression of your creative freedom.

Chances are you have experienced many people—your past and present partners, for instance—who have lost touch with their natural sexual essence. Maybe you were with a weakened man who lacked direction, humor, integrity or "spine." Or perhaps you have been with a hardened woman who was reluctant to let down her guard and open her heart, breath and body in love.

The motivation to achieve a 50/50 Relationship is so strong today that few people are simply relaxed in their native sexual essence, allowing their unique emotional and sexual offerings to flow spontaneously and without fear in Intimate Communion. Instead, people of today are more balanced than the stereotypical macho men and submissive women of yesterday, but we are still dissatisfied.

In a well-intentioned effort to achieve inner balance and 50/50 Relationships, we have inadvertently neutralized our intimacies. As a result, we are craving the dynamic play between the Masculine and Feminine. We have become fascinated by substitutions, including tear-jerking emotional dramas and wildly passionate sex scenes on TV, at the movies, in books and in our secret dreams.

A WHOLE PERSON IS NOT NECESSARILY A NEUTRAL PERSON

If deep down you long to be swept off your feet, to be entered by a strong, sensitive and confident lover, then you have a more Feminine sexual essence. If deep down you often long for your partner to open to you, to respond to your desire with total trust and passionate surrender, then you have a more Masculine sexual essence.

Moment to moment, we are always free to act more Masculine or Feminine. Even if we are completely confident and relaxed in our natural sexual essences, we probably enjoy incarnating more Masculine energy at certain times and more Feminine energy at other times. But this is not the same as developing a false sexual character based on long-term fear and resistance.

Most of us who are striving for a 50/50 Relationship have been hurt in the past and are healing ourselves by balancing our own internal Masculine and Feminine. For example, after a divorce, you don't want to ruin another marriage by forcing your partner to follow your commands. So, you learn to balance your strongly directional Masculine energy by cultivating your more receptive Feminine energy.

Nor do you want to become dependent on someone only to lose them, as well as losing your self-esteem and financial support, when they leave you for another partner—someone who can "give them what they want." So, you learn to balance your trusting Feminine energy by strengthening your Masculine energy, your ability to discipline yourself, cut through obstacles and achieve long-term success on your own.

After being wounded by a past relationship, we often try to balance ourselves, which is healthy—as long as we don't forget that if we hold on to "balance" too long, we begin to appear more Neutral, rather than Masculine or Feminine.

If your sexual essence is *truly* Neutral, rather than more Masculine or Feminine, you very naturally would prefer a friendly partnership based on sameness rather than a sexually passionate intimacy based on attractive differences. If you have a naturally Neutral sexual essence, you really are most happy financially supporting your partner half the time and being supported by your partner half the time, or perhaps splitting all costs and responsibilities right down the middle. One week he does the laundry, the next week she does. One week he collects the dead mice from the traps, the next week she does.

Some of us have chosen a 50/50 Relationship because we naturally have a more Neutral sexual essence. Others of us have chosen a 50/50 Relationship to avoid being hurt.

In a 50/50 Relationship based on self-protection, we often act to achieve friendship and equality by establishing clear boundaries and remaining (falsely) sexually Neutral, rather than passionately Masculine or Feminine—as is true of our essence. Thus, we negate the enlivening energy of sexual polarity that probably attracted us to each other in the first place.

Furthermore, in such a 50/50 Relationship, we often act to achieve independence and self-sufficiency by claiming our personal, separate space, rather than by yielding our sense of separate self and relaxing into trustful heart-union with our loved one.

The very action of concentrating our efforts on achieving 50/50 sameness and independence with our partner often neutralizes the sexual polarity and weakens the trust that serves as the attractive force and foundation in our emotional and sexual play together. It is certainly necessary to achieve independence and mutual respect in intimacy, but it is also necessary to *then* let go of our defended boundaries, our guarded stance and our belief in the myth that a 50/50 Relationship will fulfill the desires of our deep Masculine or Feminine sexual essence.

It is essential that today's men and women grow into wholeness, beyond old roles of power and powerlessness. Equality is absolutely essential—but it is a phase, not an endpoint. Fairness and equitableness are only necessary prerequisites to the practice of Intimate Communion. For many men and women today, the 50/50 Relationship is just a step toward getting what they really want.

SURRENDERING AS SLAVE OR LOVER

Most of us feel a real fear of stepping beyond 50/50. It feels very risky to give up our boundaries, to trust so much that we are willing to become absolutely vulnerable—and yet vulnerability is necessary if we are to give and receive with an open heart in Intimate Communion. We have all been hurt before, and none of us want to be hurt again. But the fact is, we *will* be hurt again. When your heart is wide open, you are vulnerable to being hurt by those who don't return your love: intimate partners, children, parents and friends. But you are also open to something else. When you are no longer protecting yourself, you are open to giving and receiving love in its most powerful and sublime form.

Many of us have experienced sexual occasions that can only be characterized as "ecstatic." The love flows so powerfully or the pleasure is so intensely sublime, that the memory of it is burned into our hearts forever. Perhaps we felt total oneness with our partner, as if our two bodies were dissolved into a single heart of breathing joy. Or maybe our love shone as bright light. Or we experienced rushes of delicious energy running up and down our body. Or we felt like we were being filled with so much love that we would burst open, exploding our boundaries in a silent shout of love.

Whatever we *did* feel in such a moment, it is clear that what we did *not* feel was guarded, closed or resistant. This kind of love is available only to an open heart.

We may, of course, experience this ecstatic sense of loving and oneness in a non-sexual moment, too. Perhaps you have felt a sense of no-separation while gazing into an infant's eyes. Or maybe you forgot yourself in a moment of seamless rapture while beholding a beautiful sunset or while looking out over a snowy mountainside. Some may have felt a divine sense of unity while reading spiritual literature, or while praying or meditating.

In each of these moments, whether sexual, with our children, in nature or while praying, we have let down our guard. We have allowed ourselves to experience a deeply pleasurable oneness with something, someone or some Divine Presence.

A key to the awakening of Intimate Communion is surrender, or letting down our guard. This is also the opposite of resistance. But since many of us have worked so hard just to get equality into our relationships, we are afraid that if we surrendered completely, even for a moment, we might lose all the ground we have gained.

What is the difference between "loving too much" and surrendering into spiritual ecstasy? It is also the difference between a slave and a free lover. It is the difference between whether you are hoping to *get* love or are relaxed with no boundaries, *as* love. It is the difference between a moment of Dependence and a moment of Intimate Communion.

This difference is often misunderstood, especially by people who are yet unwilling to let down their guard. To them, all surrender is negative, a sign of weakness. But for those who are willing to surrender their hearts to love, ecstasy awaits. It is true that a slave surrenders—but so does a freely ecstatic lover. And the difference is crucial. The difference is whether you are surrendering because you are fearful and dependent on getting something, or whether you are surrendering as a free sign of your recognition of oneness, joyfully giving your gifts of love.

Remember that each stage of a relationship—Dependence, 50/50 and Intimate Communion—is also a style of relationship. And we can shift from one style to another, moment to moment, regardless of the stage in which the relationship usually is.

To understand this further, imagine that you were Leah making love with Paul. In a moment of ecstatic sexual passion you plead, "I'm yours! Take me! I'll do anything you want!"

Is this moment an example of Dependence and powerlessness? Is it a moment of well-planned 50/50 equality? Or is it a moment of blissful surrender in Intimate Communion? What is the difference between the gift of ecstatic surrender and the pain of submissive self-denial?

If you were Leah in a moment of *Dependence*, locked into your role as a good wife, your inner Masculine voice would remain silent. It wouldn't be heard at all. However, your inner Feminine voice would say, "I want to feel loved. When Paul holds me so tightly I feel wanted. I will do anything he says so that he will always love me."

If you were Leah in a 50/50 moment, your inner Masculine and Feminine voices would both be free to speak. In a 50/50 moment, your priority is equality. Everything has got to be 50/50.

Your inner Feminine might say, "I feel like letting go. It feels good to be vulnerable in his arms like this. But can I trust him? Am I throwing my power away?"

Your inner Masculine would say, "I don't want to lose control. I like to follow my own direction. I don't want him to feel like he could boss me around. I may do what he wants me to tonight, but then tomorrow night he does what I want him to do. Then we have a fair, 50/50 Relationship."

If you were Leah in a moment of *Intimate Communion*, you would be uninhibited in your loving, willing to let go of all resistance in the deep fulfillment and expression of your unguarded heart.

Your inner Feminine would say, "Aahhh. I feel Paul's love and I want to receive him deeply. I want to open as much as I can and feel his love deep inside my heart. I trust the love overflowing in my heart, and it is ecstatic to open to this powerful flow of love with no boundaries, with no defense. I surrender to the flow of love. I *am* love."

Your inner Masculine says, "What a pleasure it is to relax, let go and trust Paul. I can trust and enjoy the force of love I feel, because I can feel the deep truth of the love that is moving us in this moment."

In a moment of Dependence, Leah is thinking that by giving up her own needs and attending to Paul's, she will gain his love. In a 50/50 moment, Leah is carefully guarding the independence of her separate self by not surrendering completely. But in a moment of Intimate

Communion, Leah is surrendering, not so much to Paul, but directly to love, *as* love, confessing and celebrating love with her whole body, heart and mind. This is most important to understand: Leah's opening to the force of love becomes her gift to *herself* as much as to Paul.

In Intimate Communion, Leah's surrender is an invitation for Paul to yield his sense of separateness and commune deeply in the act of loving. The gift of Leah's surrender draws Paul beyond his angular Masculine world. Through her Feminine gift, Paul is drawn heart to heart into direct relationship with Leah's heart and into the present flow of love. He yields his position, just as Leah has surrendered hers.

Their separateness first becomes vulnerable embrace. And then the membrane of their touch dissolves, so that Paul and Leah melt into each other. Finally, even their surrendered union is pervaded by so much love that they forget themselves, forget each other and yield even further, dissolving into the bright fullness of love itself with no boundaries. In Intimate Communion, the awakened Feminine essence is a living invitation to love.

Paul may or may not be able to surrender into love as deeply as Leah. But in either case, Leah's practice of Intimate Communion is not to withdraw, not to withhold love, but to literally breathe a deep and sweet breath, relaxing into every inch of her body, allowing her love to radiate. The more that Leah practices opening her breath and body, giving love rather than closing down, the more she becomes a vehicle through which love can flow, and the more her life is a gift for everyone in her presence. The more she is willing to surrender her tension and trust love, the more her old wounds heal and her old resistances to love melt. This is how Leah's heart blooms in the present moment of Intimate Communion, regardless of what changes in her relationship with Paul may occur in the future.

WHAT DOES INTIMATE COMMUNION
LOOK LIKE?

In the practice of Intimate Communion, each partner discovers, day by day, what true gifts he or she would like to offer in love. Intimate Communion may *look* like an old-style Dependence Relationship, with the woman giving gifts that were conventionally considered "womanly" and the man giving gifts that were conventionally considered a "man's job." Or Intimate Communion may *look* like a 50/50 Relationship, with the man and woman dividing all the responsibilities down the middle, sharing in the housework, family and financial responsibilities equally.

Or Intimate Communion may *look totally different*, with the woman taking two lovers and the man spending six months of the year in a monastery in Tibet!

We have very few models of relationships based on the practice of Intimate Communion, so some people don't understand the attraction toward such practice.

In a Dependence Relationship, men and women don't really understand why someone would be willing to risk losing sexual, financial and family security for the greater self-integration and self-fulfillment of a more mutually autonomous 50/50 Relationship. Just so, in a 50/50 Relationship, men and women don't really understand why someone would be willing to risk *everything*, including a sense of personal self-fulfillment in life and in relationship, for the unbounded heart-truth of infinite love in the practice of Intimate Communion.

If a woman is dedicated to the practice of Intimate Communion, she will only trust a man who is committed to Truth more than he is to pleasing her—after all, how can she trust a man who can be swayed from his true path by the smile of a beautiful woman, even if it is her own?

If a man is dedicated to the practice of Intimate Communion, he will only trust a woman who is willing to devote herself to divine love, even if that means she is not entirely "his own." He is turned on by witnessing her devotion and open-hearted surrender to universal or divine love. He trusts that she is committed to a life of communion with the divine, rather than merely committed to the 50/50 ideal of the shared "good life," perhaps renovating an old barn and spending time together with family and friends in the countryside.

In the practice of Intimate Communion, the intimate partners do whatever it is they feel is truly necessary to magnify the expression of love and freedom in their lives. They do what feels like true service, rather than mere self-pleasuring or shared consolation. They relax into their native sexual essence, whether it is more Masculine, Feminine or Neutral, and give their inherent and creative gifts that are spontaneous, loving and irrepressible, without concern about the way their gifting looks in the eyes of people who are inclined toward Dependence or 50/50 Relationships.

THE RISK OF SPONTANEOUS LOVE

A Dependence Relationship is about power struggles, suppression and sexual roles. "Don't you tell me what to do! I'll do whatever I damn please." Who gets their way is more important than giving the gift of love.

A 50/50 Relationship is about sharing, equality and achieving a 50/50 division of responsibilities and roles. Therefore, communication is more important than the freely offered gift of love. For instance, if the woman gets upset and goes into her room, shutting the door and saying, "Leave me alone," then that is just what the man should do— walk away and give her space, regardless of how the force of his love would otherwise move him. In order to achieve equality, partners learn to honor each other's words and boundaries.

A 50/50 man is careful not to be a macho brute. So he holds back his Masculine force and direction, and instead always follows his partner's requests, even when his heart says to do otherwise. He is afraid to follow his deepest truth or assert his real desires in love because he doesn't want to be too pushy.

A 50/50 woman is careful not to make herself vulnerable to hurt and abuse. She never quite lets down her guard, even when her heart is moved to open completely so that she could give of herself without hesitation in love with her intimate partner. She may love her man, but she is afraid to surrender and trust love because she doesn't want to give up her sense of safety and independence.

In a moment of Intimate Communion, nothing is more important than surrender into the mysterious force of love, not even so-called communication between separate but equal partners. Intimate Communion involves dropping our boundaries and trusting the spontaneous wisdom of love. For instance, if a hurt woman goes into her room and shuts her door, but her man is truly moved to embrace her, should he trust his love and enter the closed doors to her room and to her heart? It's a risky thing to do, but what are his alternatives?

We are all going to die. Everyone we love will be dead one day. Their fragrance, their warmth, their smile, will be gone forever, and we will be alone or dead ourselves. Any embrace may be our last. Why hold back our loving? If this breath, right now, were your last, what gift would you be willing to give your intimate partner? What is stopping you now?

6

The Search for Love and Freedom

THE SEARCH

We are all trying to win something. Some of us want to make a lot of money. Some of us are hoping to find a lover or a lifetime companion. Whatever it is, once we get it, we hope things will be different. We hope we can finally relax our search after we have won our prize. But there is a surprise in store for all of us: It is impossible to win our prize, once and for all. A key discovery in Intimate Communion is that we cannot win; we can only dissolve. And in the moment of dissolution, what remains is that for which we have been hoping all along: unbounded love and effortless, abundant being.

To make this discovery, we must understand our present search. And to practice Intimate Communion, we must understand that the Masculine and the Feminine tend to search in different ways. The Masculine searches for freedom. The Feminine searches for love. By understanding our own search and that of our partner, we prepare ourselves for the practice of Intimate Communion.

Each of us, man and woman alike, animates both Masculine and Feminine energies. However, the majority of men animate more Masculine energy than Feminine and the majority of women, more Feminine energy than Masculine. There are, of course, many exceptions to this. For ease of illustration, I will take the liberty of assuming, in many of the examples throughout this book, that the man is animating more of the Masculine energy in the relationship and the woman is animating more of the Feminine. In homosexual and bisexual relationships, and in heterosexual relationships where the man animates more Feminine energy and the woman animates more Masculine, the dynamics of the Masculine and Feminine energies would be the same, but the genders of the example characters might be different.

HOW THE MASCULINE GROWS

The essential Masculine style of search is that of the warrior, the hero or the visionary. The Masculine force is one-pointed, directional and guided by a vision of freedom. Masculine energy cuts through any obstacles that are in its path. Nothing deters the Masculine from its goal of freedom. However, not every man uses his Masculine energy to search for freedom in the same way.

The way a man searches for freedom depends on his particular needs, which typically change through his life in three stages. Just as we can understand intimate relationships in terms of the three styles or stages we looked at in earlier chapters—Dependence, 50/50 and Intimate Communion—we can view a man's needs in terms of the three styles or stages through which he grows.

First-stage needs are about gaining something, like food, money, sex, power or fame. A first-stage man tends to form a Dependence Relationship with his woman.

Second-stage needs are about self-improvement, authenticity, being in touch with your inner wisdom and creating a Garden of Eden on earth. A second-stage man is interested in forming a 50/50 Relationship with his woman.

Third-stage needs are about letting go of self-definition, relaxing your endless search for completion, feeling through the tension of this present moment and surrendering your limits on openness, as each moment arises and dissolves in love. A third-stage man enjoys a relationship with his woman based on the practice of Intimate Communion.

The Masculine force looks different depending on which type of need is most important to a man. For instance, a first-stage man is searching for freedom by trying to get something. Since his search is an effort to gain something, he is offended when someone asserts that he doesn't have something, whether it be brains, bucks or babes. The first-stage man is an acquisitional man. He sees freedom as something to *get*. He is a car mechanic dreaming of his own garage. A predator on Wall Street. A doctor with a Mercedes and a mistress. He is a man whose goal is somewhere outside of his body, outside of this moment, and he is going to get it. First-stage victory involves acquiring the sacred object—the cash, the car, the country—that is out there to be had. The first-stage man is a man of acquisition, of gain and of enlarged self-image.

A second-stage man looks quite different from a first-stage man. The second-stage man is not out to conquer his enemies; he is out to conquer his own limitations. He is not looking to gain more of something; he is looking to improve who he is. He doesn't want *more*, he wants *better*. He seeks freedom by transforming himself and his world, not by overpowering and acquiring things and others.

The second-stage man battles his own demons and emerges victoriously whole, balanced, a hero of self-integration. If he is afraid of heights, he learns to sky-dive. If he is shy of intimacy, he uses therapy to help him grow beyond blocks he developed in childhood. He seeks to transform his self-understanding through the study of philosophy or esoteric spirituality. He wants to transform the outer world from a battleground into a Garden of Eden. Whereas the first-stage man tries to become a hero of *acquisition*, the second-stage man tries to be a hero of *transformation*.

The first-stage hero stands victorious atop his mound of wealth, slain enemies and respectful subordinates. The second-stage hero stands victorious atop his mound of self-control, internal mastery and impeccable action. He has won—he is completely his own master, authentic and whole, fully responsible for his own happiness. He is free to go where he wants, when he wants. He is free to love whom he wants, perhaps a woman or two, or maybe just himself. The second-stage man is a free spirit, a Renaissance man of the new age, a man of inner evolution and outer adventure—an adventure not of gaining personal wealth, but of creating a more utopian way of life.

The second-stage man is also singularly deluded. At least the first-stage man is up front with his wants: He wants big bucks and big breasts. The second-stage man often hides his own emptiness and his own needs, even from himself. He has practiced meditation for 10 years, traveled all over Asia and India, is a certified aikido master and psychotherapist, and, essentially, nothing fundamental has changed. He still feels unfinished.

Things are a little easier than they used to be, but still, he is not free. He is still locked in his own fears. He is still bound by the fear of death, the fear of separation, the fear of failure. Furthermore, he is older now, and he doesn't have the energy or determination he once had. He has created a comfortable place for himself in the world and although he is embarrassed to admit it, he doesn't want to risk losing too much. But he has no choice. His evolving Masculine energy moves him to take a good look at his life and face the consequences of truth.

Suddenly, the second-stage man opens his eyes and sees his life as he has settled for it. He feels his own dullness, his own fear, his own mediocrity, and he begins to burn inside. His precious self, which he has worked so hard to master, feels like a clench. His life, which once seemed so easy, now seems like a tedious burden. His relationships and career weight him with false obligations. He is afraid to let go of it all, but the constant knot in his gut is becoming too much to bear.

It is a helpless situation. He is absolutely unsatisfied. The breakdown of hope and the recognition of futility have brought him to the edge, and he has no real choice: He releases into the abyss. He succumbs to a crisis. His self-sufficiency and self-worth fall to zero.

If he stays in place without adding consolation to his suffering, if he remains an open-hearted warrior even at zero, then a miracle will manifest. Because he knows he can depend on nothing, he has freed himself from all false support. Because he has outgrown the first-stage need to depend on something outside of himself, as well as the second-stage need to depend on something inside of himself, he is vulnerable to grace. His reduction to nothing has rendered him helpless, but not without help.

Without looking, without trying, a spontaneous force of life begins to become obvious. It is the same mysterious force that beats his heart, moves his thoughts and illuminates his dreams at night.

Since he has felt the futility of letting his life be dictated by others as well as by his own endless thoughts, he is now open to being lived by another force, the force of truth, the force that has always lived him and is living him now. Whatever he may call this force, it is the force of existence itself, the direct and unmediated flow and feeling of being.

It is who he is, even when his friends and concepts fail him. It is the one who witnesses his dreams at night and his thoughts and actions during the day. It is the force of being or consciousness that is constant throughout all of his experiences. It is who he is, always, but it controls nothing.

In the crisis of futility, he realizes that his inside world and his outside world are obviously beyond his control, and that death is inevitable. So he does the only thing he can do. He surrenders, sacrificing all experiences, inner and outer, into the one force that creates, sustains and dissolves all of his experiences.

The third-stage man is rested in the fullness of this force. He is lived by this force, *as* this force. Thus, his actions are spontaneous truth. His home is the fullness of love or non-separation.

When the third-stage man forgets his home and temporarily wanders in search, he always wakes up to the same moment: this living moment, now, spontaneously arising, luminous as the objects within it and conscious as the witness of itself. He realizes that this living moment is always appearing to itself. This moment is neither dependent on him nor independent of him, but arises, spontaneously and consciously, inclusive of him.

His search is always dissolved in this intuition of non-separation, of unity, of love. He stands as the free consciousness in which this moment arises. The fully mature third-stage man recognizes that his nature is freedom itself, always transcending, witnessing and including that which arises.

HOW THE FEMININE GROWS

An essential Feminine principle is that of opening to love. The Feminine nurtures, gives life and dances in sensual joy—although sometimes Feminine energy is also wild, fierce or chaotic. The Feminine can shine with radiance or can appear dark and mysterious. The Feminine is the force of life altogether: the healing force of nature, the life-giving force of earth, as well as the force of destruction, which reabsorbs that to which it has given birth.

The Feminine force is not goal-oriented and directional, so the Feminine heroine is not a warrior who cuts through obstacles. Rather, she is a goddess who opens doors with love. A Masculine warrior slices through impediments to freedom and truth; a Feminine goddess shines with love's radiance, opening passageways to the heart.

The Masculine is primarily struggling with Himself, moving beyond His own fears and learning to master the unknown terrain. The Feminine is primarily moved by Her need for love. She is also yearning for a way to release the love in Her heart.

Her whole life is about opening and loving: giving love and receiving love. Her primary suffering and Her primary joy are in love relationships, usually with an intimate partner, but also with Her children, Her friends or with God.

The Masculine is essentially alone, until He is dissolved in free consciousness. The Feminine is essentially in the play of relationship, until She is dissolved in free love. The Masculine warrior wields his sword of truth. The Feminine goddess dances in the garden of love.

Just as the first-stage man is always looking for a bigger sword, the first-stage woman is always hoping for more love—to give and to receive. When her intimate relationship is not working, she thinks it might be her fault. Maybe she isn't giving enough love. Maybe she is expecting too much. Maybe she needs to give it another chance.

Love is her motive, and the first-stage woman will do anything for it. She will give up her own needs, her own power, her own authority. She will give them up to her children, her husband or her teacher, in her desire for what she thinks is love. If love brushes her life, she opens to it and out flows her energy and attention to the object of her loving. She finds it difficult to accept her own needs, her own power, her own identity, because she so readily opens her boundaries in the hope of love.

Abandoning her own center, the first-stage woman seeks to fill herself with an imitation of real love. To fill her vacant heart she eats ice cream, chocolate and cookies. Perhaps she watches soap operas or reads romance novels.

True love seems always out of her reach: "Maybe I don't deserve love." She settles for anything that offers the potential for love: "Maybe in *this* relationship, there is a chance. Even though he abuses me, I think he could change. I just want him to say that he loves me."

Eventually, her pain becomes too great. She will no longer do anything in exchange for the potential of love. She will not give up her personal identity and her personal needs. Even though she wants an intimate relationship, she is determined to stand her ground. This is the second-stage woman, the woman who, temporarily, focuses on loving herself.

The second-stage man is devoted to self-improvement rather than acquisition; the second-stage woman is devoted to loving herself rather than to giving up her own needs—supposedly for the sake of another—in the hope of receiving love. The second-stage woman is no longer dependent on the love of another, just as the second-stage man is no longer dependent on things and people outside of himself.

The second-stage woman stands whole, frequently in the company of other second-stage women. She is no longer needy of men. In order to free herself from a Dependence Relationship with a man, she cultivates her own internal Masculine energy. She learns to assert her needs clearly, to direct herself with her own guiding hand, to see herself through her own loving eyes instead of through the eyes of an external lover. She is her own person. She has taken responsibility for herself.

The Feminist voice is one voice of the second-stage woman,

celebrating her free womanhood with her sisters. As a cultural shift, women who had been following men's directions have learned to depend on their own internal voice and sense of direction. They no longer merely follow a man's lead; they allow themselves to be leaders. Such women have liberated themselves not only from men but from their own self-doubt.

Just like their second-stage male counterparts, second-stage women are independent, self-responsible and dedicated to internal and external transformation. In fact, it is at the second stage that men and women are most alike. They are both dedicated to self-responsibility. They are both interested in self-definition and respecting personal boundaries. They both, therefore, want to create a 50/50 Relationship.

The words "surrender" and "sacrifice" raise their hackles, second-stage women and men alike. The second stage is all about personal power, self-authenticity and making one's stand as an individual: worthy, strong and not dependent. The second-stage woman and man speak loudly: I follow no doctrine, I am my own woman/man/person.

Because whole personhood is so important to second-stage men and women, they often attempt to balance their internal sexual energies. The man cultivates his inner Feminine energies and the woman cultivates her inner Masculine energies. The man may grow his hair longer, wear an earring, speak softly, smile a lot, express his feelings and be cautious not to assert his opinion too strongly: "Whatever." The woman may cut her hair, wear less sexy clothes, use less make-up, travel widely and speak with confidence.

A 50/50 Relationship is often uniquely lukewarm between second-stage men and women. Why? Because although mutual self-responsibility is a lot more whole than mutual dependency, it is a lot less passionate than mutual abandon in love.

Mutual self-responsibility, by itself, makes for a boring intimate relationship. It makes for a good friendship, which is a step up from a good slaveship. Yet it does not allow for the full incarnation of the Masculine and Feminine forces as two magnetic poles.

Second-stage men are often afraid to love their women freely. For instance, a second-stage man often listens, becoming dull and inattentive, as his woman talks to him. He may have no real interest in what she is saying, but he feels he should listen, or at least try.

Yet her real desire is for a deep connection in love, not for a passive audience. He can choose to give her love directly, passionately, with no hesitation: "Enough talk. I love you." Second-stage men are so devoted to their inner balance that they are afraid to sweep a woman off her feet with the kind of uncompromising love that could fill her deepest desire for intimacy.

A second-stage woman, on the other hand, is often so cautious of losing her center that she is afraid to love a man freely. She doesn't trust that he will honor and appreciate her openness. She is afraid to give a man the kind of devotional love that wants to overflow from her heart. Both the second-stage man and woman are cautious not to let go of their own boundaries or to trespass beyond the emotional boundaries of their partner. They are "safe" men and women.

We have already looked at how a second-stage man may grow into a third-stage man, but what about a woman? Just as a second-stage man may come to realize that he still feels incomplete and unfinished, a second-stage woman may come to realize she is still searching for love. Her heart is still yearning. She still feels a void, whether she is in a mutually self-responsible 50/50 Relationship or not. For most women, sisterhood is not enough, and a second-stage man is safe but not sufficient to pierce the deepest caverns of her heart.

Just as the second-stage man is reduced to zero in the abyss of absolute futility, the second-stage woman is reduced to zero in the black hole of her deep need. At the very center of her life, something is missing. Her independent strength does not fill the emptiness inside her, nor does her 50/50 Relationship.

What can she do, when neither relationship nor aloneness fills the need in her heart? She must let go of her relationship and her independent stance, both, and be sucked through the black hole of her need before she can emerge like a butterfly with wings of love. When the second-stage woman dies, the third-stage woman is born. The third-stage woman no longer searches for love, but rather breathes love, relaxes in love and radiates love.

The third-stage man lets go of everything for the sake of true freedom; the third-stage woman lets go of everything for the sake of true love. She is no longer dependent on external love. She is no longer relying on her self-love. Rather, she *is* love incarnate.

Her mood is not needy, nor proud, but devotional. Her hand is not clinging, nor holding off, but blessing. She does not love like a "wife" should. She does not love like a "person" should. She loves; she is not fearful nor cautious, but abandoned in love.

In a Dependence Relationship, a first-stage woman *seduces* a man, body to body. In a 50/50 Relationship, a second-stage woman *interests* a man, mind to mind. In the practice of Intimate Communion, a third-stage woman *enchants* a man, heart to heart. In Intimate Communion, attraction includes the mind, but quickly the mind disappears in love. In Intimate Communion, attraction is expressed through the body, but quickly the body becomes transparent in radiant energy.

The third-stage woman is not shy about her enchanting power of Feminine love; nor is she careful to maintain her personal identity. She knows that she *is* love, and so she practices giving love, moment to moment, in the ecstasy of surrender. This is the practice of the third-stage woman: to give love, to be of the disposition, "I love you," since love is her true nature.

The first-stage woman is her man's woman. The second-stage woman is her own woman. The third-stage woman is love, in the form of woman. Her identity is not derived from her man, nor from her self. Her need for self-identity is virtually gone, so bright is the shine of her love.

She wanted this unending love from a man, and no man could give her what she wanted. She wanted this unending love from herself, and she couldn't give herself enough love to fulfill herself perfectly. Now she has sacrificed her search for love because she has gained the knowledge of love. She feels deeply, at her core: She *is* love. She knows that she is either *being* love and *giving* love, or she is collapsing.

The third-stage woman knows there is no ultimate relationship to seek, no perfect self-acceptance to achieve. She understands that she will never receive enough love from a relationship nor from her self-acceptance. But she doesn't need to anymore. She has discovered that when she is in the disposition, "I love you," her life is filled with love. She has realized that when she wants to *feel* love, all she needs to do is *give* love. In fact, that is the only time she feels love—when she is loving.

Her search for love is over. She may forget love, but her remembrance is always the same: I am love, and I love you. In this present moment, she practices feeling her body being lived, her breath being breathed and her heart being opened by the radiant love that naturally wants to flow from her heart. She allows herself to be the movement of love in this present moment. She is the dancing energy of love.

THE GIFTS OF MASCULINE AND FEMININE LOVING

Through practice, a man grows stage by stage into the fullness of free consciousness, serving his woman with the Masculine force of love.

When she is lost in her mood or feeling abandoned, he calls her present with humor and passion, and he opens her heart with his pervading and uncompromising love.

Through practice, a woman grows stage by stage into the fullness of the dancing energy of love, serving her man with the Feminine force of love. When he is trapped in his mind or feeling burdened by life, she enchants his heart and enlivens his spirit with her powerful healing energy and radiance of love.

Through the three stages of intimate relationship, man and woman serve each other with their unique forms of Masculine and Feminine energy. In a Dependence Relationship, the first-stage man gives Masculine energy to his woman in the form of money, sweet affection and security. The first-stage woman gives Feminine energy to her man in the form of sex, admiration and nurturing care.

In a 50/50 Relationship, the second-stage man gives Masculine energy to his woman in the form of insight and self-discipline. The second-stage woman gives Feminine energy to her man in the form of intuition and healing.

In the practice of Intimate Communion, the third-stage man gives Masculine energy to his woman in the form of fearless persistence in truth. The third-stage woman gives Feminine energy to her man in the form of ever-radiant, heart-opening love.

By growing through the stages of intimacy, both men and women eventually realize they cannot win: The Masculine never *acquires* absolute freedom and the Feminine never *receives* absolute love. Rather, through their unique gifts, men and women serve one another to grow beyond their illusions of security, need and self-identity. They serve to magnify one another's ability to let go, stop seeking and breathe freely *as* love and *as* freedom, in this present moment.

Finally, in the practice of Intimate Communion, we understand that there is no need to win anything or anyone. Our bellies soften and our hearts relax. Unarmored, unstriving, feeling into the living, naked radiance of this present moment, we *are* that which is always being given. We are the mysterious force of free love, spontaneously arising as man and woman, recognizing itself, touching itself and dissolving in union with itself in the short drama of our lives.

7

The Use and Abuse of Sexual Substitutes

SEXUAL SUBSTITUTES

In our search for emotional and sexual fulfillment, we often seek out and make use of non-human sources of Masculine and Feminine energy. Sometimes we approach these sources consciously, though often we are unaware of the extent to which we indulge in non-human sexual liaisons. By understanding the healing, as well as the weakening, power of sexual substitutes, we can learn to strengthen our own sexual essence by their proper use. Furthermore, we can cultivate a full flow of sexual polarity in our chosen intimacies, rather than "leaking" our sexual flow with substitutes throughout the day.

THE GEOGRAPHY OF SEX

You feel *her*. She is moving all around you, caressing your skin. Her breath tickles your ear and her warm scent touches your nose. You press your tongue against her and her sweet juices spill, dripping down the corners of your mouth, mixing with the beads of sweat on your neck and chest.

At another place and another time, you were with *him*, learning a new skill from him and loving every minute of him. His energy was so strong and supportive that you felt energized by him. Every day, he offered you many opportunities for making money, introducing you to new friends and clients, staying up late at night with you, giving you an extra push to go beyond yourself and strive for perfection. He entered your life completely. You could feel his intensity inside of you, providing a kind of driving rhythm that helped you move through the day. In the evening, he would offer you fine restaurants, movies, theater or dancing. He was always willing to show you something new and was never more than a phone call away.

Who are these wonderful friends, she with her fragrant juices and warm caresses and he with his round-the-clock support and exciting plans for your future? They are not fantasies. They are not even people. They are, in fact, places. They are the silky smooth waters and sweet fruits of Hawaii and the buzzing, stimulating evenings and intensely productive energy of New York City.

We often unknowingly relate to our surroundings in a sexual way. Just like human beings, places can be more or less Feminine, Masculine or Neutral. More Feminine places, like Hawaii, embrace us in warm arms and wash away our concerns with their radiant beauty. More Masculine places, like New York, move us with their directional energy and strong intent. We may not think about it, but sometimes we look to a place for the sexual energy that we may not be receiving in our intimate life.

We are especially prone to geographic sexuality when we are not "getting it" from our human intimate partner. Perhaps you are single or involved in a depolarized relationship with a partner who no longer gifts you with his or her strong sexual essence. Especially in 50/50 Relationships, we may begin to crave strong Masculine or Feminine loving, since we often do not get it from our partners. When our own sexual essence is not coupled in a fulfilling polarized relationship, we often unconsciously seek sexual energy in all kinds of un-acknowledged ways.

By becoming conscious of the principles of sexual geography, we can gain an understanding of how we unwittingly use places as sexual substitutes. We can discover how these unconscious geographical "affairs" affect our intimate relationships, often preventing us from growing beyond the emotional-sexual stalemate of a 50/50 Relationship. If we begin to rely on sexual exchange with our surroundings, rather than relearning to gift healing sexual energy with our intimate partners, we may retard our growth from a 50/50 Relationship to the practice of Intimate Communion.

On the other hand, sometimes your partner is unavailable for a legitimate reason, or perhaps you don't currently have a partner. If you have a strongly Masculine or Feminine sexual essence rather than a Neutral one, you will feel like a single pole of a magnet uncompleted by a partner, wanting to attract and be attracted. You desire to be in a polarized relationship with the opposite sexual essence, but you are temporarily unable to connect with such a person.

In this case, you can learn to *consciously* embrace the place of your choice like a lover, taking a trip to the snow-peaked mountains, a quiet lake or perhaps a special city. In this way you can heal and rejuvenate your stressful or weary sexual essence, especially when your intimate partner is unable to give you what you need for one reason or another. This kind of "affair" is often beneficial to all involved, no matter what stage of relationship in which you are involved.

HAVING AN AFFAIR WITH A MASCULINE
OR A FEMININE PLACE

When you want or need the company of the Feminine, go to a place like Hawaii. Her abundant plant life surrounds you in tropical greens and every shade of red. Her soft beach sand clings to your toes like a lover's teasing kisses, reminding you of a day of wild ocean caresses and the sweet juices of guavas, mangos and papayas. Your cares and concerns are washed away as you relax every inch of your body in Her sensuously swirling waters, which sometimes gently lap at your navel and sometimes suck you in beyond your control.

Wherever you live, the Feminine is found in any place that is radiant with natural, rejuvenating energy, a place that feeds you with life rather than drains you, a place that magnifies the shine of your heart rather than challenges your ability to succeed. If you are in Denver, for example, you can go to a nearby river for an afternoon smile with the Feminine, who is always waiting for you, ready to receive a dip of your foot or a plunge of your whole body. Her singing birds and soothing ripples surround you in an embrace of refreshing relaxation. If you don't have an intimate partner who willingly gives you the sensual and nurturing energy of the Feminine, don't starve: Her welcoming arms await you somewhere nearby.

If you want the company of the Masculine, go to a place like New York City. His intense energy will fill you to the brim and you won't be able to escape His massive and towering skyscrapers. You will learn to cut the mustard fast, because, although you're offered every possible opportunity for making it, He also keeps on going whether you are with Him or not. Night and day He persists in His mission, like a locomotive churning steam to reach some great destination, and all you need to do is learn how to ride. Underneath His apparently stoic shades of gray asphalt, gray suits and gray buildings, lurks one of the most powerfully active places in the sophisticated worlds of art, commerce and science. And it is all there, offered to you on a plate—if you are good enough to make it.

The Masculine takes His stand all over the world, not just in New York. The quality of the Masculine can be found in many places, from rocky plateaus to air-conditioned offices. There are mountains to climb, deserts to cross, stock markets to beat and real estate to sell. You are in the company of the Masculine any time you are competing—with yourself, with other men and women, or with the challenging terrain. His energy aligns your purpose like a compass needle, pointing your attention toward the goal of the moment. As you resonate more and more with the Masculine, you become focused, goal-oriented and willing to cut through any obstacles to get to where you want to go.

Although you may not live in Hawaii or New York, you can look at these extreme examples to help you understand whether you relate to your surroundings more as the Masculine or as the Feminine, or as a combination of both. Hawaii nurtures you. New York tests you. Hawaii invites you into her healing nature. New York challenges your capacity to think and act. If you have been working hard and your mind, body and heart desire to be soothed and rejuvenated by powerful and healing life-force, then go to Hawaii. If you are waiting for your lucky break, preparing your career for the big league or ready to meet your mark and finally do it, then go to New York.

SEXUAL SUBSTITUTES CAN WEAKEN YOUR ESSENCE

Sexual geography is real. You can go to certain places to be healed and enlivened by the energy of the Feminine, and to certain other places to be moved by the energy of the Masculine. Wherever you go, the sexual geography of the place will affect your behavior, rhythms, ambitions and relationships. Our entire lives are affected by our chosen geographical consorts. And that is why we have chosen them: Often without knowing it, we desire the company of a non-human source of Masculine or Feminine energy because we don't have a human companion who gives us what we want.

We often choose a place to live because we do not have a partner, or because we are not getting enough Masculine or Feminine energy from our intimate partner to fulfill our deep sexual needs. So, we accept a substitute. Instead of becoming the kind of partner that would evoke deep sexual communion in our intimacies, we take the easy way out and have a non-human affair. By doing this, our own sexual essence becomes weakened. Our relationships become less sexually polarized and we become more dependent on sexual substitutes.

Particularly in 50/50 Relationships, we often become dependent on sexual substitutes in order to satisfy the lack we feel. After all, it seems far less demanding to do something like go to the beach or pour our energy into our career than to deal with our intimate relationship. Coupled with a non-human substitute, our sexual essence has less opportunity to grow in a polarized relationship with our chosen partner. We begin to settle for an intimate life with far less passion and depth than we know is possible. We drift closer and closer to a Neutral relationship, even if our true sexual essence is more Masculine or Feminine.

Instead of depending on substitutes for a sense of satisfaction, we could learn to reclaim, rejuvenate and breathe life into our true sexual essence. An enlivened sexual essence shines as a gift, acting like a beacon to attract an appropriately polarized intimate partner, or serving to "turn on" our present partner, evoking a more potent emotional-sexual force in him or her. When we are no longer dependent on substitutes, then our essence is free for the practice of sexual polarity in Intimate Communion. We can give and receive enlivening gifts of love with our partner, instead of settling for a daily lack of the Feminine or Masculine and seeking substitutes to fill the void.

FEMININE SEXUAL SUBSTITUTES

Like many people today, suppose you are in a 50/50 Relationship where you and your partner work so hard at Masculine-type jobs that by the end of the day you are both too stressed out to offer each other any Feminine energy. Neither of you experiences enough of the enlivening, healing, sensual energy of the Feminine. So you may want to "get a little on the side." What does it feel like when there isn't enough Feminine energy in your life?

Basically, your everyday routine gets stale. You both come home from work exhausted. Who's going to make dinner tonight? Who is going to pick up the kids? Neither of you has the energy to do much of anything.

Finally you get into bed together. Your partner wants a massage. Oh, great. Well, okay. You give a little massage, and then turn over so you can receive a little. But your partner is snoring. You're out of luck. No healing and delightful Feminine energy for you tonight.

When you don't get enough Feminine energy, you become weary and emotionally dry. You feel lifeless inside and you begin to crave someone to nurture you, cook for you, massage you, enchant you and delight you. You demand more and more of this Feminine energy from your partner, and if you don't get it, you turn to other sources. You may look for an affair with the Feminine in a non-human form.

Alcohol and many drugs are one kind of Feminine substitution. Any drug that softens your edges, soothes your mind, relaxes your body and opens your heart is providing you with Feminine energy. The Feminine caresses and enchants you, whether She comes from a relaxing marijuana joint, a few cold beers or a warm injection of heroin.

On the other hand, the quality of the Masculine is found in any drug that pushes you forward, brings you into your head and motivates you to accomplish your goal, cutting through any obstacles that may lie in your way. Drugs like caffeine, amphetamines and cocaine give you that Masculine edge and forward thrust. As with any substitute, when we are regularly coupled with a drug, our sexual essence is less avail-able for deep union with a chosen intimate partner.

Besides looking for the Feminine in smoke, drink or pill, you might also look for the Feminine in human form, either as friend or lover. If you are extremely developed in your Masculine, always pushing, analyzing and directing other people, you will be most attracted to a partner who embodies the radiant, healing, enlivening and even wild aspects of the Feminine. A partner like this will dynamically balance the Feminine you lack. It is not unusual, for instance, for a mega-level super-businessperson to take a radiantly beautiful but not-so-driven partner as a consort, just as you might decide to go to Hawaii rather than New York to relax in its sensual and healing Feminine energy.

A man might also substitute one or more casual "friendship" rela-tionships with women for a deep commitment to love in a polarized intimacy. His Masculine essence is somewhat completed and partially satisfied in the subtle exchanges of sexual energy he gets from spending so much time with his woman friends, even if all they are doing is talking together. It is as if he has many superficial "sexual" relationships, rather than a deeply engaging and committed practice in intimacy.

Over time, his sexual presence diminishes—it is being "leaked" and compromised in his casual relationships. This is, of course, as true for women as it is for men. Unconscious sexual substitutes, even in the form of the subtle sexual satisfaction we get from spending time talking with opposite-sexed friends, can act to weaken our sexual essence and lessen our gift as a potential partner in the practice of Intimate Communion.

Let's take this even further. Imagine that a man has chosen not to visit Hawaii, but to live there. He has even arranged his life to have a daily tryst with his tropical source of Feminine energy: his life revolves around surfing, or kayaking, or hiking. He enters her wild and radiant waters or jungles daily.

Ask a surfer sometime: "If you could have the perfect wave, every wave, for three months, or the perfect intimate relationship every day with a woman for three months, which would you choose?"

A surfer, or someone like him, already has a source of Feminine energy, in the form of the water. What experience can a human woman offer him that he does not already get from the ocean? He is bathed and nurtured by Her. He rides with Her ups and downs. She is unpredictable, always fresh and alive. Sometimes She lifts him into glory, into the perfect moment of intimate union. Sometimes Her moods almost drown him, bashing him into the rocks or carrying him so far away from land that he wonders if he is crazy to be with Her.

Why would such a man make a commitment to a single human woman who has her own needs? Why burden himself, he might wonder, with a deeply committed relationship when most of his needs for the Feminine are already satisfied by a big, wet, radiant Feminine source who is always there for him, open to him, ready to give him the ride of his life?

Surfers, skiers and other Masculine-essence men who embrace the wild and living forces of Feminine nature are among the least likely men to commit in full presence to intimate relationship with a human woman. The reason a Masculine-essence man chooses a Feminine woman (or man) as an intimate partner, rather than a more Masculine woman (or man), is because he wants to embrace, and be embraced by, the Feminine. He wants to commune with the Feminine in intimacy.

He desires to enter Her deeply and move with Her energies, like a dedicated surfer. He is ready to be healed by the Feminine source and he is also ready to master Her moods and dangerous currents. If he is already embracing, mastering and being healed by Woman in the form of nature, it will take a very special human woman, a woman who is more of a woman than his watery source of Feminine force, to attract him away from his commitment to the surf. Ask any woman who has tried.

MASCULINE SEXUAL SUBSTITUTES

Imagine that you are a woman who has just been divorced. While married, you played around with developing your artistic talent, had a few low-key showings at local galleries and even sold a few pieces. But now you are single, and you want to make art your career. So you move to a big city and find an agent, making contacts in the art world, learning from other artists and being inspired by showings, museums and the hubbub of the city night life. You have moved to the big city for the energy of the Masculine: directional, persevering, passionately active and directed toward successfully achieving a goal.

In effect, you are having an affair with the city, just like a surfer is having an affair with the ocean. You allow yourself to be moved by the energy of the city. You say to yourself, "I am here for a purpose. I am going to achieve my goal. I am going to take advantage of the resources the city offers me."

And then you meet a man.

Something clicks between the two of you the very first time you meet. But you are on your way to an appointment and don't have time to chat. A few days later when you meet him at the museum for lunch, you open your schedule book and pencil him in for dinner at Chez Renée next Saturday night. Saturday afternoon comes and you remember about an important gallery opening that evening. You really should attend. So you call him up and ask him to meet you at the opening-night party instead of at the restaurant.

He shows up at the party with a big bouquet of flowers for you, and your heart melts. But suddenly, out of the corner of your eye you see Mr. Bigmoney, one of the city's greatest patrons of the arts. You don't want to miss this opportunity, so you grab your date by the arm and whisk him over to Mr. Bigmoney for a conversation.

The evening continues and later your date turns to you and says, "Look, I'm here to be with you. Do you want to be with me or are you going to schmooze with everyone else here at this party?" You look at him, take another sip of coffee and say, "Sorry. I shouldn't have brought you here. I'm busy now. I'm on a roll. I'll call you tomorrow."

A woman's commitment to her Masculine mission may frustrate a man who would like to be the main source of Masculine energy in her life. A non-human affair is not much different from a human one. It is exciting for the participants, and yet the jilted partner feels cheated.

A surfer's commitment may be to the undulating waves. A body builder's commitment may be to the smooth curves of his own body, a skier's to the slippery slopes and a sailor's to the mysterious sea. Likewise, a businesswoman's commitment may be to the upwardly mobile energy of the big city. Its thrust moves her toward the big score. And, just as a weight lifter's commitment to his curvaceous image in the mirror might frustrate a woman who would like to be the cherished object of his affection, a businesswoman's devotion to her Masculine mission frustrates a man who would like to be the main recipient of her devotion.

In a place like New York, men may feel frustrated because their potential mates are all having sex with the hard and fast energy of the city, being filled by its upward mobility and skyscraping vistas, taken by the arm and led from one golden opportunity to the next. In a place like Hawaii, women may be frustrated because their potential mates have a prior commitment to the surf, the warm soft sand, the lush and fertile valleys of fruit trees and river. No matter what city you live in, no matter what career you are engaged in, you may find your partner in a more or less sexual relationship with his or her place and profession.

IN THE COMPANY OF *MAN* AND *WOMAN*

If you are guided by your schedule book and challenged to perfect your mental sharpness, self-discipline, financial dealings or artistic skill, then you are keeping the company of the Masculine.

When men keep the company of the Masculine, they become more Masculine and therefore more polarized in intimate relationships with women. For instance, after making a killing on the stock market or a touchdown on the football field, a man is all charged up, full of his Masculine power and very ready to share it with his woman.

However, when women keep the company of the Masculine, they tend to lose connection with their natural Feminine sexual essence (unless, of course, their natural sexual essence is Masculine). By opening themselves to the energy of the Masculine all day, by running Masculine energy through their body all day, they become less full of Feminine radiance and more full of Masculine direction. A woman who has just made a killing on the stock market will probably express more Masculine energy than Feminine: She's more likely to raise her clenched fist and shout, "Victory!" than she is to relax into every inch of her body and radiate Feminine force.

A woman who runs Masculine energy through her body all day begins to desire external Feminine energy to complete her, just as a man does. She desires the Feminine to come to her at the end of the day: a relaxing massage, a warm bath, a delicious meal or any other form of Feminine, enlivening energy to ease her mind, fill her body with life and caress her spirit.

Trouble may begin if she regularly desires this Feminine energy from her intimate partner. She wants her man to listen to her more, support her in her quest for success, nurture her tired edges with his affection and breathe life into her weary soul. In effect, she wants more Feminine force from her man. This is fine, temporarily, or even permanently if her partner's sexual essence is naturally more Feminine. But when we consistently want our partners to give us sexual energy that is not native to their sexual essence, we are asking for trouble in our intimate relationship.

In the company of the Feminine, on the other hand, women become more Feminine—as witnessed in the lively, colorful, enchanting dress and attitude of women of the tropics. Women run Feminine energy through their bodies whenever they are in the company of the Feminine force. After spending time laughing with her close women friends, walking in a flowered meadow, dancing to her favorite music or expressing her personal creativity, a woman is full of the Feminine force and quite ready to be with her man.

But men become depolarized by the Feminine's constant companionship. A man who drinks beer or smokes marijuana all day, surfs all day or plays his guitar under the trees all day, is less likely to have the strong directional integrity it takes to make a long-term commitment with a woman. This kind of depolarized man is caricatured in the stereotypes of the dreamy pothead, the beach bum or the love 'em and leave 'em musician.

To strengthen and enliven your emotional and sexual core, spend time in the company of the sexual force that is the *same* as your native sexual essence. If you must spend a lot of time in the company of the opposite sex (in human, geographic or professional form), make sure to rejuvenate yourself by spending equal time in the company of your native sexual force. If you have a Masculine sexual essence, spend substantial time in the company of only men or in some arena of challenge, self-discipline and focused directionality, in the form of a sport, a meditative practice or a goal-oriented giving of your creative gifts. If you have a Feminine sexual essence, spend substantial time in the company of only women or in the powerful flow of natural life-force, dancing to music, moving in nature, allowing your body to spontaneously express your creative gifts and making passionate love.

As long as we take care to nourish our emotional and sexual core with the force of its native energy, Masculine or Feminine, we can spend our workday being as Masculine or Feminine as we like with no ill effects, regardless of our native sexual essence or our gender.

THE RESULTS OF SEXUAL GEOGRAPHY

What happens to the intimate partners of driven businesswomen and undirected men? The Masculine and the Feminine are always found together, embraced in a dynamic play of filling and being filled, giving and receiving, guiding and energizing one another. If he doesn't do it, she will. If a creative but undirected man doesn't give his woman Masculine energy, then she will develop it for herself. If a successful but stressed-out woman doesn't give her man Feminine energy, he will create it within himself, or seek it elsewhere.

We forget how sexually extreme a place can get. New York is so Masculine that the sight of a hurried person in a gray business suit looking at his or her watch while stepping over a piece of trash is so common, it is barely noticed. What would it be like to find on the streets of New York a woman in a bikini, her skin oiled with lotion and beaded with fine sweat, wearing a lei of flowers around her neck, walking slowly to an unseen rhythm, smelling the flowers and greeting every stranger with a smile and radiant eyes? This is a common sight in a place as Feminine as Hawaii, where a hurried person in a business suit totally ignoring his or her surroundings would draw sympathetic smiles from the vacationing people splashing on the tropical beach.

Understanding sexual geography allows us to predict what aspects of intimacy will be easier or more difficult, depending on where we live. In a Masculine place like New York, both men and women will have more difficulty connecting with the Feminine. In a Feminine place like Hawaii, both men and women will have more difficulty connecting with the Masculine.

Men and women in a place like Hawaii are surrounded by the Feminine all day and night. Therefore, men always have an option to human Feminine companionship—the surf, for instance—and women are always competing with these other Feminine sources for their men's attention. Thus, the dress in Hawaii is extremely Feminine, sensual, colorful and revealing of the body's curves: a woman must be quite a woman to stand out as Feminine in Hawaii. And this is difficult for a woman whose non-goal-oriented, beach bum partner forces her to work hard all day in her Masculine just to get by financially.

Men and women in a place like New York City are surrounded by the Masculine day and night. Therefore, women always have an option to human Masculine companionship—they can embrace their schedule book and cellular phone—and men in such places are always competing with their women's career ambitions and one-pointed schedules. The dress in New York is extremely Masculine, well-planned, functional, sometimes even protective and often purposed for success. A man or woman must be quite Masculine to make it in New York. And this makes it hard for a man to find a woman who will commit to being his source of Feminine energy.

OTHER SEXUAL SUBSTITUTES

The Masculine and Feminine energies are not only found geographically; sometimes we substitute a child for a sexual partner. We may not actually have sex with the child, yet we use the child to subtly satisfy our need for the energy of Masculine or Feminine. For instance, when we allow our child's developing career or talent to guide the decisions in our lives, we are relating to our child as a directional, or Masculine force, and this often causes jealousy between parents: "You give our son more attention than you give me."

We relate to our child as the Feminine force when we depend on him or her to share loving touch and spontaneous laughter, whenever we emphasize the child's beauty and ability to enliven us and bring pleasure into our lives. Sometimes our child becomes our most willing and immediate source of intimate Masculine or Feminine energy. This could be a natural form of delightful sharing, or perhaps a source of jealousy between intimate partners. More rarely, it could escalate into overt forms of sexual abuse.

We may also attempt to satisfy our need for the Masculine or Feminine by unconsciously embracing animals, fantasy companions or favorite objects as our source of subtle sexual flow.

For example: He is her protector, her longtime companion, her committed partner. She confides everything to him and he never flinches. He is present with her through her most difficult times, always supportive and sensitive to her needs. She enjoys feeling his strength as they wrestle, yet she knows he would never hurt her. He's obstinate and he might interrupt her phone calls or even wake her from a deep sleep to get what he wants, but she always feels appreciated. She loves her German shepherd, her most loyal consort.

Another example: He loves to admire her smooth and well-shaped form. He worships the lines of her body, soaping her with his own hands, trailing suds down her front, along the beautiful curves of her sides, finishing with long strokes up and down her rear end. In public, he is very jealous and keeps an eye on any man who stands too near her. But when he is alone with her, he loves to turn her on and feel her purr in response to his ministrations, his expert fingers gliding across her well-lubricated inner parts, as he alternately heats her up and cools her down. He looks forward to spending weekends with her, sometimes going to the beach and showing her off to his friends, although his wife often gets upset at the amount of time, money and energy he puts into his new car.

If you notice that your partner or potential partner has chosen an emotional or sexual substitute, be wary. His or her sexual essence may already be compromised or absorbed into a non-human polarity. It is not always easy to break old habits of sexual substitution, freeing our essential energy for taking the next step beyond a 50/50 Relationship, so be forewarned.

Your Masculine partner may have chosen to lavish attention on a substitute source of Feminine force in the form of surf, car or boat, marijuana, music or many other forms of sensuality, beauty and rejuvenation. If so, He will be less likely to commit to giving you His Masculine love and receiving your Feminine love in an intimate relationship.

Your Feminine partner may have chosen a substitute source of Masculine force in the form of a career, schedule, animal, city, mission or in any other way of filling Her life with purpose, direction and goals. If so,

She will be less likely to commit to giving you Her Feminine love and receiving your Masculine love in an intimate relationship.

BEYOND SEXUAL SUBSTITUTES

A woman's career rarely penetrates her heart and fills her with the same kind of love and emotional fulfillment that a good man would— a man whom she could trust, a really good man full of passion and loving presence. And a man's search for the perfectly formed wave, the perfectly formed biceps or the perfectly formed powdery slope may distract him from his life's deep purpose, as will the obsessive search for a perfectly formed woman. We must outgrow our misplaced searches before we are willing and able to practice love in Intimate Communion.

The key to intimacy is love, and the key to love is trust. A man or woman who is having an affair with a sexual substitute is less likely to be totally present and committed to human love. Therefore, he or she is not fully trustable. You don't expect that a partner like this will be fully committed in love with you, since he or she is too distracted by a sexual substitute. Your partner may even seem unwilling to let go of the substitute and commit to your relationship, surrendering himself or herself in vulnerable embrace with you rather than with career, child or golf club.

If you are not getting what you want from your partner, then you probably aren't moved to give your sexual essence as a gift to him or her. You think, "As long as my partner withholds, I will withhold." In this kind of stalemate situation, we often try to set up a 50/50 Relationship so at least we are getting our "say," our fair share of responsibilities and money. And besides, a 50/50 Relationship is safe. We are rarely required to reciprocate sharing with our partner from the vulnerable depth of our sexual being—which works out fine, since we resist giving our sexual essence as a gift to a partner whom we don't trust will reciprocate.

RESISTING SEXUAL ENERGY

The deep exchange of human love in a sexual relationship is often difficult because most of us have resistances to the demands of sex and love. One of the main reasons we replace human intimacy with substitutes is because of this resistance to deep sexuality; however, very few of us would admit this. Nevertheless, very few of us regularly surrender ourselves to the point of perfectly vulnerable sexual union with our chosen partner. How many of us, on a regular basis, hold our partner close to our heart, looking deeply into his or her eyes, merging with him or her, surrendering through him or her, opening so wide and giving so deep we are both, man and woman, dissolved in the bright bliss of love?

This is not a metaphorical question. Almost all of us resist relaxing into completely vulnerable sexual embrace with our partners. We are either afraid of "getting screwed" or we are afraid of the commitment to love.

Perhaps in our childhood we were screwed over in some way, either literally in the form of sexual abuse, or in a less literal, but equally real way, in the form of emotional abuse. We have learned to protect ourselves. We have learned not to let anyone inside of us. Our hearts are always guarded and we have developed a hard exterior.

But inside, we long for love. We long to be touched. We long for the Masculine or Feminine to touch our hearts.

Two Masculine aspects of the world are "control" and "penetration." If for some reason we resist the Masculine, we will resist being controlled or penetrated. For instance, when we are near a sharp and angularly forceful person, we might sit with tense shoulders, crossing our arms and closing off our chest to protect ourselves from being entered. Or, we might be frightened by overt signs of anger. When our partner yells or grabs us abruptly and with force, we may freeze up and close down, shutting ourselves off from our partner's penetrating Masculine energy.

There are other ways to resist the Masculine. For example, some women refuse the Masculine by refusing to be "pinned down" by a man's requirements. These women will attract, and be attracted to, more Feminine men—men who do not make strong demands. "I'm not going to let any man tell me what to do," she may think to herself, or even say out loud.

In fact, her refusal of the Masculine may be so thorough that she is always struggling with discipline and self-discipline, which are expressions of the same Masculine force. She may look self-disciplined on the outside, but her secret life is shot through with obsession: She sticks to an impeccable schedule at the office and then eats a quart of ice cream in the privacy of her home. She dreams of a man she can totally trust, and yet she tells her friends that men are not worthy of her. She hates to be told what to do, yet spends her evenings reading romance novels filled with forceful, passionate men sweeping flushed, swooning women off their feet. Her Feminine sexual essence would like nothing more than to be cherished and loved by a strong man, yet her personality defends her against the Masculine force.

If you are a man considering a woman for an intimate partnership, remember this: The way she responds to control, the way she relates to discipline, will be the way she relates to your Masculine force. If she fights discipline, expect a battle. If she resists control, expect resistance in relationship.

On the other hand, a woman who willingly responds to healthy discipline and self-discipline, and who gladly relinquishes control when she knows it is to her benefit, has a good relationship to the Masculine force. She is not a pushover, but neither is she so resistant to guidance that your Masculine force will always meet with anger and refusal.

And what if you are a woman, considering a man for intimate partnership? A man relates to the life-energy of the whole world the same way he will to your Feminine force. If he feels burdened by the world, you can be sure he will often feel burdened by you. If he relates to the world as a source of pleasure, you can expect that he will desire to be pleasured by you. If he plays with the world more often than he seriously tries to participate in its depths, he will enjoy your relationship as two playmates might, but he is unlikely to enter your inner chambers and unfold your deepest potential.

If he treats the world as a challenge, so he will treat you. And a man who approaches each moment with strength and integrity will approach you in the same way. But don't expect a monkish bookworm to match you belly-to-belly in your ever-changing dance, swooping low and jumping high with you in rhythm to the music of your heart. The relationship a man has with the life-energy of the world is the same relationship that he will have with his woman's Feminine force.

A man who resists Feminine energy, who resists the flow of life by over-controlling and trying to organize the signs of chaos or wild energy around him, will do the same with his intimate partner. If he fearfully tries to "intellectualize" himself away from the threat and requirements of the real world, so he will with his woman. If his bedroom must be perfectly ordered, he will expect the same of his woman's emotions. And if he is haphazard about his surroundings, he will be equally nonchalant about his partner's feelings. By understanding our partner's—as well as our own—sexual relationship to the world, we can better predict and work with the dramas that may arise in our intimacies.

BECOMING CONSCIOUS AND TRUSTABLE LOVERS

We have examined the play of sexual polarity with human as well as non-human sources of Masculine and Feminine energy. By using the principles introduced, you can continue your exploration on your own, as a practitioner of Intimate Communion. Each relationship is unique; none of the guidelines we have looked at will be true for everyone. It is up to you to experiment and find what works best in your practice of intimacy.

In any case, nearly everyone has had an affair, at some time, at some place, with a sexual substitute, and so have our intimate partners. Perhaps it was a short-lived kiss with a refreshing bottle of beer or a long-term engagement to the challenge of medical school. Perhaps we kick and scream and refuse to submit to discipline—or maybe we all too quickly open ourselves to the whims of supposed authority figures. Perhaps we try to keep the messy, complicated world at arm's length, standing above it, aloof and uninvolved—or maybe we instantly lose ourselves to the first delicious moment that comes our way.

We are surrounded by the Masculine and Feminine forces in many forms. Understanding how we relate to these great sexual energies serves our ability to be conscious and trustable lovers—capable of a fully polarized relationship, founded in the practice of Intimate Communion.

8

The Masculine Way

THE CORE OF THE MASCULINE
IS DIRECTIONALITY

Through many years as a consultant for individuals and couples, I have seen this pattern over and over: One partner in an intimacy, the one with the more Masculine sexual essence, is moved primarily by his or her direction in life, or mission. The other partner, with the more Feminine sexual essence, is moved primarily by his or her emotions in intimate relationship.

Both partners are influenced by both factors, their direction and their intimate relationship. It's just that the Masculine sexual essence gives priority to "life direction" and the Feminine sexual essence gives priority to "intimate relationship."

What I am calling "direction" here, and what might also be referred to as the Masculine's personal "truth," "mission," or "goal," is the most important thing in life to the Masculine sexual essence. Historically, the Masculine has very frequently been willing to lay down His life for the sake of truth, goal or mission.

I have seen through the lives of my clients, time and time again, that it is only *after* the Masculine sexual essence is aligned with its true mission that this person was able to participate in intimacy with full commitment.

MISSION IS THE MASCULINE PRIORITY

To illuminate the Masculine way more fully, I am going to combine aspects of my relationship with my long-time intimate partner with the lessons I have learned from years of working with other couples. I will use this "combined" intimate partner, who I will call "Ophelia," as an example of a typical partner with a Feminine sexual essence, just as I will use myself as an example of a typical partner with a Masculine sexual essence.

In actuality, of course, each individual is unique and always changing, so the real picture of the Masculine and Feminine forces is far more complex than the relatively simple images presented here. Still, I think it is useful to consider how the Masculine and Feminine may be lost and how they may be found, even if this consideration cannot take into account the uniqueness of each and every person.

Over and over I tried to be as concerned about our relationship as Ophelia was; but I wasn't. Perhaps it would be more accurate to say that I wasn't concerned in the same way as she was. I was far more concerned about the direction of our lives, the big picture, than I was about how I was feeling this moment with Ophelia.

This is not to say that I wasn't concerned at all about our relationship. On the contrary, I thought about Ophelia more than anybody else, and of all my relationships, ours was far and away the most important. It was just that *where* we were going occupied my attention more than *with whom* I was going.

I have come to discover that this is true for every person, man or woman, who has a Masculine sexual essence. And the more Masculine the essence, the more true it is. The core of the Masculine sexual essence is directionality, or where we are going.

Because Ophelia did not seem to prioritize life in the same way, I began to feel like I was self-centered compared with her. It seemed that she was so concerned about me, about our relationship, but I was more concerned about what we were doing, where we were going and how I would accomplish my mission.

Over time, though, I began to realize a more full truth: We were both self-centered. Whereas I was concerned about where we were going, both with our practice of Intimate Communion as well as with my "life-mission," Ophelia was concerned about how she was feeling in our relationship. She was occupied with her emotions (which were tied primarily to the "tone" of our intimate relationship). I was occupied with my direction and quest (which included our relationship but also many other aspects of my life).

The Feminine sexual essence is moved primarily by the flow of love in Her relationships, and the Masculine sexual essence is primarily concerned with His overall direction in life—that is, His goal or life-mission. In my case, this became most obvious when I was involved in a major project. If I was procrastinating or unclear of my goals with the project, then my energy was constantly sapped by my lack of clarity, and Ophelia suffered my lack of energy for our relationship. I couldn't really be with her, fully present. Part of me was involved with the project, consciously or unconsciously, trying to work out my clarity and direction.

However, when I was clear about my direction, then I was able to "really work when I was working" and also be completely present with Ophelia when I was with her. I didn't have to actually complete the project before I could give undistracted love to Ophelia; I just had to be clear about my true direction and align my life with clarity and purpose. Otherwise, my Masculine sexual essence was divided. Part of me, a big part, was always distracted by a deep sense of incompleteness at my core.

THE MASCULINE IS MODAL

I have watched many women's futile attempts to get their men's attention while the "boys" are riveted to a football game on TV. "Why can't he just talk to me for a moment?" This is the recurring question that many women have asked me about their man remaining oblivious to her beckoning during a 50-yard field goal attempt. "Because he doesn't even hear you," I answer them. And I know, as does any man or woman with a Masculine sexual essence.

For instance, a woman with a more Feminine sexual essence must learn that her man, if he has a more Masculine sexual essence, is probably not ignoring her; he is just totally focused, absorbed in a mode. In his reality, he isn't hearing her call and then choosing to ignore her. Her voice never even registers in his conscious awareness while he is in another mode. It is as if he is asleep and dreaming. His attention is totally involved in a certain mode, a certain realm, outside of which there is nothing; he could hear his lover's voice calling to him if she speaks loudly enough to penetrate his dream mode, but he would have to leave the dream realm to really hear her and respond—and who knows if he would ever be able to return to the same dream?

In the same way, for anyone with a Masculine sexual essence, the waking state is divided into well-defined modes—namely realms that don't seem penetrable from the outside. These modes can seem rather one-dimensional to the Feminine: the football mode, the business mode, the driving-the-car mode and the intimacy mode are some of these modes. The more Masculine the sexual essence, the more impervious each mode is to the outside world: "Can't you see I'm busy? Please don't bother me right now."

For the Feminine sexual essence, however, modes are not nearly as rigid. A person with a Feminine sexual essence can quite easily flow between watching TV, talking with a friend and working on a project—all at the same time. The flow of Feminine attention is fluid: "Sure I'm busy, but I don't mind being interrupted. How are you?"

This is one of the Feminine's greatest strengths—and weaknesses. She can flow from one task to another easily, and thus can also be distracted rather easily, getting absorbed in a telephone conversation or a visit with a friend rather than finishing the writing project that needs to be finished.

Masculine energy, though more rigid than the Feminine, is also less distractible. Masculine modality can be a real gift. It allows a man or woman to persevere through obstacles and distractions that would veer a less Masculine person from his or her path. The extreme Masculine does whatever it takes to reach a goal without being moved from its tracks—whether that goal is watching a football game, writing a novel, making a million dollars or realizing enlightenment. This ability to achieve a goal without being distracted should be honored by both men and women as a valuable aspect of the Masculine way.

At the same time, men and women must realize that this Masculine gift—of persisting in one mode until the goal is reached—needs to be balanced by the Feminine gifts of flow and bodily sensitivity. There is a time to work, and a time to smell the roses. There is a time to remain alone in a room, focusing with total concentration, and a time to roll around in a disheveled bed, laughing and playing with your lover.

This balance between Masculine focus and Feminine flow can be achieved in two ways: within a person, or between two partners. Usually, it is easier for a person with a more Neutral sexual essence to achieve this balance within himself or herself, alternating between work and play, between focus and laughter, between the mission and the flow of love.

However, if your sexual essence is either toward the Masculine or toward the Feminine, it often feels more natural to trust your partner's native gifts. After you have achieved a 50/50 wholeness on your own—that is, after you are able to be either focused in your Masculine or flowing in your Feminine—it is often very pleasurable to relax into your native pole in Intimate Communion and enjoy receiving the other side as a gift from your partner. In this way, the Feminine partner is like Hawaii and the Masculine partner is like New York, gifting each other with unique qualities of Feminine radiance and Masculine direction, respectively.

THE MASCULINE IS
LOOKING FOR TROUBLE

The Masculine sexual essence is looking for trouble. That's how it finds its purpose. It sees a problem and wants to fix it. In fact, it often sees a problem and wants to fix it even when there isn't one.

Once upon a time, I viewed Ophelia's emotional states as problems to be solved. To my eyes, she would be moping around the house, so I would try to talk with her about it, asking her a lot of questions, hoping to get to the bottom of it.

I can vividly remember one particular time that Ophelia was literally storming around the house, slamming doors, angrily bashing things around in her bedroom and the kitchen. I had been in my study working for several hours, and after a few minutes of hearing all the bangs and crashes, I came out to see what was going on. As soon as I saw Ophelia, it was obvious that she was really angry about something, so I started to ask her questions, hoping that by finding out what it was that made her angry, we could get to the bottom of it and solve the problem. My natural response—in fact, my loving response—was to try to fix her.

Ophelia, however, *hated* to be fixed. She didn't like when I went into the "time to fix Ophelia" mode. In fact, the more I asked her what was wrong ("Is it because of so-and-so?"), the more angry she seemed to get.

What she wanted was to feel my love, to feel my acceptance, to feel my caring for her—my overall embrace of her. But what she felt was my prod and poke, looking for a loose screw here, a stuck emotion there. She felt my questions, my frustration, my push to get to the bottom of her "problem."

Since I love Ophelia, I wanted to help her. And because I have a Masculine sexual essence, the way I tended to try to help was by trying to solve her problem. Why only give her love and acceptance when I could get to the root of the problem and solve it?

More often than not, love and acceptance were what she wanted to feel. On this occasion, as on many others, the "problem" was simply that she wasn't feeling my love. I was so involved in the project on which I was working that Ophelia felt like my project was more important to me than she was. But the more I tried to figure out her problem, the less she felt my love and the more she felt my analytical dissection of her life, or her "problem." Ophelia didn't want to be fixed; she wanted to be loved.

So, now I have learned to give her love directly first, through my loving embrace and touch, through my loving gaze into her eyes, my loving words of praise for everything I appreciate about her. Then, after the force of love is flowing full and free between our open hearts, we can discover if there is really anything that needs to be "fixed."

When the Masculine truly understands the Feminine heart, He puts aside the need for questioning and problem-solving, instead embracing His intimate partner with the caring force of His love. He might sing to Her, or dance Her around the room, or gently stroke Her arm, or say how much He really loves Her; however done, He will continue to give His sensitive, persistent and playful love until Her heart opens and Her face shines with happiness. Then, if there are details in Her life or in their intimate relationship that they need to deal with, they can do so without confusion; at Her core, and in the feeling-tone of their intimacy, love is flowing fully. Rather than trying to "fix" Her, he can apply His Masculine sense of mission to dealing with their lives in the world.

It is important for men and women to realize that often the Masculine sexual essence expresses its real love by trying to solve a problem, just as the Feminine sexual essence often tries to solve a real problem by offering emotional support. Men, especially, could learn that trying to solve her "problem" does not necessarily feel like real love to a woman with a Feminine sexual essence. Women, especially, could learn that trying to offer emotional support does not necessarily solve the problems that the Masculine sexual essence is really trying to fix.

However, we must honor these gifts as they are if we are to accept the Masculine and Feminine sexual essences as they are. The next time you feel your more Masculine partner trying to fix you, thank Him for His love and tell Him you don't need to be analyzed right now; in this moment, for instance, you need to be hugged. Chances are, He is only loving you anyway, though expressing it in Masculine form. Over time, He will learn that what you really want is love, not fixing (although even then, He may treat His embrace of you as a way to fix your emotional problem).

THE MASCULINE SEEKS RELEASE

"I want out of here!" This is the essential Masculine plea. When the Masculine is in a bad mood, He wants out. He feels constrained, weary, trapped and burdened by life, responsibilities and relationships. He seeks freedom from all this "stuff" of life. He wants out.

For a man with a strong Masculine sexual essence, life is not simply a given fact. Rather, it is a problem to be solved or an art to be mastered. It is a struggle. Therefore, when such a person feels burned out, tired and weary, His first desire is for release. He wants to get out of this "place" that requires so much work. He wants to be released from the burdens of life and relationship, for example through beer, TV, philosophy or meditation.

In intimate relationship, this tendency to want "out" can be misunderstood. For instance, a woman with a more Feminine sexual essence is tending to either doubt love or enjoy love. So when her partner wants out, she immediately assumes that he doesn't love her, and that is why he wants out. But very often, he does love her. He is just feeling trapped by the constraints of life, and so he is reacting to the feeling of being burdened by wanting out. He wants to feel release—not necessarily an end to his intimate relationship.

The Masculine tends to feel trapped when He is in a bad mood. He tends to feel trapped by life and relationship; that is, by the Feminine aspects of the world. Therefore, the Masculine tends to blame the Feminine for His feeling of constraint. He seeks release from this constraint and often tries to find this release by getting away from the Feminine, or by blaming Her or abusing Her in some way.

Just as the Feminine in a bad mood will always tend to feel unloved by the Masculine, the Masculine will always tend to feel burdened or constrained by the Feminine. The Feminine seeks more union with the

Masculine in an effort to relieve Her sense of being unloved. The Masculine seeks release from constraint in order to relieve His sense of being weary and burdened. All relationships between a more Feminine person and a more Masculine person will include this drama: the Feminine seeking to fill Her sense of emptiness and the Masculine seeking to release Himself from constraints.

THE MASCULINE LIKES THE EDGE

The Masculine likes the edge. Even as a form of relaxation, even as a form of recreation, the Masculine often prefers a challenge to a free ride. Driving the car a little faster than necessary. Watching boxing matches, football games and action movies. Competing on the tennis court, the backgammon board and at the poker table.

This is not because the Masculine always has to prove Himself, or because "men enjoy violence." It is because the Masculine comes alive at the edge, when challenged.

If I am in my Masculine energy, I don't like watching boxing matches because I like to see men get hurt; I like boxing matches because two men are competing with themselves and with each other, completely at their edge—the slightest loss of edge and the feedback is immediate. I don't like cop movies because I like to see people get shot. I like cop movies because they are usually stories of men taking on a challenge that demands their absolute best and tests their edge. They either meet the challenge by going beyond themselves and exceeding their personal limitations, or they die.

People who have an extremely Masculine sexual essence don't compete with each other in order to see who is better; they compete because they like competition itself. They like to test themselves. They like being on the edge.

This is where the Masculine flowers: at the edge. This is where the Masculine feels His purity: at the edge. This is where the Masculine discovers His real strengths and His real limitations: at the edge.

For boys transitioning into manhood, many cultures around the world and throughout history have provided an initiation ritual. This initiation virtually always involves the boy's edge being tested. It may involve him going out into the jungle by himself, stalking and then killing a tiger, or else not coming back at all. It may involve long periods of fasting, or wandering, or bodily mutilation, or terror.

In virtually every case, at the initiation rite's core is the boy's confrontation with personal limitation, with possible death, with inevitable fear. Here, he discovers the core of his true Masculine sexual essence, the part of him that really comes alive at the edge: his source of unshakable confidence in his ability to face—without collapsing—the real confrontations of life as well as his own limitations.

Such a boy, having passed through this initiation, can stand erect, whole, strong and open-hearted, knowing both the reality of his limitations and the reality of his deep resources. Even in the midst of fear, he has discovered that he has a tremendous capacity, far beyond his conventional assumptions, to live at the edge, or die trying. And because he has tasted his limitations, he knows that one day he will, indeed, die, and so will everybody he knows. His confidence and Masculine power are grounded in this humbling reality, and therefore his strength is tempered with true compassion.

He has both exceeded himself in victory and also knows that, in truth, he is not ultimately the victorious one. It is at his edge that the realization of authentic confidence and true surrender becomes most profound. And it is to this edge that the Masculine continues to return, whenever such a realization needs to be had.

In our modern culture, we have very few real challenges for which a man could honorably risk his life and taste the vivid exposure of his essential courage and compassion—his ability to offer his all at the edge of infinity. As a modern culture, we have war. We have the financial arena, wherein a man's financial life or death can be at stake (and often a man will act as if his financial life *is* his life). And we have sports—rituals of challenge in which heroes are the ones who really go beyond themselves, who can go beyond even what is considered possible. Those who can take the pressure and excel, who can "survive" the unpredictable and often dangerous challenge on the field, are accorded the benefits all Masculine heroes of all time have been accorded: money, women and glory.

But heroes, too, die. So the true Masculine hero holds onto nothing, abiding in the ecstasy of ungraspable infinity, not the pumped-up fullness of temporary accomplishment or victory.

ANGER, PASSION AND THE FREE MAN

Michael is a friend of mine, a good man who has never really been happy with the women in his life. He says he knows what he wants: a radiant, sexy, lively woman. But women like this don't seem to be interested in deep intimacy with Michael. They may want to be his friend, talking and sharing their thoughts with him, but Michael wants more than friendly conversation. He wants a passionate lover, not just a good friend.

"The women who do want to be my lover are nice people, but they aren't as wild and sexy as I would like. The women who are really glowing and full of life never seem to go for me," Michael often laments.

A basic principle of sexual polarity is that you will always attract your sexual reciprocal. Michael is well aware of what this means: He must not be putting out very strong Masculine energy, since he is not attracting radiantly Feminine women. Yet, Michael insists that he *is* Masculine. He says he has a successful business and a brilliant mind.

Michael is blind to his own demonstration, unable to feel the tone of the character he projects.

He and I recently had this conversation:

Michael informs me, "I was going to go on a 10-mile hike into the wilderness this weekend."

So I ask, "Why aren't you going? It sounds great!"

Michael answers, "My friends who were going with me are leaving early, and it would take me a day to catch up with them."

"So?" I wonder out loud.

"So, the main reason I was going was to socialize with my friends. I don't want to hike alone."

"Why didn't you ask them to wait for you?"

"Well," Michael continues, "I didn't want to push them too strongly. They had already made their decision, it seemed, and I didn't want to make them angry at me."

"Why should they get angry at you for asking them to wait?"

"Well, actually, I'm a little angry at them for going. But I try not to express anger, and I try not to make others angry."

"Why?"

"Because anger, violence, hate—I'm trying to grow beyond all that."

Michael is an emotionally castrated man. He has lost touch with the fullness of his Masculine sexual essence: He is afraid to be alone, he is afraid to assert his desires, he is afraid to feel and express his own anger, and he is afraid to receive anger from his friends. Although Michael might have a successful business, his intimacies will stop short of fulfilling him. Why? Because he is afraid of incarnating the full Masculine force, which includes anger, and even the passionate force of caring penetration, which can sometimes seem too aggressive.

Anger and passion are different expressions of the same Masculine force. You cannot negate one without negating the other. If a man disowns his anger, then he also disowns his Masculine passion. If he is afraid to express his anger, then he is afraid to express his passion. If his woman attempts to squelch his anger, then his passion will be likewise squelched. A man without the ability to be freely angry is a man without the ability to be freely loving: uninhibitedly passionate and alive.

Michael doesn't attract radiant, uninhibited women because his Masculine core isn't free and uninhibited. He suppresses his free flow of Masculine energy because he believes gentle is better than powerful, receptive is better than penetrating and friendly sharing is better than bold passion or delicious submission. He has denied himself the incarnation of the full Masculine force. And so he will attract women who likewise deny themselves the incarnation of the full Feminine force.

Inside, Michael's Masculine core desires to embrace a Feminine woman, but this core desire is blocked. From the outside, Michael seems to be very loving, sweet and nurturing, but not very assertive, confident or passionate. As a result of being Masculine at his core, but less Masculine in his expression, Michael doesn't attract the kind of intimate partner that he wants. He attracts women who have more warrior in them than goddess.

Many modern men and women have witnessed the "low" or dark side of the Masculine force and have decided, quite correctly, that such energy is often aggressive, suppressive and destructive. Therefore, they have decided certain aspects of the Feminine energy—soft, sharing and nurturing—are better to express than potentially aggressive Masculine energy. In doing so, many men, such as my friend Michael, have ceased expressing the entirety of their true Masculine desires—sexually, emotionally and even creatively. They have thrown the Masculine baby out with the destructive bathwater. They have chosen, consciously or unconsciously, to express less Masculine energy (to be less directional and demanding, for instance) than is true of their natural sexual essence.

Thus, they attract women who do not fulfill deepest the desires of their true sexual core. They attract women less radiantly Feminine than they truly desire, because they are putting out energy that is less Masculine than their true sexual core.

The sexual energy that you express always attracts its reciprocal. Therefore, weak Masculine energy attracts weak Feminine energy. Likewise, wild and radiant women are attracted to their reciprocal in confident, passionate men—men who are not afraid to assert their love and desire.

A key to emotional and sexual fulfillment is to behave true to your sexual essence. If your sexual essence is Masculine, then you have no choice but to be freely expressive of your Masculine force or to be unhappy. And to be freely Masculine, you must feel free to express all your Masculine qualities, which may include confident directionality, the desire for solitude, a passion for being on the edge, or a desire for experiences of extreme release.

Today's relational landscape is littered with lost men who have weak Masculine energy and hardened women who have weak Feminine energy, complaining that their partners don't give them what they want. It is time to reclaim the fullness of Masculine and Feminine, and attract the kind of partner who can fulfill our true desires.

DIS-EASE OF THE MODERN MAN

To better understand the Masculine's native gift in the practice of Intimate Communion, we must first understand the dis-ease that plagues modern men. Many men today have lost touch with their sexual essence. They may appear competent enough, but at their core they are weakened. They have lost touch with their humor and their certainty, in love and life. They have become uncommitted and undirected, or have adopted a false mission in order to make money or distract themselves from their underlying fear.

A key aspect of the Masculine sexual essence is its sense of true direction, or mission, in life. Thus, a man who has lost touch with his Masculine sexual essence becomes undirected and ambiguous at his core, and he seeks a mission in external sources. His life may begin to revolve around a football team, a business enterprise or a political cause. He may become obsessed with himself, with his personal projects and even his car; but at his core, he is lost.

In his deepest thoughts, he knows he has swerved from his course of true integrity. Such a man will only be able to give ambiguous love, for he fears that a commitment with a woman may cost him the freedom to do what he really wants to do when the time comes to do it. Therefore, it is necessary for a man to find his strong and true purpose, and align his life with integrity, before he is really capable of being fully present in intimate relationship.

STAGES OF DIRECTIONALITY

When the partner playing the Masculine pole in an intimacy does not animate the native directionality of the Masculine, the more Feminine partner begins to lose trust, and the passion in their intimacy diminishes. For example, if a man becomes too ambiguous, too wishy-washy or weak in his direction, his woman may begin to feel disappointed, or even angry at him, though she may still love him.

It should be obvious that although love is enough for a fulfilling friendship, love is not enough for a fulfilling emotional and sexual intimacy. Many times I have heard a concerned woman or man say, "I love my intimate partner, but it just feels like something is missing." That "something" is quite often the full flow of polarity between Masculine and Feminine sexual essences.

When two people commit to the practice of Intimate Communion, they are no longer merely responsible for themselves. They are also responsible for contributing their gifts in the ongoing practice of intimacy. This responsibility is not a moral sense of duty, nor is it part of a legal contract. It is the responsibility inherent in love—the same responsibility that moves us, quite naturally, to serve anyone we love, like our children or our friends. In Intimate Communion, we commit ourselves to practicing such service in emotional and sexual union with our intimate partners, just as in a 50/50 Relationship we commit ourselves to practicing self-responsibility and not becoming dependent on our partner.

The Masculine gift of directionality, which may be either present or lacking in intimacy, looks very different in each stage of relationship. In a Dependence Relationship, first-stage directionality is often expressed as a financial quest. The more Masculine partner is expected to "provide for the family" and to "put the bread on the table." In a Dependence Relationship, a woman may feel that her man depends on her to be always nurturing and sexy, and a man may feel that his woman depends on him to be always successful and strong in the world. And, in such a Dependence Relationship, their feelings may be correct. They may, in fact, depend on each other for sex or money because neither of them are yet whole in themselves.

In a 50/50 Relationship, two whole and independent people place more emphasis on creativity than on the accumulation of finances. Someone with an attractive second-stage Masculine is someone who knows how to create a good life. This probably includes stable finances, but may also include artistic creativity or the desire to improve the quality of life in many ways: community life, intellectual life, political life and spiritual life. The emphasis in a 50/50 Relationship is on getting *better*, rather than on getting *more*. Therefore, the second-stage Masculine's ability to "cut through" and persevere toward a creative goal is highly valued.

In the practice of Intimate Communion, appearance, finances and creative talents are still important, but the most important criterion of a potential intimate partner is his or her ability to *practice* spiritual maturity, rather than physical, financial and creative maturity. In Intimate Communion, the Masculine is valued for His ability to bloom any moment into love, even a difficult moment. The third-stage Masculine may use any means, from humor to anger to sensitive touching, but His communication is always the same: "Let's face this moment without turning away. Let's be fully present in direct relationship with one another. Let's allow the spacious love in our hearts to dissolve our resistance so that we may breathe fully and relax into our natural openness together."

To offer this kind of third-stage Masculine gift, a man or woman must be aligned with his or her highest priority, moment by moment, rather than be weak and ambiguous in intent. Only then is a person with a Masculine sexual essence capable of being fully present in intimacy without being distracted by his or her unfinished business. And only an undistracted Masculine partner can fully "touch" the Feminine partner's deepest heart-desires with steady and loving Masculine presence.

MID-LIFE CRISIS AND THE VISION QUEST

At one point in my life, I had finished with a major scientific research project, and I was emptied of purpose. Having finished with something that occupied me for years, my life was no longer driven by the same engine. That particular motive had exhausted itself after coming to fruition for me. I didn't know what to do with my day-to-day life.

I wasn't confused at all. I simply had finished my business, and no other business made itself obvious. The core of my life has always been spiritual practice—understanding myself and growing beyond fear into greater love—but the everyday details of my life change over the years, as do everyone's. And at this point, it was not obvious what the daily routine of my life was going to be, now that I had finished the project I had been working on for years.

So, what did I do? Did I spend more time with Ophelia now that my work was complete? No. I went into a mountain monastery in the South of France to practice intensive meditation. I was sealed in a small cell with a mattress, a meditation cushion and a toilet, and once a day, food was placed on a shelf I could reach from the window. I would stay in that cell, contemplating the nature of consciousness, until it became obvious I had other business to attend to.

Meanwhile, in California, Ophelia was growing concerned. Did I still love her? After all, there I was, sequestered alone, thousands of miles from her. Over the weeks, she created a scenario in her mind in which I no longer loved her. She grew frustrated and angry toward me.

I was really enjoying my time in the monastery, and I was also loving and missing Ophelia. In fact, even though I had remained in silence for the better part of a month, on her birthday I arranged for a remote telephone to be brought to my monastery cell so that I could wish her a happy birthday from across the earth. I dialed her number and waited to hear her sweet voice.

"Hello?" Ophelia answered.

"Hello, love! Happy birthday!" I greeted her warmly.

"Hello," she said, rather curtly.

"Ophelia, are you okay?" I wondered.

"No. I'm not. What do you expect?" she answered.

As the strange conversation went on, it became clear that in my absence she had conjured a feeling that I no longer loved her, and then responded to my "abandonment" with anger. All the while, I was enjoying deep meditation in the monastery, and certainly not abandoning Ophelia in my heart—although, obviously, I was choosing to be apart from her physically for this period. Ophelia felt like I was just choosing to be apart from her for the sake of being away from her; she felt I was rejecting her.

To someone with a Masculine sexual essence such as mine, choosing to be apart from my woman is rarely a rejection of her, but more often reflects a need to discover something on my own. The Masculine sexual essence most often discovers itself in solitude, rather than with an intimate partner.

Periodically, a man (or woman) with a Masculine sexual essence realizes that his life has become cluttered with unauthentic burdens, obligations and habits. In order to purify himself of a false life, he often must temporarily abandon all habitual relations in order to find his true core, the core with which he has lost touch. He most often discovers his true core in solitude, or in the company of other men (or people with a Masculine sexual essence).

The Feminine sexual essence often prefers emotional support and loving company during times of crises and life-change (and sometimes the Masculine does, too). But more often, a man (or woman) with a

Masculine sexual essence needs to let go of everything old, rediscover his true purpose and authentic way of life, and then re-engage his relationships in a new and refreshed way.

Our culture does not really allow people to do this; therefore, we have the so-called "mid-life crisis." During a typical mid-life crisis, a man begins to feel that he is in an unauthentic situation. He no longer feels authentic in his job, in his intimacy, with his family and friends. The only real option that our culture offers is quitting or changing jobs, getting a divorce and moving to another part of town—which are just what men often do during a mid-life crisis.

But if we honored that the Masculine discovers Himself in solitude, we would support men (or anyone with such a need) to temporarily abandon their worldly responsibilities, including their intimate relationship, and commit all of their energy and attention to rediscovering their true purpose, their authentic way of life. Then they could return to their family and intimates renewed and refreshed—full with their heart's desire. Or perhaps they would discover that they needed to change their intimacy in order to live an authentic life.

In any case, a man returns from a successful "vision quest" full of authentic commitment and inner integrity. Such a man's choices are aligned with his true desires, and so whatever he chooses to do will ring of truth, rather than be driven by old habit or fear.

It is important that people with a more Feminine sexual essence come to understand this Masculine need. If this need is not met, then the man will seek to "refresh" his Masculine core in some other, less permanent, ways.

He may seek a sexual affair, frequently with a younger woman who is "fresh" and "alive" (who appreciates and trusts his "manhood")—the very qualities that he would discover for himself, in a much deeper way, if he were to engage in a successful vision quest or retreat.

Surprisingly, the Masculine best achieves clarity about what He wants in an intimate relationship when He is on His own, outside of the intimate relationship! Most men discover their authentic desires in solitude, or perhaps while being challenged and supported by other men. Then they can re-enter the play of intimacy and express their love, now that they are refreshed.

In my own life, I have found that when I am feeling dissatisfied with my intimate relationship, it is virtually always because I have lost touch with my true purpose. When my life veers from authenticity, all of my life feels false, including my intimacy. The solution is not to end my intimacy because it no longer feels alive. The solution is to rediscover my core desires, my authentic purpose and my direction.

I do this best in solitude, or with other men who are doing the same. Then, having *realigned* my life, I can return to my intimacy refreshed. I no longer am looking for Ophelia to make my intimate life authentic. Rather, everything I do is now drenched in authenticity and integrity. I return to Ophelia to discover whether or not our relationship—our new and present relationship—is congruent with my deeply felt sense of authenticity.

I have always found that my relationship with Ophelia takes a quantum leap after these periods of solitude or vision questing. Our old patterns are gone. We see each other with new eyes. I am full of authentic direction and clarity. And when I embrace Ophelia, I do so because I really choose to do so, because my love for her is strong, not because we just happen to be intimate partners.

If more men and women understood this process, I am sure there would be a lower incidence of divorce. If you have a Masculine sexual essence and you feel like your life and intimacy are no longer authentic, and you notice yourself attracted to more "refreshing" Feminine forms, do not get a divorce! Instead, take care of your business and arrange for a real vision quest. Don't just leave your family and goof off. Rather, liberate yourself from all your worldly obligations and commit every ounce of your energy and attention to discovering your authentic vision of life.

Do whatever it takes. Rent a cabin in the mountains and remain in contemplative silence. Join a men's group committed to discovering authenticity. Fast and chant for days on end, like American Indians do. Wander the countryside while contemplating your true nature, like Hindu *sannyasins* do. Study scriptures like priests and rabbis do. Go on a fishing trip with your men friends, and seriously consider what the hell you are doing with your life!

Whatever you do, don't return until you can do so with authenticity. Then align your life and your relationships with your sense of authenticity. Allow what is no longer appropriate in your life to fall away. Whatever you do discover to be part of your authentic life, embrace without hesitation. Find out if you can create an authentic intimacy with your partner, now that you have planted your staff of clarity in the ground of your true purpose. If you can, then do it for real. If you can't, end it for real, and do whatever most serves your growth.

Remember that true growth is *always* marked by increased openness and ability to love. If it is time for your intimate partnership to come to an end because you have outgrown it, then you will most likely feel a mixture of pain, grief, sadness and love, as if your lover had died. If, however, your intimacy ends with much conflict, hardness, emotional closure and lack of communication, then you have probably *not outgrown* your relationship; you are just bailing. Don't leave a relationship until it falls away from you in love, if that is possible for you.

Anyone with a Masculine sexual essence must temporarily leave the daily habits of an intimate relationship in order to rediscover its own authenticity. As men and women, we must learn to allow and even support this need. With proper guidance, men don't necessarily need to get divorced or find a younger girlfriend in order to feel alive. They just need to rediscover their reason to live, their true purpose, their real heart's desire. If we can encourage and guide this process with humor and care, we can move our intimate relationships to their next step.

It is important, though, to discriminate between a true quest and the desire to merely shirk commitment and responsibility. When is a man merely running away? Hiding? Escaping from his past, his burdens, which he himself has created?

When a man seeks isolation in order to create more comfort in his life, he is probably hiding. A true vision quest is not comfortable at all. A true vision quest is an ordeal. It involves facing your real fears as well as your real desires. When a man is on an authentic vision quest, he is stripped of all distraction and faces the true color of his bones, the true sound of his heart, alone, without work or woman to occupy him.

However, when a man leaves an unpleasant situation to enjoy the immunity of solitude, he is only escaping growth. He is avoiding responsibility. He may think he is starting over, but nothing has really changed. He is just removing himself from the game he is already failing.

A true vision quest involves leaving the usual games of life, such as work and intimacy, long enough to reconnect with the authentic desires at your core, your real direction in life. Then you can return to the games of life and transform them into expressions of your highest gift.

A false escape from responsibility involves removing yourself from pain and constraint and seeking an easier situation with less pressure, perhaps by entering a new relationship or changing jobs. You have merely traded games; you haven't transformed the game of your life into an artful expression of your real gift.

A true vision quest cuts through the accumulated fat of unauthentic responsibility and motivation to reveal the moist certainty of your real heart, which can then shine through the game of your life and illuminate every step you take with the authentic light of your highest gift.

A false escape is more like changing clothes, refreshing you somewhat but not really changing your presence in the world or transforming the way you play the game.

In authentic solitude, or in the company of other dedicated men, the Masculine is stripped to its heart and bone. Here, a man (or woman) can discover his true purpose without distraction or consolation. Then, putting his flesh back on, returning to the daily game of work and relationship, he is centered in his own heart, and the concentric circles of his certainty and openness emanate outward, encompassing his career, his woman, his children and his every choice in life.

VARIETIES OF MASCULINE T-SHIRTS

At a party, it is not unusual for women to want to dance and for men to want to sit and watch, or talk seriously with one another while the women are going wild on the dance floor. The Feminine is *in* life and wants to move with the energies of life. The Masculine is *transcendental* to life, and wants to be free of life, outside of it, watching it perhaps, but not caught up in the chaos and flow that seems so native to the Feminine sexual essence.

In a first-stage moment, a man (or woman) with a Masculine sexual essence transcends life by avoiding emotions and attempting to stand above his partner and the flow of life. He doesn't want to get involved. He would rather watch TV and read the newspaper than talk with his woman. He would prefer to enjoy the realm of "perfection"—the perfect basketball shot, the perfectly answered crossword puzzle— than the "imperfect" realm of relationship, emotion and life. While his woman sips champagne to enjoy the dance of life more, he guzzles beer to numb himself to the hell in which he feels trapped.

A first-stage man may express his transcendental perspective by wearing a T-shirt that says, "Life sucks, and then you die." Of course, to some extent, he is right. Even the Buddha taught that life is suffering and impermanent—but then he also taught how to realize the truth of timeless freedom, not just how to drink beer and temporarily escape the pain.

Unlike the first-stage man, the second-stage man transcends life by worshiping mind. He loves to think about things, as if there were an answer to life that could be formulated through thought. He loves to question life and entertain various concepts, perspectives and philosophies. The second-stage man enjoys serious conversation, and often chooses an intimate partner based on shared philosophies and outlooks on life. He loves the "perfection" of good art, a fine bottle of wine and an elegant theory.

The second-stage man often attempts to create a personal realm of perfection, a Garden of Eden on earth. He may become involved in politics, or create a community where like-minded people can live together, or renovate a beach house where he can retreat in his personally designed paradise of comfort.

Furthermore, the second-stage man is either struggling with trying to figure it all out, or thinks that he *has* figured it out. He may wear many T-shirts that express his transcendence, his ability to rise above: "Life's a Beach"; "Visualize Peace"; "Question Authority"; or "Live Your Dream."

The third-stage man transcends life by realizing his true nature as well as the true nature of life itself. Although he may work to improve life, his moment-to-moment practice is to recognize life's inherent perfection—not in the details, but in the "perfect" witness of life itself: consciousness. He may say, "Life sucks," and then smile broadly. He may say, "Life's a beach," while remembering and empathizing with the millions of starving people who suffer each day on earth. The third-stage man experiences life as a temporary school, a place where each of us can learn to love fully and let go fully.

Of course life sucks; the third-stage question is, can you feel your true nature, the inherent perfection of consciousness, and thus transcend the suffering inherent in a place where everybody dies? Of course you can work to create a comfortable utopia on earth; the third-stage question is, can you also feel the tremendous suffering on earth with an open heart? Can you creatively improve life circumstances and still love without self-protection?

A third-stage man might wear a T-shirt that says, "Already free." He practices finding his happiness prior to his experiences, transcendental to life, yet inclusive of life. He recognizes that life is what it is: half pleasure and half pain, if you are relatively lucky. And even so, what is born eventually dies, maybe sooner, maybe later. What you can create can be destroyed—*will* be destroyed. This is the reality of life.

A third-stage man realizes that it is ultimately fruitless to try to escape life and relationship, or to try to improve life and relationship, as if such improvement will lead to true happiness.

In a third-stage moment, you realize that you cannot find truth either *in* the world and relationships, or *out* of the world and relationships. However, you can relax into and as your true nature, which *is* happiness—whether or not your world or relationships are pleasant. Your true nature is already free, already transcendental, already happy, already loving.

Liberated in the truth of his own being, a third-stage man might still renovate a beach house or go out drinking with his friends; but he won't be seeking happiness by such activities. He will be *expressing* happiness. He is already rested in transcendental happiness, in his true nature, in the space of awareness that always *is*, regardless of the flavor of experience.

SAINT BOGART

In the movie *Casablanca*, Humphrey Bogart's character was saying good-bye to the woman he loved, but whom he would never see again, as she was about to board a plane. He was obviously suffering, obviously in love, obviously wishing they could live together forever. But circumstances necessitated her departure. Bogart's character knew this. And he accepted this fate, even as his heart was an open wound.

In this moment, he lent his Masculine transcendence to the woman he loved, whom he would never see again. He said something like, "You and me don't add up to a hill of beans."

This is a quintessential expression of Masculine transcendence. Our personal experience doesn't mean anything in the scheme of the universe. Our intimate relationships, which seem so important to us, are barely a flash of dim light in the total radiance of the cosmos. Even all of humanity is but a moment; it will all come to naught in the eventual explosion of the sun.

Life doesn't amount to a hill of beans.

A first-stage man suffers this realization and tries to temporarily escape his pain through TV, alcohol, cigarettes, sex or work.

A second-stage man suffers this realization and works to improve his life through increasing his knowledge or building a creative and comfortable living situation. Life may not amount to a hill of beans, but he is going to try to find some answers, or at least enjoy the goods of life while it lasts.

A third-stage man suffers this realization and no longer seeks happiness by trying to gain knowledge or experience. Through suffering, he has gradually realized the futility of such seeking. Through grace, he has glimpsed his true nature, which is also the nature of the world, the spacious awareness and energy that transcends the particularities of life. He practices the moment-to-moment remembrance of that which already transcends the ups and downs of life. And he realizes that who he is, is already that one. He is *already* free.

When you wear a wristwatch all the time, it is easy to forget it. After a while, you are no longer aware of it on your arm. Because it is an unchanging aspect of your experience, you don't notice it. In the same way, who you are is who you *always* are, and is therefore very easy to forget. You—whoever you really are—are an absolute constant in your experience, and therefore go unnoticed, like a watch you always wear on your wrist.

However, when you finally do feel who you are, you realize that what you have always sought is actually who you always already are. Once you wake up to your true nature, you can begin the practice of remembering who you are, recognizing your true nature, whether your experience of life is presently pleasurable or painful. And you realize the transcendental perfection of your true nature is what you have been trying to replicate through drunken oblivion, TV absorption, deep intimacy, peaceful politics or a beautiful house on the beach.

A third-stage man practices the moment-to-moment recognition of his transcendental nature, who he truly is all the time, regardless of how big or beautiful his hill of beans.

This expression of the transcendental Masculine sexual essence is something a "Saint Bogart" would say. And that's why this scene in *Casablanca* is so memorable to so many people. Love transcends relationship. "I love you" is simply true, even if the heart is broken by the inevitable ending of relationship. The third-stage Masculine sexual essence is able to stand free and loving in the midst of such incidents, transcending such incidents in open awareness and love.

In Intimate Communion, the Feminine often teaches the Masculine that it is possible to be totally free and loving within life and relationship:

She demonstrates that you don't need to get out of life and relationship to be truly happy.

The Masculine often teaches the Feminine that it is possible to be totally free and loving whether or not life and relationship continue: He demonstrates that you don't need to hold onto life and relationship to be truly happy.

MASCULINITY, PURITY AND DEATH

Throughout history and around the world, men's clubs have sought to create a "pure" place, undisturbed by attractive, wild and chaotic Feminine energy. Historically, the academic "ivory tower" was a men's club, where the pure forms of ideas, mathematics, theories and concepts reigned supreme. Women have also been historically excluded from many spiritual men's clubs populated by Christian priests, Zen Buddhist monks, Hindu swamis and Jewish rabbis. These gatherings have always been characterized by a sense of purity, perfection and mystical transcendence. That is, they have approximated the unchanging stillness of death or the "beyond" more than the ever-changing unpredictability of life.

Of course, there have been clubs and goddess-cultures that have embraced both the Masculine and Feminine—both the deathlike and lifelike aspects of experience. I am only pointing out this observation: Those clubs that have excluded women have traditionally been dominated by the Masculine preference for non-change and perfection. That is, they have sought to re-create on earth a stark and formal version of that which transcends life on earth: death, or that which is beyond life.

The Masculine sexual essence is at home in death. It sometimes even courts death, both of itself and of others, as a form of pleasure: hunting, warring, race-car driving, etc. And if the Masculine sexual essence is not courting literal death, it is often courting a mystical death, an ego death, the ending of desire through spiritual practice.

Furthermore, even when a man (or anyone with a Masculine sexual essence) is strongly involved in life and relationship, he still seeks to re-create "death." In sex, he looks forward to that "little death" of orgasm, after which he can lie in a state of peace, free of desire, and fall asleep into sweet nothingness (often to his woman's dismay). In finances, he looks forward to "making a killing." In football, he hopes that his team "murders" the other on the field.

When men drink alcohol, it is often in an effort to create a feeling of oblivion, happy release and death-like bliss, rather than to enjoy the sensations of life more. It is a male ritual around the world to gather together and use some drug to the point of "losing it." In fact, such drug or alcohol use is often a kind of Masculine initiation, dividing the men from the boys. Who can be "at home" as the mind dissolves, the body numbs, and a death-like state of happy release from life approaches?

The first-stage Masculine is addicted to the non-responsible "freedom" of death, whether brought on by the bottle, the needle, the TV or the orgasm.

The second-stage Masculine is often tempered by the inner Feminine and thus does not admit His desire for the extreme death-like state. He often settles for virtual disembodiment: the world of heady theories rather than bodily sensuality, the realm of thinking rather than the realm of feeling. The second-stage Masculine often prefers good conversation to football, "sharing" to "wild" sex.

The third-stage Masculine is committed to practicing "death" while alive. That is, whether engaged in life or not, He remains aware of that which transcends life. Whether having sex or not, He remains full in the bliss that transcends bodily sensations. Whether in relationship or not, He is already free, as if already dead, fully responsive in relationship but deeply indifferent at the same time. A third-stage man practices the recognition of consciousness. He recognizes that consciousness is his true nature. It is that which is always true, always present, unaffected by experience and changeless even as his life continues to change.

Recognizing his true nature as consciousness, the mature third-stage man is already free, as if already dead, even while engaged in the play of life. He is already full before, during and after sex. He is already at peace, whether winning or losing the current game. Death is his home— not the empty death of denial, but the spacious, undefined infinity of perfect openness, "unclinging" awareness and unthreatened love.

This is the same "space" that the first-stage Masculine attempts to approximate through alcohol and orgasm, and the second-stage Masculine attempts to approximate through thinking and creative adventure. All men are only seeking to approximate whatever glimpse of perfection, of truth, of spacious peace, that they first experienced. They may try through money, sex, knowledge and creativity, but they will fail to re-create it.

They will fail because it cannot be created; it can only be recognized. It is *already* their true nature and their core. They *are* the spaciousness, the vastness, that they seek to experience through all the little deaths and releases they continually arrange for themselves. The third-stage man knows this, and thus practices the direct recognition of the part of him that is already dead, already indifferent, because it is already only witnessing life, never threatened or changed by life. Then, he practices remembering that part of him, relaxing into it, being it, even while lovingly embracing life.

Eventually he realizes he has always only been that one, that consciousness, already free of birth, change and death. Then he has truly relaxed in his home, *as* his home. The pleasurable sense of release he has experienced through beer, orgasm or thinking is just a tiny experience of the home he truly craves—the home where, paradoxically, he is already. In the third stage, he simply practices relaxing beyond his attention enough to recognize it.

THE MASCULINE EDGE GROWS THROUGH THE STAGES

Just as the Feminine learns the truth of love, stage by stage, the Masculine learns the truth of death. Stage by stage, He courts the edge and learns to transcend His fear of loss and death.

The first-stage Masculine edge is experienced during a challenge with an outer opponent, an "other": other stockbrokers, other football players, other chess masters, other countries. The object is to be a winner rather than a loser.

The second-stage Masculine edge is experienced during a challenge with your self: fighting your own inner demons, facing your own dark side and discovering your true inner resources. The object is to emerge a master of your own life.

The third-stage Masculine edge is experienced during a challenge of self-sacrifice: The point is not to survive, not to win and not to become a master of your own life, but to discover that which cannot die. You are not struggling to be victorious over an outer opponent or an inner demon; you are struggling with your own illusion that you *can* be victorious.

The third-stage Masculine hero is one who has "already died," who is completely willing to relax as the consciousness beyond the arising experiences of life and so no longer has anything fundamentally to lose, or to gain, by life. Therefore, this Masculine hero is truly free. His freedom is not limited to the football field or the arena of His own psyche; He has realized Freedom itself. He has realized his true nature: who He is before any particular experience comes, and after any particular experience goes.

Until a man (or woman) has recognized his true nature, he will always seek elsewhere for a sense of freedom. He will rationalize, "After I have enough money in the bank to live off the interest, then I will feel free." Or, "After I truly understand my psyche and write a book about it, then I will feel free."

But true freedom, the only freedom that cannot be threatened, is inherent to our being. In any moment, all we have to do is know who we are and we will know that who we are is never confined or threatened by experience, but only witnessing experience, no matter how pleasurable or painful such experience may be. We are already free, right now, in this moment—but we only know this freedom when we know who we are, who we always are, rather than getting lost in the details of the moment. And this ability to know who "I am" is what we cultivate in the practice of Intimate Communion.

The Feminine struggles to find love. In the first stage, She looks outwardly for another to love Her in a Dependence Relationship. In the second stage, She looks inwardly to give *herself* the love she wants, in a 50/50 Relationship with a partner who is doing likewise. Finally, in the third stage, She discovers that when She is not looking *for* love She can relax *as* love—and then practice being love in Intimate Communion.

The Masculine struggles to find freedom, and this struggle usually takes place at his edge. In the first stage, He attempts to find freedom by facing outward and mastering His financial edge. In the second stage, He seeks freedom by turning inward and attempting to master His psychological edges, His personal fears and His inner demons.

Finally, in the third stage, He realizes that His edge is an illusion. In fact, *He* is an illusion. Now, His edge is the practice of this realization, the moment-to-moment recognition that His essential fear—death—is based on a false presumption: that He is a separate something that can die.

In the practice of Intimate Communion, the Feminine realizes that whether She feels loved or not, She can always give love; that, in fact, She *is* love, although Her emotional clouds may be obscuring Her true nature, just like the sun's constant shine may be temporarily obscured by clouds. Therefore, in Intimate Communion, the Feminine gift is the gift of love, and this gift must be practiced.

In the practice of Intimate Communion, the Masculine realizes that whether He succeeds or fails in life, He is free; in fact, His true nature is freedom itself. He realizes that his thoughts and experiences come and go, and that He is always the witness of them, and always has been. He realizes that His true nature as consciousness always remains unaffected by experience, and this is obvious in any moment He remembers or recognizes His true nature. When He forgets His true nature and begins to mistake Himself for something that he experiences—such as His experience of money or creativity—then He suffers the inevitable pain of loss, since any experience that can be gained can also be lost.

In Intimate Communion, the Masculine gift is freedom and the Feminine gift is love, whether given by a woman or a man. The Masculine practices by realizing His true nature in spite of His experiences of gain and loss. This practice is His "edge." The Feminine practices the remembrance of love, surrendering into Her true nature *as* love, in spite of Her experiences of love and rejection.

9

The Feminine Way

THE FEMININE IS THE FORCE OF LIFE

The Feminine force is much more than womanhood. The Feminine is the force of life itself, and you can experience it in many ways.

Your favorite music is playing, and without thinking your body begins to move. Your arms arc through the air, your hips sway, your eyes close. Your body and the music seem to be one, moving gracefully with no separation. The dancing is spontaneous, unrehearsed, as if the music itself were the blood moving through your arms, legs and torso. Such is the dance of the Feminine force, the dance of love with no goal, the bodily celebration of life.

You are sitting at your desk trying to finish a crossword puzzle, thinking hard. The world outside of you seems not to exist as you focus mightily, searching for an answer to the puzzle. Suddenly, a gust of wind through your window carries the fragrance of gardenias from the garden. Your body relaxes and you let go of your concentrated effort as you sit back in the chair, inhaling the sweet smell of flowery delight, and smiling. Your breath becomes deep, your forehead smoothes and your shoulder muscles soften. The fragrance reminds you of life and unburdens you from your mental efforts, refreshing your smile and gratitude for the earth. Such is the Feminine reminder, the blessing of sensual joy and rejuvenation.

For a moment, allow yourself to feel your breath entering and leaving your lungs. Hold your breath, and notice how the desire to breathe becomes greater and greater, until finally you surrender to the force of breath itself. You will eventually give in to the desire to breathe, the desire to live. This is another aspect of the Feminine force of life, the energy that moves you to breathe.

Feel your heart. If you relax and sit quietly, you will be able to feel your heart pumping. You may also feel blood pulsing through your arms and legs. This constant circulation of life-blood is another aspect of the Feminine force—the energy that moves the blood through your body.

If it is possible from where you are sitting, listen to the wind blow, or watch the trees sway in the breeze. Everything in nature is in motion. If you looked at a handful of soil under a microscope, you would see millions of little organisms moving around. Water is moving up and down the trunks of trees and the stems of bushes. And within every drop of water, there are millions more little creatures constantly swimming. Nothing alive is ever really still and unmoving. Everywhere, life is motion.

Our bodies, our senses and the living earth are all manifestations of the Feminine force. She—the Feminine force—is the force of life. All that is attractive in life, and all that is frightening in life, are but aspects of Her dancing form. Volcanoes, rainbows, nipples, flowers, hurricanes and blood enchant us and repel us. The Feminine is not just manifest as women, as the female gender, but is alive as the entire living world.

When we allow ourselves to relax, to enjoy the living world of sights, sounds, smells and relationships of all kinds, then we allow ourselves to be intimate with the Feminine force. When we allow ourselves to feel—not only our own emotions but the "music" of the world around us—then we allow ourselves to move with the Feminine force.

Sexuality itself is a quintessential expression of the Feminine, a full-bodied relational dance of love, sensuality, feeling and creation. It doesn't matter whether you are a man or a woman; sexuality is an expression of the Feminine force of embodied love. How you relate to sexuality, the degree to which you feel free or restrained, reflects your attitude toward the Feminine force in general.

The energy that moves life is the force of the Feminine. She is unstoppable. She is the source of all life, the mover of blood, the breather of breath, the flow of the river's water. The Feminine *is* life. We can feel Her moving and living in any moment we are open to Her, or *as* Her.

THE CORE OF THE FEMININE IS RADIANCE

Imagine you are sitting on your porch, worrying over your mortgage payments. A hummingbird whizzes by and catches your attention. The bird zig-zags from flower to flower. As you gaze at the beautiful flowers—golden marigolds, red tulips, speckled foxgloves—you forget all about the mortgage. Instead, you smile at the beauty of the flowers, the bird, the sublime vision of natural glory. Your body relaxes and your heart opens. Your life has been graced, for a moment, by the radiant beauty of the Feminine force.

Driving along the freeway, you look up and behold a perfectly formed rainbow, alive with brilliant and subtle hues, ephemeral, glowing in midair. Amidst the speeding cars and concrete, in the middle of a gray and ordinary day of work, the rainbow is a blessing of splendor—a shining vision of the radiant Feminine mystery.

Radiance is at the core of the Feminine. Whether appearing in the vision of a flower, a rainbow, a man or a woman, there is a certain mysterious quality of grace, shine and beauty that can best be described as "radiance."

As our body ages, it may begin to wither. Our youthful, healthy glow may fade as our skin wrinkles and our hair thins. But if we are truly happy inside, then age brings with it a maturity, a depth and a power that only magnifies our radiance. Regardless of our outer appearance, our inner shine can glow brightly, and it is this radiance that is at the core of the Feminine.

Most of us are very aware of this shine, at least superficially. The cosmetic industry is very aware that radiance is at the core of the Feminine, and very attractive to both men and women. Make-up is advertised to make a woman's skin "glow," to add "luster" to her hair, to "brighten" her eyes and to "gloss" her lips. In a word, make-up is used to enhance Feminine *radiance*, if only superficially. Likewise, jewelry and clothing may enhance the shine of the Feminine's inherent radiance.

But it is the inherent radiance of love itself that is the true Feminine core. It can be enhanced or accentuated through the use of beautiful clothing, jewelry and make-up. It can be supported through maintaining good health and grooming. Yet there is only one way to truly magnify the inherent radiance of the Feminine: Love.

When your heart radiates love, you are radiant. Everyone has witnessed the transformations people go through when they fall in love. They seem to shine. They walk into a room and the room gets brighter. Love itself is a brightness that not only shines through a person's smile and eyes, but actually radiates into his or her surroundings.

How, then, do we magnify our inherent radiance? By relaxing into our loving heart. We must learn to let go of our resistances, and give love. Each of us will follow a different path of growth, but all true paths are paths of love. They are not paths *to* love; they are paths *of* love. Step by step—whether through therapy, intimacy, service or meditation— we practice opening our hearts and loving. As we do so, our shine be- comes brighter and brighter. The core of the Feminine is this brightness of love. And it is this radiance that the Masculine finds most attractive.

The Masculine looks to the Feminine for completion. Thus, the more strongly the Feminine shines, the more such a person will fulfill his or her Masculine partner's desire for completion, even without doing much else. A truly radiant person doesn't seem to have to *do* much to attract a partner, except radiate! And that radiance is very real, tangible and valuable.

THE FEMININE IS THE FORCE OF ATTRACTION AND ENCHANTMENT

Like a star, the moon, a flower or a sunset, the Feminine attracts and enchants us, opening our hearts to beauty and love.

We seek the Feminine when we go on vacation, often choosing places of extraordinary natural beauty in which to bask in Her enchantment. While contemplating the majesty of the Grand Canyon or the endless blue of the ocean, we are drawn out of the knot of our little problems. Even the glimpse of a beautiful man or woman attracts us out of our little world, so that we might feel enchanted for hours or days by his or her attractiveness.

It may be the way a man says something, or the look in a woman's eyes, or the way the clouds drift through the sunset sky, but whatever it is, the Feminine force of attraction makes us sigh, smile and relax. Men and women highly value this enchanting quality of the Feminine, in other people as well as in nature.

But I am not talking about mere physical attractiveness. I am talking about the inner beauty, the healing radiance, that shines so brightly from a happy heart. Such beauty is native to the Feminine, regardless of the particular physical appearance *through* which it shines. Tulip or rose, orange sunset or red sky, a nubile 17-year-old or a wise and graceful 60-year-old—the enchanting quality of the Feminine can shine just as brightly.

Not everybody is physically beautiful. Not everyone looks like the models who pose in popular magazines. And even those who are gorgeous in their younger years may become wrinkled, saggy and gray in their older years. This process of aging is completely natural, and it has nothing to do with true Feminine attractiveness.

For several months while I was writing this book, I lived on the Indonesian island of Bali. While I was there, I established a friendship with a Balinese family who owned and operated a little restaurant with three bamboo tables, and where I frequently ate. The family consisted of three sisters and their mother. The three sisters, all in their early 20s, were extraordinarily beautiful. Any one of them could have been a magazine cover girl. Two of the sisters were, in fact, professional models. Their bodies, their faces, their hair—everything about their appearance was captivating. I could hardly eat, their beauty was so enchanting.

For the first few weeks, they were the only people I saw at the small restaurant. Then one day, their mother came out from the kitchen into the dining area. I will never forget that moment. The three beautiful sisters were sitting in the dining area, talking. Their mother walked out and began talking with them. I was shocked by what I saw.

The mother was about 60 years old. Her brown skin was wrinkled from the sun, and she was clearly no longer a young woman. But her beauty was incomparable. From the mother's eyes shone a rare light of love, compassion and humor. Her every move was filled with an "otherworldly grace." She looked at me, and her smile lit up my heart. I couldn't believe it. As beautiful as her young daughters were, this old woman was far more beautiful.

It wasn't her physical appearance but her disposition that so enchanted me. She was so relaxed, so loving, so happy, so wise and so radiant that I felt like bowing in honor of her Feminine fullness. Her daughters were but small buds compared with the fullness of her flowering. Perhaps one day her daughters would achieve the graceful depth of Feminine maturity that their mother had, but for now, they were just good-looking girls. However, their mother—old and wrinkled as she was—inspired awe by the depth and fullness of her Feminine force. My heart widened at the sight of her and continued to do so every time I saw her over the next two months.

The Feminine *is* beautiful. The Feminine *is* radiant. Physical attractiveness could express an aspect of this radiance, but it doesn't last, and even while it does, it's only skin deep. However, the Feminine force in people is always attractive, loving and radiant, if it is rightfully honored and allowed to show itself in its unique fullness. A star need not hide its shine, no matter how "unnoticed" it feels.

WHY THE FEMININE WANTS TO BE NOTICED

In general, the more Feminine a person's sexual essence is, the more he or she will desire to be noticed as attractive. This is a natural sign of a more Feminine sexual essence.

If you have a Feminine sexual essence, then you are particularly sensitive to this quality of attractiveness, both your own and others'.

You are sensitive to whether you feel attractive, like a twinkling star or a glowing sunset—or whether you don't. It's painful to feel unattractive, or even unnoticed. Why? Because attractiveness is one of the native Feminine gifts. And we are only truly happy when we are giving our native gifts.

In our Masculine-dominated culture, this concern with attractiveness is often viewed as self-centered or petty. However, sensitivity to attractiveness is actually a natural recognition of the power, depth and beauty of one of the qualities of the Feminine force.

FEMININE RADIANCE IN MEN

The Feminine force is active in men as well as women. Male rock stars, models and body-builders—in fact, all men who cultivate their attractive radiance—are attempting to enhance their Feminine shine, their power of attraction and enchantment. Thanks to our modern cultural movement toward a 50/50 balance of Masculine and Feminine qualities, modern men are "allowed" to acknowledge their Feminine qualities more than in the past.

The popularity of men's hair styling salons and exercise spas, as well as manicures and cosmetic surgery for men, has increased dramatically over the last 20 years. Thankfully, it is now okay for men to be concerned with their attractiveness, just as it has been okay for women.

It is possible, however, for this trend toward men's reclamation of their Feminine to affect their intimacies. A client, Ann, once told me of her frustration with her boyfriend, Jon.

Jon spent quite a bit of money and time on his fancy wardrobe. When Jon and Ann prepared to go out together, Jon was usually late. He would stand in front of the mirror for what seemed to Ann like forever, making sure his hair was perfect, picking every little piece of lint off his new jacket and massaging men's moisturizing cream into his face.

Ann didn't feel particularly fulfilled by Jon's over-concern with his own attractiveness. She definitely liked the fact that he cared about his appearance, but she wished that *she* was the recipient of Jon's praise and adoration of Feminine attractiveness, not his own image in the mirror. Without thinking about it, Ann began to feel frustrated, wishing that Jon was more in his own Masculine energy, naturally attracted to *her* Feminine energy, rather than being so preoccupied with his own Feminine radiance.

A liability of some of today's men is that in seeking a healthy balance toward 50/50, they begin to give their own Feminine gifts of attraction and enchantment more appreciation than those of their intimate partner. It is one thing for a man to grow from a macho slob to a clean and attractive gentleman; it is quite another for a man to cherish his own attractiveness more than that of his chosen woman.

FEMININE, MASCULINE AND THE BODY

You've seen her. Maybe on a deserted beach as she happily slips out of her confining bathing suit and dives gracefully into the ocean, luxuriating in the feel of the water against her skin. Or perhaps it was on a dance floor, where she seemed to be the dancing expression of a universe happy to be itself. Or maybe you saw her walking down the street, not moving as purposefully as everyone else, but instead, moving with a Feminine ease and sensual relaxedness.

The Feminine lives in the world of sensation, the world of the body, the world of unseen connection to the flow of elements and natural forces. Any person, man or woman, who is thus connected to the world around him or her has a highly developed Feminine.

You have also seen someone who is animating extreme Masculine energy. Oftentimes you've watched him heading to his office. Eyes pointed straight ahead, never looking off to one side or the other, he strides purposefully, along the shortest straight-line route from where he is to where he's going. Nothing can distract him. He doesn't even seem to be aware of his body or the world of relations that surround him.

A man (or woman) in his extreme Masculine is likely to merely *use* his body, perhaps with the spare grace of efficiency; but for him the body is either irrelevant or, at best, a tool to help him accomplish whatever his current goal is. In fact, such a person only becomes conscious of his body when he is sick or in pain, when it becomes an obstruction to fulfilling his mission.

But the Feminine is inherently alive in the body. Whether in man or woman, the fully incarnated Feminine *is* loving sensuality, connectedness and full-bodied flow in the realm of sensations and life. People like this are a delight to behold. They remind each of us of the mysterious and unseen forces that exist within and around us that move our bodies and our feelings, but from which most of us are distracted by our preference for our own Masculine relationship to the world: goal-oriented, mental and sharp, as if we were cutting through a world of obstructions rather than dancing in a world of energy and sensation.

RELATIONSHIP IS THE FEMININE PRIORITY

To a woman with a Feminine sexual essence, relationship is a priority. If her relationship is going great, then she is essentially happy at her core, and she can deal with other difficulties that may arise, say, at work. When she is happy in her relationship, when she feels the flow of love, it shows: the Feminine shines. But when she is unhappy, it also shows.

For a woman with a Feminine sexual essence, her intimate relationship is *central* to her emotional being. Her whole emotional disposition is affected by whether her relationship is full of joy or full of pain. The tone of her intimate relationship colors her day, her work and her conversations with her friends. It is as if the color of her intimate relationship, whether light or dark, shines through the rest of her life, through her daily activities and her ability to function.

Not so for the Masculine. When He is out the door, His relationship is behind him. At work He is able to focus and concentrate, regardless of whether or not He and His partner had a fight in the morning.

It is as if the Feminine has a sensitive "relationship meter" in Her heart that is always sensitive to whether or not love is flowing in Her intimate relationship. When love is flowing, Her whole life lights up. When love is not flowing, a shadow is cast on Her day, at Her job, with Her friends and when She is alone. The meter in Her heart is always sensitive to how Her relationship feels to Her.

The heart-meter of the Masculine is tuned to a different frequency. The Masculine meter asks, "Is my quest, my mission, going well?" If a man with a Masculine sexual essence gets stuck for a few days trying to solve a problem he is working on at the office, his whole life might be colored by it. No matter how loving his partner is, he will be self-involved and unable to fully respond to her until his mission is restored. He may not be capable of sexual arousal for months if he perceives that his creative or financial quest is failing. However, once he feels that he is successfully back on track, suddenly his intimate life springs back to life. His whole life is colored by how his mission is going; whereas, for a woman with a Feminine essence, her whole life is colored by how her intimate relationship feels.

Without understanding this fundamental difference between the Masculine and Feminine sexual essence, it is easy to misunderstand our partner's needs. For instance, when a man with a Masculine essence is heavily depressed, it most likely has nothing to do with his partner. There is very little she can do directly for his mood, except give him support on his quest by empowering his mission with her love.

A woman with a Feminine sexual essence will naturally tend to feel that something is wrong with the relationship when she feels her partner is depressed day after day—after all, an unloving intimacy would be the most likely cause of *her* depression. But Masculine happiness is far more affected by a smooth or difficult life-mission than by a smooth or difficult intimate relationship.

In a similar misunderstanding, when a man with a Masculine sexual essence notices that his partner has been "down" for several days, he is all too likely to ask in a clinical fashion, "What's wrong?" Because his heart-meter is not as sensitive to relationship as the Feminine's, he may genuinely be confused as to the source of her unhappiness. After all, the only thing that would make *him* so depressed would be some kind of failure in his professional or creative life. So he will try to "fix the problem," and ask her all kinds of pointed and impersonal questions, with the good intention of trying to ferret out the cause of her lack of happiness and come up with a "cure"—usually some specific action that he recommends.

Yet, if he truly understood the Feminine heart-meter, he would put aside his questions and problem-solving and embrace his intimate partner with the caring force of love. He would be fully present with her, since her Feminine core will respond most strongly to the flow of love. Then, if there is anything to talk about, they can do so with their hearts already full. Whereas the main concern of the Masculine is direction, the main concern of the Feminine is relationship.

THE FEMININE STAYS TOO LONG,
THE MASCULINE LEAVES TOO SOON

In bed, heated by passionate loving, the Feminine opens, vulnerably, willingly, to the Masculine. The Masculine enters more deeply.

But also in bed, stung by impatient and abrupt words, the Feminine closes, unwilling to be open to the Masculine. The Masculine turns away and leaves.

Whereas the Masculine is either going deeper or pulling away, the Feminine is either opening or closing.

At the first sign of difficulty in their relationship, the Masculine and the Feminine both become concerned. The Masculine, in man or woman, questions if He should be in the relationship at all, and wonders whether He should leave before things become too committed. The Feminine in man or woman, instead of questioning whether She should continue in the relationship, contracts and closes Herself off from Her partner. If the Masculine softens and offers His love again, the Feminine gradually opens, though it may take days.

This is the cycle of the abused Feminine: opening when loved and closing when hurt, but rarely changing directions and leaving the relationship altogether. Cycling through good times and bad, opening and closing, the Feminine tends to stay in the relationship—sometimes too long for Her own good.

The Masculine tends to leave a questionable relationship too soon. The Feminine tends to stay in a questionable relationship too long.

Anatomically as well as emotionally, the gesture most native to the Feminine in intimacy is one of opening or closing. The Masculine, however, is either interested in entering more deeply or withdrawing and leaving. This is why it is often so difficult for a woman with an extremely Feminine sexual essence to leave a relationship, even when her friends tell her that the relationship isn't good for her. The direction away is not easy for her. She may close down when hurt, but then over time, as her partner offers her more love, she opens again. Any person, man or woman, with a Feminine sexual essence is unlikely to break this cycle of opening and closing, and leave an inappropriate relationship for good.

The key for a woman (or man) with an extreme Feminine sexual essence is to cultivate her own Masculine. Then, in addition to her heart's native Feminine ability to open or close, she will develop her Masculine ability to change direction and leave, if that is what is best.

MASCULINE AND FEMININE FORMS OF ADDICTION

Since the Feminine lives in the world of sensation and bodily participation, She tends to become addicted to an increase of sensual experience, perhaps through tasting delicious sweets, purchasing beautiful clothing or experiencing frequent social or sexual sensations. If the Feminine becomes addicted, it is usually to ways of *filling* Her sense of emptiness.

The Masculine, on the other hand, is more at home in "death" than in life, in the mind than in the body. He tends to become addicted to reducing sensation, *emptying* Himself and releasing Himself into void-like "perfection." He gets addicted to drinking to the point of numbness and forgetfulness, to achieving orgasm in order to empty Himself into sleep, or to working so hard to achieve professional perfection that He neglects His relationships and emotional life.

Addictions are always attempts to achieve a substitute version of the feeling of true love or true freedom. The Feminine becomes addicted to filling Her sense of emptiness, to approximations of truly fulfilling

love. The Masculine becomes addicted to releasing His sense of constraint, to approximations of truly liberating freedom. Whether through
the substitute love of food-induced fullness or the substitute freedom
of drug-induced oblivion, the Feminine and Masculine are only trying
to discover the truth of Their disowned core.

MASCULINE, FEMININE AND DEPOLARIZATION

Whereas Feminine support of Masculine direction is received as a
great gift, Feminine mistrust of Masculine direction can be a devastating
source of depolarization and tension. If you don't believe me, try telling
a man with a Masculine sexual essence how to drive a car, or that he
should stop and ask for directions because he is lost. Very little is more
depolarizing to such a man than for his direction to be criticized or
mistrusted by his intimate partner.

The core of the Masculine sexual essence is directionality, just as the
core of the Feminine sexual essence is radiance. If you have a Feminine
sexual essence, you can feel how instantly depolarizing it would be if
your intimate partner were to tell you that you are looking run down,
worn out, less than radiant: "Hey, honey, do you think you could put
on a little more make-up? You are looking rather dull."

To tell a man with a Masculine sexual essence that he is lost—to
question his direction, whether it is his financial, creative or spiritual
direction, or even just his ability to find his way in the car—has the
same depolarizing effect as telling a woman with a Feminine sexual
essence that she is drab, wrinkled or not very radiant. It causes an almost
tangible collapse, repulsion or contraction to occur.

Never tell a man with a Masculine sexual essence that he is wrong
and never tell a woman with a Feminine sexual essence that she is ugly

if you would like to enjoy, rather than murder, sexual polarity. Instead, invite the Masculine into a new and better direction by inspiring, supporting and attracting him. Evoke the Feminine's radiance by praising, appreciating and cherishing her.

At work, feel free to criticize anyone's direction or appearance; if necessary after all, at work your professional goals are much more important than maintaining sexual polarity between colleagues. The same is true in all other domains of interaction between Masculine and Feminine, be they politics, science, art or finances: Outside of the intimate relationship, those with a Masculine sexual essence must be willing to receive criticism of their direction, and those with a Feminine sexual essence must be willing to receive criticism of their radiance, if such criticism will truly serve the situation at hand.

But within intimate relationship, you must decide whether such criticism is worth the inevitably depolarizing effects. It is often much better, and just as effective, to describe your feelings rather than directly criticize your partner's direction or radiance.

For instance, if you don't agree with the direction in which your Masculine partner is investing money, you could say, "I get nervous when I see where your money is going," instead of, "You are making a bad investment." Likewise, you could say to your Feminine partner, "I really enjoy when your skin glows and your eyes shine," instead of, "Today you look particularly old."

Of course, there are many moments when instant communication is more important than maintaining polarity. In these moments, people should say to each other whatever is effective in order to get the point across. They should know, however, that a price will be paid if they directly criticize their partner's sexual core. Also, a price will be paid if the spirit moves you to speak and you don't.

Since the core of the Masculine sexual essence is directionality, anything you do to demonstrate trust and support of your Masculine partner's direction will turn Him on, and anything you do that demonstrates criticism or mistrust of your Masculine partner's direction will turn Him off—immediately, and rather extremely. The same holds true for the Feminine partner's radiance or attractiveness.

By understanding this natural dynamic, we can consciously choose how to serve ourselves, our partners and our relationships, rather than being stunned into asking, "What did I say that upset you so much?" or, "Why can't you accept the fact that sometimes you are wrong (ugly)?"

THE MASCULINE SPEAKS WORDS, BUT THE FEMININE HEARS MOOD AND TONE

"Damn it! Why can't you for once just *listen* to what I'm saying. Hear my words. I just told you that I love you!" He is yelling at her, his face red, veins standing out from his neck. She sits on the bed, her arms clasped around her knees, which are folded up against her chest. She's looking down at the floor.

She isn't really listening to what he is saying. All she can hear is the furious tone of his voice, his sharpness, his anger. She sees the rigidity in his body as he points his accusing finger at her. What he says isn't as important to her as how he is saying it.

He is taking great pains to spell things out for her. It is obvious that he is picking his words with great care, making sure that he says exactly what's on his mind. He gets more and more frustrated as his carefully chosen words seem to make no difference at all. In fact, she seems to be closing down more and more. She feels like she is being bombarded with anger and sharpness. She is protecting herself from the pain that his tone represents to her. She can't even hear his words through the angry energy that he is focusing on her.

What he doesn't understand is that while the Masculine lives in a world of concepts and perspectives, the Feminine lives in a world of bodily communication and energetic sensation. Exactly what he is saying makes much less of an impression on her than what his body and emotional tone are communicating.

It is to this domain, the domain of the body and sensation, that the Feminine invites the Masculine—away from the heady world of good points and articulated examples, and into the feeling world of tangibly transmitted mood and touch.

If he would only realize this and change his mode of expression, she would be much more receptive to him. Instead of trying to tell her how much he loves her, attempting to argue her into believing him, he would just relax and give his love to her directly. If he would only touch her arm with love, rather than point his finger at her, she would feel his loving acceptance. If the tone of his voice carried love rather than anger, she would hear him. If his eyes said love rather than frustration, she would feel his care for her. The Feminine hears, sees and feels through the body. No matter what he thinks he is communicating through his words, what she is receiving is the message of his body and emotional tone.

THE MASCULINE SPEAKS "DO," THE FEMININE SPEAKS "FEEL"

Imagine a woman with a Feminine sexual essence talking with her man, who has a Masculine sexual essence.

She says to him, "I feel lonely."

He responds with, "Well, why don't you cultivate more friendships?"

She says something about her feeling and he responds by suggesting she do something about it. She communicates an emotion and he communicates an action.

He says to her, "Do you want to go visit the Smiths tonight?" He asks her about an action.

She responds with, "I'm feeling anxious about my new job." She shares her feeling with him.

"Yes," he says, "but do you want to go to the Smiths tonight, yes or no?"

The Masculine prefers to communicate in terms of action and analysis, but the Feminine prefers to communicate in terms of feeling. Therefore, a man often wants to know what his partner wants to do; that is, which path she wants to take. But she often answers his questions by describing her current feeling or emotion, rather than by stating the action she wants to take.

In the same way, when she asks him how he is feeling, he often answers by telling her what he wants to do.

She asks him, "Are you angry at Bob?" That is, she asks about his feelings.

He answers, "I want to punch him in the nose." He tells her what he wants to do, what action he wants to take.

At another time, she asks him, "Do you love me?"

And he answers with something like, "How can you ask me that after everything I have done for you?"

To the Masculine, actions are the proof of feelings. So a man often thinks that it should be obvious to his partner that he loves her because of what he *does* for her. For the Feminine, however, actions are secondary to the flow of feelings: No matter what the Masculine does, his woman may not *feel* His love. She is sensitive, moment to moment, to the emotional flow between them. In terms of what She feels in *this* moment, it is irrelevant to the Feminine essence what He has done for her in the past.

Furthermore, to the Masculine, emotional flow may actually be sec-ondary to physically expressed love, to love in action. That is, a woman may be loving her partner without limits, but if she doesn't do something for her man that expresses love physically, he may not feel her love.

She may say, "Can't you feel how much I love you?"

And he may say, "If you loved me, you would have (or wouldn't have) done such and such."

THE FEMININE FLOWS,
THE MASCULINE GOES

The Feminine has a certain way of getting things done. Suppose a woman with a Feminine sexual essence is packing for a camping trip. She goes into the kitchen to fill the water bottle, sees there's some oat-meal on the counter, and puts it into a pot to cook. The phone rings, so she answers it in the other room. As she's talking she sees unpaid bills on her desk. She hangs up, pays them, and notices a note with the phone number of a friend who is leaving town in a few days. She calls her up, and so on. Eventually she makes her way back into the kitchen, sees the water bottle on the counter and remembers that she was packing for her camping trip and making oatmeal.

Suppose a man with a Masculine sexual essence is packing for the same camping trip. He sits down and makes a list of all the things he could possibly need for the trip. He figures out into which backpack pocket each of the things is going to go, and then he moves purpose-fully through the house collecting all the items. While he is moving from the bedroom to the hall closet he doesn't even *see* the rest of the house that he's walking through. As he probes through the boxes in the closet searching for the flashlight, he is so focused on his task that he might not even hear the phone ringing.

In my own intimacy, very little "gets in the way" of my actions, so Ophelia can always count on me to carry through with what I say I am going to do. She can trust that I will act with confidence and integrity no matter what may come up, even in the midst of obstructions and turmoil.

I often expect that Ophelia is also able to act and think clearly regardless of her emotions. However, because of the strength of her Feminine essence, her emotions often move her more strongly than her goals. When Ophelia says she is going to do something, I might expect her to carry through with it, no matter how she is feeling, unless I remember that her essence is more Feminine than mine. Then, I realize that Ophelia will give priority to her emotions (or her friend's and family's), rather than her current direction of action.

One day years ago, Ophelia and I were at home, each of us working in our studios. Ophelia was writing an important term paper on sacred dance that was due in several days, for a class that she needed to obtain her bachelor's degree. A friend of Ophelia's called on the phone, crying, in the midst of an emotional situation. As I watched Ophelia flow fully and immediately into the conversation with her friend, forgetting about the term paper completely, I noticed that there was a little tension in me. I realized that what was bothering me was that Ophelia had abandoned her mission; she didn't seem to care that she needed to finish her paper and only had a few days left.

If a friend in crisis calls Ophelia on the phone, crying, Ophelia will give her friend's emotions priority. She is likely to put down whatever she is doing and flow into sympathetic conversation with her friend. But if my friend was to call me in such a moment, I would automatically assess the various courses of possible action: Is it better to talk with him now or to wait until after I finish with the business at hand? Is there someone else he can call who could serve him better? What can he do about his situation right now?

In my Masculine way, I would translate the emotional situation into possible courses of action, examine each course and then choose what I thought was the best one. For Ophelia, however, there isn't even a decision to make. She automatically flows in empathy with the intensity of her friend's emotions, offering her feeling-support and not really thinking about all the alternative courses of action that are immediately possible.

In a real emotional emergency, my "directionality" could get in the way of my ability to provide needed emotional support for my friend, whereas Ophelia would be right there with no questions asked.

On the other hand, if a friend called just to chat, Ophelia would also be very likely to sit for hours and talk, completely forgetting the task that she was working on when the phone rang. I would be much more likely to explain to my friend that I was working on something important and suggest another time when I would be free to talk with him.

The Feminine in man or woman deals with what's at hand, flowing from one thing to another. Rather than following a predetermined sequence of steps allowing no distractions, the Feminine responds to the events and people that are in front of Her. The Masculine acts to achieve a goal; the Feminine responds to the immediate needs of Herself and others. Obviously, to be both effective and healthy, we must each learn to animate either Masculine or Feminine, in response to the needs of the situation. When we understand both ways, we neither denigrate nor overvalue one way or another.

One Masculine gift is the ability to persist in attunement with the big picture, the overall perspective, the long-term goal—without being side-tracked by people or "little things." One Feminine gift is the ability to stay connected with immediate reality, with the ever-changing needs of people and of life, rather than getting lost in the big picture and forgetting, for instance, that the body needs daily care or that people are not just machines you can turn on, use and then turn off.

The Masculine tends to be blind to the trees, but is good at always viewing the big picture of the forest. The Feminine tends to forget the forest, but is intimately connected with and aware of each and every tree She touches. Neither Masculine nor Feminine is complete in itself— though in the right moment, each is a perfect gift.

FEMININE FLOW IS PAID LESS THAN MASCULINE GO

The Feminine and Masculine both have their place in the workings of our daily life, and they should be honored, and paid, equally. Unfortunately, our culture still pays much more for Masculine than for Feminine skills and talents.

As a typical modern culture, America pays for analytical and goal-achieving behavior in both men and women. That is, it pays for navigating the boat, not for the flow of the ocean upon which the boat rides. Like the flow of the ocean, the Feminine is often taken for granted.

Though immensely powerful, the Feminine way is like water, flowing into the shapes of its surroundings rather than pushing ahead to have its way. Though not passive at all, the Feminine naturally embraces the dynamic shape of the moment. The Feminine senses and serves someone's real and complex needs, for example, by true healing (underpaid Feminine) rather than by cutting away a single symptom with drugs and surgery (overpaid Masculine).

The Feminine is also superior to the Masculine in any situation that necessitates flowing among a dozen tasks at once—for example, by swirling with a group of chaotic children, somehow keeping it all together yet also managing to be everywhere at once, and still imparting an atmosphere of love, trust and mutual respect rather than mere obedience to authority. Kindergarten teachers are paid less than college instructors, though I'm not sure which job is more difficult or demanding.

This Feminine dance is undervalued in our culture. Many men and women have had to forsake their more Feminine talents and develop their Masculine skills in order to succeed financially. In succumbing to this lopsided cultural demand, we have all lost. We have lost many gifts of true Feminine genius. And we have continued to tacitly support an anti-Feminine stance, which dishonors all service by women and men that is not rendered in the Masculine mode.

MASCULINE AND FEMININE IN POLITICS

In any field where long-term goals are valued over and above the quality of human relationship, the Feminine is excluded. Therefore, our political arena has tended to be Masculine-oriented, and dominated by men. Even the few exceptional women who have succeeded in gaining a high position in political office have established themselves based on their Masculine abilities. In large part, they have been elected for powers of analysis, vision and determination rather than for powers of cooperation, healing and intuition.

Understandably, a person in high political office should be able to make long-term strategic decisions whenever necessary—even when his or her intimate personal life is temporarily full of pain. So it is easy to understand why the men and women who have been elected to high office have been accorded their positions largely due to their ability to animate their Masculine. An individual in such a position may need to make an important critical analysis at any moment—even amidst personal or intimate turmoil.

The Masculine ability to switch modes—from intimacy mode to analysis mode—is very useful in political as well as corporate situations. If you are a key figure in such a situation, you are not supposed to let your emotions get in the way of your work. Your daily actions are supposed to be completely dissociated from the emotions of your personal, intimate life. And thus politics as we know it has tended to be a "men's club," populated by Masculine-oriented men and women.

Because our political decisions have been so one-sidedly Masculine, we have championed the quest for freedom at the expense of love's wisdom. We have consistently disregarded human well-being and individual need for the sake of so-called political, ideological and economic freedom.

The answer, of course, is not to downplay the strengths of the Masculine when it comes to long-term planning, clear analysis and vision unfettered by personal turmoil. However, it is now time to reclaim the Feminine way of politics, both globally and within our intimate sphere. Just as our intimate relationships have grown from situations of male dominance toward more balanced 50/50 partnerships, so must our political relationships.

Furthermore, just as our intimacies could eventually grow beyond the 50/50 Relationship to the practice of Intimate Communion, our politics could also, in time, honor the unique gifts of the extreme Masculine *and* Feminine. There *are* times when a decision has to be made that, in the short term, will result in loss of life, but in the "big picture" will yield long-term gifts for all. Decisions of this kind may be involved in policy concerning euthanasia and war, for instance. The Masculine is more at home amidst death than is the Feminine, and thus should be trusted more in the necessary moments of crisis that do occur in our lives. However, the Feminine, in both women and men, is far more attuned to appropriate action when it comes to the propagation and support of life, human and otherwise.

We must first achieve a 50/50 balance in every political arena, just as there is a necessary stage during which intimate partners should learn to split the responsibilities of their relationship right down the middle. But then we must learn to let go of our hold on "balance" and practice trusting the uniquely Masculine and Feminine gifts. Thus, when it comes to ecological, interpersonal and bodily legislation, the Masculine must learn to relinquish its control and trust Feminine wisdom *more* than its own long-term strategy.

In intimate relationships as well as in global politics, the Masculine and Feminine are *not* equally gifted at every task. Rather, after we balance the pervasive Masculine one-sidedness in intimacy as well as politics, we must let go of the need to hold fast to a 50/50 ideal. Instead, we must learn to trust each other's differences as gifts.

The Masculine must be willing to observe that, in certain situations, Feminine wisdom is superior. And the Feminine must be willing to observe the same about the Masculine. Then, based on the obvious gifts of the Masculine and Feminine, we can begin to develop a politics of trust, in intimacy as well as at a global level.

In certain moments we become blinded by our emotions, and we cling too tightly to that which must die, be it an intimate relationship, an embryo or a hero. In such moments, we must learn to trust the wisdom of the Masculine, which is able to act clearly in spite of emotional feelings.

In certain moments we become blinded by our quest for freedom: political, financial and even spiritual. We dissociate our actions from our heart, and end up with a sterile and rigidly life-suppressive political regime or intimate partnership. In such moments, we must learn to trust the wisdom of the Feminine, which is the genius inherent in relationship, bodily intuition and the natural force of life.

There are times when the Feminine does allow personal emotion to get in the way of clear thinking and effective actions; but equally, or perhaps more often, the Masculine allows clear thinking to get in the way of love. Without love, our lives are empty. And at this point in our evolution, both intimately and politically, it is time for the Masculine to lay down its analytical sword, temporarily, and allow the Feminine to heal the unnecessary slices and gashes wrought by men and women who would prefer to stand separate and think rather than participate and love.

THE FEMININE IS THE FORCE OF CREATION AND DESTRUCTION

Our culture embraces the fact that the Feminine gives birth and nurtures. After all, we have witnessed many mothers giving birth to and raising their children. But if we extend our view to include all of nature, we see that the "Mother" not only gives birth to the children of the animal and plant kingdom; she also consumes them, digests them and gives birth to more. The Great Birther, Nature Herself, is also the Great Consumer, eventually eating the very children She has generated, destroying life only to create again.

The Feminine is the force of creation *and* destruction. Any man or woman who does not embrace the destructive qualities of the Feminine is denying Her full expression.

A man with a weak Masculine is especially prone to despise and fear these qualities and may attempt to suppress the more destructive elements of the Feminine force in his partner. Such a man withdraws when his partner begins to get wild, looking as if she might "eat him alive." He acts like he is disgusted at her mood, but she can feel the truth: He is afraid. He is afraid of the destructive aspects of the Feminine force, and therefore he fails to embrace her, including every part of her, light and dark, calm and wild.

Anyone with a strong Feminine sexual essence also has a strongly wild and destructive aspect. This aspect completes the fullness of the Feminine spectrum; without it, for instance, sexuality loses its passion and becomes prissy and genteel. The fullness of the ocean includes its storms and dangerous currents. A swimming pool is safer, but it is also far less than the ocean.

After years of criticism, a woman may come to reject the "dangerous" aspects of her own Feminine sexual essence. In doing so, her sexual essence becomes partially owned and partially disowned. Her sexual core becomes weakened. Her sexual energy is suppressed. Her Feminine radiance is diminished.

Many of today's men and women have opted for the safety of neat little swimming pools of contained Feminine energy. They have done this for so long that they have forgotten the immensity, and the fury, of the uncontained Feminine ocean. But beneath the surface, the well-contained fury of the Feminine can begin to turn back on itself.

When the fury of the Feminine is contained, it becomes self-destructive. When wild Feminine storms are disallowed in relationship, they become self-contained and engulf themselves inwardly. Rather than providing the Feminine with raw power, fullness and immense energy, this furious Feminine aspect implodes upon itself, creating a black hole. Rather than radiating outwardly, it sucks energy inwardly.

A man or woman with an imploded Feminine is likely to be self-destructive, perhaps even to the point of physical disease. The solution is not merely to yell and scream and express rage, fury and unbridled power, although that might help at times. The solution is to not contain the wild Feminine in the first place.

The Feminine is never conquered; its energy is far too immense to be defeated. In our culture, suppressed Feminine fury is either turned back upon itself in a mood of self-destruction, or propelled outward in a mood of rage. But there is a third option: the wild Feminine can become "husbanded" through love, by both men and women.

For instance, by loving herself, every part of herself, a woman with a Feminine sexual essence "husbands" her own wild energy by wedding it to the energy of steady love. She provides herself with a center of loving stability around which her Feminine energy is absolutely free to move in its full range of expression. She knows that love is stable in her heart before, during and after the emotional storm.

If her partner can learn to grow beyond his fear, he too can provide a stable heart of love for her Feminine fury, neither rejecting nor consoling it, but standing free and strong in the midst of her fury, and loving.

This coupling of Masculine and Feminine power occurs both within individuals and between partners. It provides the ever-present stability (Masculine) and raw energy (Feminine) necessary for a dynamic and growing intimate relationship. Sexual passion and emotional vibrancy peter out when the Feminine is contained or when the Masculine is bent in fear. Both are necessary for the fullness of love.

When, as men and women, we are no longer afraid of drowning, the Feminine swimming pool can be liberated, uncontained and restored to its native self: the immense and glorious ocean. Sometimes it is dangerously wild and sometimes exquisitely calm. But always, the true and free Feminine is full. And so is the woman or man who is unafraid to honor and re-own every aspect of her or his wild Feminine.

THE FEMININE IS NOT
ALWAYS APPRECIATED

The Feminine force of life is often too unpredictable for the Masculine mind. She's like a gentle breeze that becomes a hurricane, then suddenly calms again into the warm and quiet embrace of a balmy summer afternoon. The Feminine force of life is often too wise for the Masculine's need to know: The mysterious energy of the evolving cosmos is always superior to our temporary scientific notions about it, which seem to become outdated and revised weekly.

The pure Feminine is the force that moves life, not the abstract logic that stands outside, analyzing and commenting about what it sees. The Feminine is more like the ocean than like a scientist or a TV news commentator. The power of the ocean does not derive from its structured expressions of analysis and logic, but from its immense depth, motion, energy and vastness. As we learn to relax into this powerful depth of living energy, our bodies become radiant with health, our relationships become rejuvenated and our minds become moved by passion, rather than by dry and rigid abstractions.

The Masculine is like a boat on the ocean, navigating the shortest route from point A to point B. But oceanic Femininity doesn't move along a single traceable line from one point to another. It flows in many directions at once—sometimes calmly, but sometimes with such a tremendous force that it could easily submerge any boat in its depths.

The free Feminine force is alive, nurturing, healing, rejuvenating and full of life, like the free-flowing ocean. And like the ocean, it is sometimes wild, unfathomable, dark, untamable and even destructive in its power.

Very few of us trust our immediate connection with nature, or the intuitive intelligence of our body. All too easily, we align ourselves with the logical world of Masculine intelligence. As a culture, we have become so Masculine that we are much more comfortable with analytical problem-solving than with ecstatic dancing! We would rather paddle around in the safety of a man-made swimming pool than learn how to swim in the immense and glorious power of the ocean. The Masculine often wants to pin the Feminine down and keep Her contained, rather than let Her flow as she will.

A married couple that came to me for counseling, Alice and Richard, personify this difference between the Feminine, which is the force of life itself, and the Masculine, which transcends life, and often seeks to analyze, contain or navigate through life. Alice wants to laugh and splash in the rain; Richard wants to hurry to his destination with an umbrella. Alice wants to spring onto the dance floor and let loose; Richard wants to crinkle his forehead and talk philosophy over brandy. Alice can't help but give affectionate attention to purring cats and frisky dogs; Richard doesn't like to risk exposing himself to fleas.

When Alice tries to express herself, Richard frequently says to her, "What do you *mean* by that? Give me an example. You're not making sense to me." After years of Richard's pointed comments, Alice has begun to feel that she is inarticulate and that Richard will "win" in a verbal argument because she can't analyze and articulate her desires as clearly as Richard. Alice's feelings and emotions flow very strongly—it is Richard who wants her to stand outside of her emotions and try to analyze and control them.

As does our entire Masculine-dominated culture, Richard suppresses the fullness of Alice's Feminine ocean. For instance, he demands that she articulate, in navigable words, every little wave of feeling that arises in her ocean of emotions. He demands a reason for why she did this, for why she did that. Richard is trying to turn Alice's spontaneously flowing ocean into a tidy swimming pool, something he can handle. And in doing so, he is denying her Feminine sexual essence its immense and innate power.

DISOWNING THE FEMININE CORE

It's Christmas morning. A 10-year-old girl sits amongst the bright wrapping paper and bits and pieces of boxes torn open with the usual abandon. She sits smiling, watching her sister posing in her fancy new clothes and jewelry, listening to her parents praise her sister's beauty, unable to identify the vague feeling of unease that she feels as she looks over the books and educational games she has received as presents.

Her mother turns to her father and says, "Aren't we blessed, dear, to have two daughters so special in their own ways?"

This little girl, whose native sexual essence happens to *actually* lie toward the more Feminine end of the spectrum, is being tacitly "shaped" by her parents' perceptions and expectations. Over time, she will likely accept the "fact" that she is a smart person, but not a particularly radiant one, for example. A girl like this will probably develop other, more Masculine aspects of her personality, her abstract analytical and organizational skills, perhaps, or her competitive edge. Of course, it's very healthy to develop the entire spectrum of qualities, Masculine and Feminine. It's just that a girl like this may overemphasize developing her Masculine energy and thereby deny, for example, her native radiance and attractiveness, as well as all the other natural qualities of her Feminine sexual essence, which remain lingering in her heart.

By denying her natural radiance and power of attraction, for instance, by numbing herself or resigning herself to a "hopeless" situation, she denies a core aspect of the Feminine sexual essence. She disempowers an aspect of her Feminine core.

An adult woman whose Feminine sexual essence has been

disempowered will tend to attract men whose Masculine sexual essence has been likewise disempowered. Such men are relatively ambiguous and lacking in confidence. In other words, if you are a woman who has denied the native radiance—or sensuality, or creative chaos, or wild power—of your Feminine sexual essence, you will probably find yourself in a relationship with a man who is afraid to take a strong stand in your lives together: He is denying the native force of his Masculine sexual essence. Your Feminine sexual essence won't be fulfilled by such a man.

The first step in attracting a partner with a strong Masculine sexual essence, or in evoking more Masculine energy from your present partner, is to cultivate your ability to trust your own Feminine core. By relaxing into your Feminine essence's native and inherent attractiveness, radiance, wildness, spontaneity and intuitive connection with life, you will empower your core, and you will shine. Then you will also automatically attract, or evoke in men, a strong Masculine sexual essence.

WHY SHOULD WE HIDE?

To grow beyond the 50/50 Relationship into the fullness of Intimate Communion, we must understand the differences between our natural sexual essence and the sexual character we may have become. Our sexual blooming has been influenced by the ways we were treated in the past by our parents, friends and lovers. We may have been praised for our Neutral, Masculine or Feminine essences, or we may have been wounded or even abused. It is important for us to discriminate between conscious sexual growth and unconscious sexual hiding.

Elaine is a woman who came to me for counseling with a deeply wounded Feminine sexual essence. When Elaine was a child, her mother often worked late at night. Sometimes, Elaine's father would come into her room and touch Elaine playfully. These episodes of touching gradually became more and more sexually oriented, and, eventually, Elaine's father was regularly abusing her sexually.

Sexual abuse is a complex and important issue, which is not the focus of this book. (There are many excellent books on the subject for those who want to research the topic further.) However, we will look at one simple consequence of this kind of abusive relationship: Anyone who suffers this kind of circumstance will probably develop a strong resistance to the Masculine force. Her father was her first source of Masculine energy, and so now as an adult, Elaine feels guilty, angry, helpless and full of pain—the same emotions she felt with her father—whenever she feels the extreme energy of the Masculine. She tends to close down whenever extreme Masculine energy is offered to her—it doesn't matter whether this energy is abusive or offered as a loving gift. Her automatic bodily response is mistrust. She doesn't feel safe in her intimacies with men.

In fact, Elaine also distrusts her own Feminine core, since it was "clearly" her femininity that attracted the abuse in the first place, or so it seemed to the little girl Elaine. After all, her brother wasn't abused— she was. She was so pretty and so nice to touch, her father used to say before abusing her. Her body has learned that its mere Feminine radiance attracts violation, and so at some level she has rejected her own Feminine essence. In different women, this kind of sexual self-rejection may take many forms, from vaginal and uterine diseases to feelings of confusion or worthlessness.

As an adult, Elaine is a compassionate, kind, intelligent and loving person, but she resists being entered by the Masculine force. And at the same time, she also suppresses her own incarnation and radiance of the Feminine force. Her sexual essence has become hidden. Her childhood memory is that Man (the Masculine force) is violent, insensitive, causes pain, crosses boundaries uninvited and is not worthy of trust. And Elaine remembers that Woman (the Feminine force) is confused, hurt and guilty—not to mention someone of whom advantage is taken. Elaine is quite able to love people non-sexually, but she is at war with the polarizing forces of Man and Woman. Deep down, her natural sexual essence is waiting to bloom. But her acquired sexual character is fearful and guarded.

Elaine is afraid that if she relaxes into her extreme Feminine, she will attract Masculine abuse and suffer painfully.

Because Elaine resists Man and Woman, her friends tend to be more Neutral in their expression, people who do not incarnate strong Masculine or Feminine energy. For example, her friend Bob is a family therapist. He is a good listener and is careful not to be too assertive or harsh. He sometimes gets very emotional, but he never gets overtly angry or violent and rarely swears out loud.

Bob did not grow up with a father who was a clear transmitter of strong Masculine integrity. His father was not even around very much. Instead, Bob absorbed the more Feminine style of loving from his mother, and he has come to view the Masculine force as distant and unfeeling, like his father seemed to be. As an adult, too, Bob has experienced that most women don't like a pushy and domineering man, so he has learned to listen and be sensitive. But his intimate partners end up leaving him because they say he is spineless and not confident of his own direction. And because Bob has lost connection with his deep Masculine essence, his sexual expression of love has become compromised, superficial and mechanical. Elaine enjoys Bob's company precisely because his Masculine energy is not particularly strong. Because of her past, Elaine finds strong Masculine energy either threatening or offensive.

Another friend of Elaine's, Maggie, is a successful dance instructor. She has her own studio in town, and many close friends. But Maggie hasn't been very lucky with the men in her life. She broke up with her husband many years ago. It seems that none of her relationships since then have lasted more than a year, and every man she has been with turns out to be undirected and dishonest in some way.

After her husband left, Maggie devoted all her energy and attention to making her career a success. Through a lot of disciplined effort, she created the life that she wanted on her own terms. But now, Maggie is afraid that if she relaxes into her Feminine she will lose her competence and independence. She remains autonomous, self-sufficient and empty in her heart.

Elaine and Maggie agree: Before a relationship can work, each partner must be whole and strong, able to be independent and self-responsible. Both of them have learned that you can't let down your guard and trust your partner. Elaine has been terrified, both consciously and unconsciously, to let a man get close to her sexually, but she has a lot of good friends, both men and women. And Maggie knows that it's better to be independent and free than to depend on some guy who is going to leave anyway.

Many women go through a stage, if not a lifetime, of wanting to feel their freedom and independence—they don't want a man to support them, or don't want to pay the unspoken price that may go along with that support. But Maggie has succeeded in the financial part of her life, and now she would enjoy finding a man who would like to embrace her as a goddess and cherish her as a woman. Yet no such man seems to be attracted into her life. A strong Masculine essence is attracted to a strong Feminine essence, and Maggie's natural Feminine essence is covered over by her highly developed Masculine energy. She has made it in the world, and will not let go of her Masculine energy. And it shows. So the men she attracts are weaker men, looking to be completed by her highly developed Masculine energy, rather than by her hidden Feminine sexual essence.

Maggie has continued to develop her Masculine side because she hasn't found a man she could trust. Trustworthy men, with a strong enough sense of direction to at least match hers, do not seem to present themselves. Because she has both a Feminine sexual essence and also a strongly projected force of Masculine energy, the energy she radiates seems to be both, half-Feminine and half-Masculine. This naturally attracts a man who is also half-and-half. Maggie continually finds herself in relationships with men who are uncertain and ambiguous in their commitment. And no such half-and-half man is going to sweep her off her feet. A half-and-half man doesn't animate strong enough Masculine passion for her to trust. And from her partners' perspectives, Maggie doesn't seem to *want* to be swept off her feet; she seems so staunchly self-sufficient and directed.

However, deep inside, Maggie's Feminine sexual essence remains unfulfilled. A core desire of the Feminine essence is to be filled with love. Because she has spent so much time developing her Masculine energy, and because men don't feel her desire to be filled with love as much as they feel her desire to be independent, Maggie must fill herself. She fills herself with sweets and social events. She fills her shelves with knickknacks and sentimental objects. Her Feminine sexual essence is yearning to be filled, and Maggie does a good job of trying to fill her own emptiness. But her attempts at self-filling are the results of a love-starved Feminine sexual essence.

Of course, Maggie does not need to let go of her creative or financial success in order to attract a good man. She can be as successful as she wants. However, if she is going to attract a man with a confident and trustable Masculine style of loving, she must be able to shift into her strong Feminine energy during moments of intimacy—opening and inviting, radiant and rejuvenating, wild and powerful. She will then attract a man with a strong Masculine, full of confidence, presence, humor and direction: a man she can trust.

Maggie will have to let go first. As long as she identifies herself with her assertiveness and her directionality, with her own Masculine, she will not be willing to animate her Feminine radiance, which is as much a part of her as her animated Masculine. If Maggie wants a man with a strong Masculine, a man who is not threatened by her success, a man in whose love she can relax, then she must trust and therefore shine her native Feminine sexual essence in order to reciprocate him. In the same way, men who want to attract a more Feminine partner must trust and strengthen their own Masculine.

Elaine and Maggie are examples of people who are not happy with the sexual character they have become, and therefore are also dissatisfied with the intimate partners they attract. They have unconsciously hidden their natural sexual essences because of pain they experienced in the past. They are suffering in their intimate lives, always repeating the same pattern of unconsciously denying themselves that which would fulfill them most. Neither of them has relaxed into her natural sexual essence.

In fact, very few of us have. To some extent, virtually all of us are hiding some aspects of our true sexual essence. We are afraid to express our true desires. We resist the sexual essences of others who secretly arouse us, or who evoke hidden aspects of our sexuality that we have rejected because of past pain or fear. We have decided that relaxing into our native Masculine or Feminine sexual essence is unsafe. We have decided that it's better to be an equal person than a hurt one. It's better to be in a fair relationship than an abusive one. It's better to be independent and self-sufficient than dependent and vulnerable, subject to loss and betrayal.

And so we seek a 50/50 Relationship that will support our desire for equality, independence and self-sufficiency. And in the process, we end up starving our hearts. We are inadvertently neutralizing the flow of passionate gifts between unguarded hearts in our intimate relationships. We are often working to achieve Neutral and fair "peoplehood" at the expense of fulfilling our deep Masculine or Feminine heart-core.

THE FEMININE CRISIS: SECOND TO THIRD STAGE

Whereas the Masculine, in men and women, is constantly hoping that His mission will satisfy Him, the Feminine, in men and women, is constantly hoping that Her intimate relationship will satisfy Her. "Am I loved? Does my partner *really* love me?" Her deepest desire is to feel loved, and thus stage by stage She lives Her life as an effort to be fulfilled in love.

Let's consider a woman who has a Feminine sexual essence. In a first-stage moment, a woman like this will often give up her own needs and desires in an effort to "get" love from her man. Over time, this does not satisfy her, and she vows to be strong, to establish her independence financially and emotionally. She develops her creative talents and gifts. She also cultivates her own Masculine energy by "buckling down" and directing her life toward career goals. She learns how to say "no" in order to stand free and independent of other people's demands, including her man's and her family's.

Emotionally, she learns to love herself, rather than to always be seeking love and approval from an outside source. Instead of seeing herself through her man's eyes, she learns to see herself for herself. Instead of wondering if she is loved, she learns to give the love she wants to herself. She does this by using her Masculine energy of abstraction and discipline to "convince" her Feminine that She is loved. For instance, she might practice affirmations over and over, repeating to herself, "I am special. I am beautiful. I am worthy of love."

Thus, in a second-stage moment, a woman uses her internal Masculine to give her Feminine the same praise that her Feminine would otherwise want to get from a man who really did love and honor her. A second-stage woman becomes "whole" and "independent" by learning to give *herself*, once and for all, the love she always hoped to get from her intimate partner in the first stage but never entirely got.

For a woman with a Feminine sexual essence to move from the first to the second stage, she undergoes a crisis: She feels that she just doesn't get the love she wants from her partner or partners. Eventually, she gives up trying, goes through a dark period of emotional suffering and yearning, and, at some point, resolves that she will simply give herself the love that she wants. This is the second-stage resolve: "I may still be in an intimate relationship, but I am essentially my own woman, fulfilling my own needs, no longer dependent on a man to make me feel good about myself. I can learn to love myself and feel good about myself, by myself."

Months or years may go by, and now this woman finds herself doubly in despair. Not only is her Feminine core unsatisfied by the lack of love she receives from her man, she is also unsatisfied by the lack of love she receives from her own Masculine; she still wants a man with whom to share love. Her heart is not overflowing with the bliss of love. Rather, even though there are good times and bad times, her heart is still yearning for more love in her life. Sometimes a man seems to love her, sometimes he doesn't. Sometimes she can love herself, sometimes she can't. Her heart might feel okay, but it doesn't feel overwhelmed by love. Her body might feel okay, but it isn't exploding in the bliss of passionate love. Her mind might feel okay, but it isn't rested in the certain knowledge of love.

The love that would absolutely overwhelm her Feminine core, that would fulfill her deep yearning, is lacking. It always has been. And so the crisis between the second and third stages begins: "I can't get enough love from him. *And* I can't give myself enough love. I am still yearning for more love. It is hopeless."

This Feminine "black hole of need" is equivalent to the Masculine's "mid-life crisis" of emptiness and inauthenticity in His life.

Eventually, a second-stage woman with a Feminine sexual essence becomes absolutely frustrated in her desire for deep and overwhelming love. Sure, there are periods in her life when she might temporarily feel this kind of love, but these periods don't last. There is always the possibility of loss of love. Always there is the fear that maybe he doesn't really love me. Maybe he won't really love me tomorrow. Maybe he'll love someone else more. And maybe I won't be happy by myself, without an intimate partner in love. This doubt of love becomes magnified to the point of heart-yearning despair in the crisis that allows the Feminine to grow from the second to the third stage.

If she can allow herself to relax into her despair without protecting her yearning and wounded Feminine heart, the yearning itself will reveal her divine nature. If she can allow herself to be absolutely open, without trying to fill the "hole" in her heart with food or talk or intimate hopes, this dark hole will eventually widen to the size of the universe. This is not a metaphorical expression, but a literal description of the Feminine Divine nature: the heart widened to infinity, in which absolute love flows with no obstruction.

It is rare for a woman to allow herself this degree of heart-vulnerability, just as it is rare for a man to allow himself the degree of self-death or ego-death necessary for the transition to a life purposed toward worship of consciousness and self-transcending service. Most women keep trying to find the right man, or keep hoping that their chosen man will give them more love, or keep attempting to love themselves to the point of happiness. But it never happens—not to the point that the Feminine heart is overwhelmed by the bliss of love, unburdened by doubt or fear of loss.

This degree of heart-openness can only be experienced by a heart with no protection, an unguarded heart open in love with no expectation of being given love in return. Such a heart is frequently wounded by the blows of unlove dealt by people and the world, but it never closes in pain. The third-stage Feminine heart may be hurt by others since it is not protected, but it is never closed by the pain it feels. Love and openness are the nature of the third-stage feminine heart, even in the midst of hurt. By always being open in love, the Feminine heart is finally pervaded by the love it always wanted. By surrendering directly to the divine force of love in every present moment, breath by breath, rather than hoping to get love from a mortal man or her own mortal self, the Feminine blooms to fullness, neither dependent on a relationship nor independent from a relationship.

Just as the third-stage Masculine realizes the inherent freedom of consciousness without needing to seek such freedom in relationship or away from relationship, so the third-stage Feminine opens in the inherent love of the Divine, in every present moment, as a practice, either alone or in the midst of relationship.

RECLAIMING THE FEMININE GIFT

All of us are in the process of learning to give love, more and more freely. The Feminine expression of love is the bodily expression of love. To the extent that your body is free to express love in relationship through touch, voice, movement and personal offering, you are free in your expression of this aspect of the Feminine force.

However, as members of a Masculine-dominated culture, most of us are not truly free in our Feminine expression. We are in denial of Her force and beauty. As a culture, we tend to deny the life of the juicy body in favor of the mechanics of the dry mind. We tend to deny the fullness of sexual play in favor of the goal of spasmodic release. And we tend to deny love in favor of work. As a culture, we tend to deny the Feminine in favor of the goal-oriented Masculine. Each of us can feel this denial in the tightness of our solar plexus and the shallowness of our breathing. And each of us can also intuit the Feminine force that waits in our heart, desiring only to be expressed in the fullness of whole-bodied loving.

Whether we are women or men, it is time to reclaim our Feminine. By doing so, we are also able to restore the intuitive, spontaneous and radiant force of the Feminine to our lives and intimacies.

TRUSTING THE FORCE OF LIFE

As we learn to trust the Feminine force of life, it begins to move our lives in ways we would never have been able to plan. How many of our significant relationships began on the basis of "chance" meetings? How would our lives be different if we fully trusted and acted upon our intuitions and feelings? How much happier would we be if we spent more time moving with the force of life, dancing, singing, making love and walking in the woods or the garden—rather than always pushing ourselves along a path that we think is leading to where we want to go?

We owe it to ourselves to acknowledge that our minds are smaller than the Feminine force of life that has given birth to our minds, the Feminine force that sustains our minds, and the Feminine force that will bring an end to our minds when the force of life no longer flows through us.

Remember: We are totally dependent on this Feminine force of livingness. It breathes us, it beats our heart, it moves our bodies and it energizes every living thing on earth, including all of nature, the shifting winds, the flowing waters, the tiny bugs, the weeds and the whales.

Our personal health as well as our intimate relationships depend on our ability to relax into the living force of the Feminine. In this moment, we can learn to relax, to breathe deeply and to feel the flow: the flow of emotions, of sexual energy, of intuitive wisdom. When we are relaxed and open to this flow of living force, it is free to flow not only within our bodies, but also within our intimate relationships.

Love is not logical, as anyone knows who has ever loved. Logic is of course very useful at times, but the logical mind is unable to fully comprehend the Feminine mystery of life in all its forms. However, when we are surrendered to the flow of life, relaxed and open to its movement and subtle intuitions, a different kind of whole-body intelligence is born. This intelligence, this wisdom of love, this genius that is inherent in a radiantly alive, open and sensitive body, is the intelligence necessary for spontaneous and skillful means within our intimate relationships. It is one of the gifts of the Feminine force.

10

Advanced Polarity

TWO MASCULINES DO NOT
MAKE A POLARITY

These days, it is rather fashionable for both men and women to animate much Masculine energy and little Feminine energy. It is more fashionable to be directional and successful in "conquering" the world than it is to be radiant and intuitively connected to the world. It is more fashionable to be a victorious hero than it is to be an ecstatic lover. Thus, almost all of us resist our partner's Masculine energy—we want to animate our own!

At the same time, most women who have come to me for counseling also want their man to have confidence, clarity, strength, direction and passion. That is, many of today's women want their men to animate strong Masculine energy, but they also want room to animate their own Masculine direction. This works fine for friends and business partners but does not allow for a full sexual polarity to develop intimacy. Two Masculines do not a polarity make. Both a Masculine pole and a Feminine pole are required for sexual polarity.

In today's world, we usually don't spend all day with our partners. One or both partners work. Therefore, we can all be as Masculine as we like during our work day—directional, analytical, butting heads with other people's Masculine energy—and still enjoy sexual polarity with our intimate partners at home. The only way we can successfully do this, however, is if one of the partners is willing to relax into his or her Feminine energy during moments of intimacy. Usually, this will be the partner with the more Feminine sexual essence. And, usually, in a heterosexual relationship, the partner with the more Feminine sexual essence is the woman (although there are also happy intimate relationships in which the man has the more Feminine sexual essence).

Over the last 30 years, some women have become so successful at animating their Masculine energy that there are very few men who are really up to playing the Masculine pole in relationship to them. Among successful women, it is very common to hear complaints about there being a lack of men who are "conscious," "evolved" or "strong" enough. And this is true enough to be said. So far, culturally speaking, women have spent more years than men actively growing from the first stage into the second stage. For the most part, women are ahead of men in the evolution through the stages.

It is now time for men to reclaim their wholeness, as women have been doing for years. Only then will we have a population of whole men and women who can truly match each other as intimate partners.

But there is another, more insidious problem. Although there seem to be more women currently ready to move from a 50/50 Relationship to the practice of Intimate Communion than there are men, there are, indeed, some men who are quite ready. And these men are often not attracted to the so-called "whole" women who have cultivated, and in many cases are holding onto, their Masculine energy. A Masculine man who is ready for the practice of sexual polarity in Intimate Communion will be looking for a woman who offers gifts springing directly from her Feminine sexual essence. He has no need for gifts from the Masculine; he already has his own.

Women who have developed their Masculine and men who have developed their Feminine must learn to relax into their native sexual essence if they are to attract partners who can possibly fulfill their deepest desires in sexual polarity. Otherwise, men will continue to complain that the women they meet are "ballbusters" and women will continue to complain that the men they meet are "wimpy New-Age men."

Most men really enjoy being with a successful woman—if she can also relax her edge, put down her sword, and open her body, mind and heart in intimacy with her trusted man. Most women really enjoy being with a sensitive man—if he also directs his life with clarity while offering his cherished woman strong and confident love, sweeping her off her feet with his passionate embrace and presence.

Successful women and sensitive men are a big improvement over suppressed housewives and macho jerks. But we must not forget the law of polarity. We must not forget that we will always attract the reciprocal of the energy we put out.

If you are a woman and you put out "successful" and directional energy, you will tend to attract an ambiguous man who lacks Masculine energy and thus wants to be completed by your directionality. If you are a man and you put out "sensitive" or nurturing energy, you will tend to attract a more angular woman who lacks Feminine energy and thus wants to be completed by your nurturing qualities.

CHOOSING AN APPROPRIATE PARTNER

Sexual polarity is stage-specific. The kind of qualities you tend to look for in your ideal intimate partner are different depending on whether you are more interested in a relationship founded on Dependence, 50/50 or the practice of Intimate Communion.

When one partner grows and the other partner doesn't, polarity will decrease and the relationship will feel obsolete. For instance, when one partner shifts from wanting a Dependence Relationship to wanting a 50/50 Relationship, then the other partner must shift, too, or the flow of polarity between them will decrease and become dissatisfying. What qualities do we look for in a partner, stage by stage?

In a Dependence Relationship, you are a slave to the force of sexual polarity and you are bound to your own sexual needs or the needs of your partner. You are a woman who gives your man sex in the hope of feeling loved, or you are a man who pays all the bills in order to keep your woman sexually available to you. You are each giving something primarily because you are afraid of the loss of the other.

A first-stage man who wants a Dependence Relationship should choose a woman who is willing to take care of his sexual and family needs as long as he is willing to take care of her emotional and financial needs, and vice versa for a woman who wants this kind of relationship. This kind of arrangement can work out fine for a lifetime, and provides a very stable foundation for the flow of love and sexual polarity, as long as both partners remain committed to their predefined roles.

In a 50/50 Relationship, you temporarily deprioritize sexual polarity, and instead place an emphasis on developing good communication, hoping to establish an equitable balance of power. You are tired of the hidden or overt power struggles of a Dependence Relationship. The last thing you want to do is surrender your boundaries of safety and become vulnerable to another, vulnerable to suffering. Instead, you hope to explore the sensual delights of mutual sexual play and simultaneous orgasms with a partner who is also your best friend.

Second-stage men and women should choose partners who are

already quite whole and autonomous, willing to establish an intimate relationship on the basis of sharing, equality and mutual respect. Their sexual polarity together will be more flexible—and less certain—than polarity in a Dependence Relationship, since both partners in a 50/50 Relationship are dedicated to balancing their own internal Masculine and Feminine energies, and then presenting this kind of balanced or more "even" energy to their partner. By choosing a partner who shares a common vision of a fulfilling lifestyle and who is willing to communicate his or her thoughts and feelings honestly, second-stage men and women can provide themselves with supportive companionship for their lifetime journey of growth and self-integration.

In the practice of Intimate Communion, you learn to master the dynamic force of sexual polarity, gifting each other from your deep sexual core and surrendering your resistances to the point of ecstatic oneness and unguarded love—not merely independence and self-integration. In the practice of Intimate Communion, the play of polarity becomes a form of love-transmission in which you move beyond your personal boundaries.

For instance, your sexual play becomes an intentional embodiment of the universal force of Masculine and Feminine energy. Bodily entwined, attracted beyond separation, your sexing ultimately becomes a mutual contemplation and realization of love beyond form.

In Intimate Communion, polarity is about total surrender in love, in truth, in God. In Intimate Communion, a man is turned on by a woman who is willing to devote her entire life to surrendering her self to the point of absolute love and bliss, and who is willing to throw out anything that stands in the way of such surrender: including money, sex and a Utopian lifestyle, if necessary. A woman is turned on by a man who is absolutely committed to surrendering everything other than the perfect realization of love, truth, God. Any man who is oriented to something else—even the achievement of good communication and a happy community of loving friends and family—simply does not turn her on as much.

Each of us is on a unique journey through the stages, and therefore we are each turned on by a different kind of man or woman. As we grow, the *kind* of man or woman who turns us on changes. If we grow and our present partner does not grow, or vice versa, then we will experience a loss of sexual polarity and trust. By respecting the stages of growth, we can avoid blaming ourselves or our partners for the loss of sexual polarity in our relationship. We can understand that this loss of polarity happens whenever one partner grows and the other partner does not.

SHIFTING STAGES, SHIFTING FANTASIES

Since sexual polarity is stage-specific, and because these stages can shift from moment to moment as well as from year to year, our responses to sexual polarity can be confusing.

After being wounded in intimate relationship, for instance, we may become very needy and shift into a moment of Dependence—even if, for the most part, we are capable of a 50/50 Relationship or the practice of Intimate Communion. In a moment of Dependence, we will suddenly find ourselves attracted to people with whom we wouldn't usually consider being intimate—gorgeous airheads, muscular dorks, famous celebrities just passing through—because suddenly, we are aroused by the first-stage style of polarity.

On the other hand, we may experience incredible sexual union with a person during a third-stage moment of Intimate Communion that is temporarily induced by religious ecstasy, a drug or even a near-death experience, only to find that we share nothing in common—and don't even like the person—a few days later, when we settle back into our second-stage lifestyle.

Sexual polarity is not beyond the grasp of our understanding; we can work with it and even master it, if we are willing to observe our lives closely as we grow stage by stage and learn the laws of this pervasive natural force. In intimacy—as opposed to friendship or business—opposite poles attract and like poles repel. If we are willing to own our unique sexual essence, rather than try to be someone else, then we will attract our true reciprocal, someone who enlivens and fulfills our deep sexual core. Stage by stage, the Masculine is looking to be loved via Feminine energy and radiance, and the Feminine is looking to be loved via Masculine presence and consciousness. The art of sexual polarity is all about giving these natural Feminine and Masculine gifts, from our hearts.

WHEN I WANT OUT

When I am in a typical Masculine bad mood, feeling weary and burdened by life, I want to be released from it all. When Ophelia feels my mood, she can respond in two general ways.

One way is that Ophelia may feel my desire to be released and respond by feeling rejected, feeling that I want to leave her company. She may be right. She may also feel that I don't love her, but then she would be wrong. The Masculine sexual essence often wants to be released even while fully in love.

Whether I love Ophelia or not, when I am in a mood of feeling constrained, I want out. I want out of constraint, not out of love. And this is a key to how Ophelia can serve me to let go of my mood.

The other way that Ophelia can respond—the way that serves

me—is by recognizing that when I am in a typical Masculine bad mood, it is not *her* that I want to be released from; I want to be released from my sense of being burdened, weary and trapped. By understanding this, Ophelia can choose not to withdraw from me because she feels rejected; instead, she can actually melt my bad mood by serving to relieve my feeling of constraint.

How does she do this? Men and women must find their own way to serve each other by experimenting. I know that if Ophelia takes five minutes to "untrap" me, I can re-approach her with refreshed love, and I can face the details of life with renewed energy and happiness. I am untrapped most by physical release. Ophelia can release the tensions in my body, perhaps by massaging me. She can release the burdens of my mind by drawing me into mindless delight through her touch and humor. Ophelia loves to dance; she can also release my sense of being burdened by transforming my experience of life into one of beauty, by dancing for me.

It usually only takes about five minutes of Ophelia's time to grace my life with her radiance, beauty and loving energy. Then, I am relieved of feeling crunched by life. My energy is renewed by Ophelia's Feminine energy. My Masculine sexual essence is strengthened and polarized, and so I naturally enjoy being challenged by life, being at my edge and solving problems. Also, my heart is connected to hers by the potent arc of sexual polarity that now flows between us.

Ophelia serves me by rejuvenating my Masculine sexual essence when I am feeling tired or burned out. She can only do so, however, when she feels that my desire to be released is not a literal desire to be released from our relationship, but is rather a desire to be released from my own sense of being constrained.

I may erroneously attribute this sense of constraint to my relationship with Ophelia. And if Ophelia responds to my mood by getting moody herself, then I will feel confirmed: "Ah yes, it *is* Ophelia who burdens me. Now I have to deal with her mood as well as mine!"

But when Ophelia is strong enough in her practice of Intimate Communion to recognize that my mood is self-generated, then she does not take it personally and she can serve to help me out of my mood. She can rejuvenate me and polarize my Masculine sexual essence with her radiant gifts. In a short time, I will feel strong again, ready to meet the challenges of life in a creative and humorous way, without feeling crunched. Ophelia's love can help me realize that my desire for release is actually a rejection of the creative challenge of life, including the creative challenge of relationship.

WHEN DOES THE MASCULINE APPRECIATE THE FEMININE GIFT?

When I am focused on my mission—writing this book, for instance—all my energies are concentrated on my purpose. Suppose Ophelia notices that I have been working for hours, and she brings me a glass of water. An hour later she prepares a snack for me. I would have to say that, of the many gifts Ophelia offers me, her loving support of my purpose is one of the most fulfilling. When Ophelia serves my mission, when she brings me a glass of water, so I don't have to break my concentration, I feel immense gratitude and appreciation for her. Her Feminine gift of loving energy turns on my Masculine sense of purpose—as well as magnifying the flow of sexual polarity between us.

However, if I was to take a detour from my purpose in that moment to thank her and express how much I appreciate her, then that would defeat the whole gift; rather than supporting and inspiring my mission, she would be distracting me from it, if even for five seconds. Her Feminine gift would suddenly feel like a burden to my Masculine directionality and mission.

This may sound like a small issue, but in my counseling of other couples I have observed over and over that it is a great source of misunderstanding. If the Masculine has to cease moving in the direction of His purpose—if He has to get off the track, so to speak, even for a few moments—then He feels the Feminine as a distraction or a burden rather than a gift.

When Ophelia brings me a glass of water, it is not the water per se that is the gift I receive. When Ophelia brings me a snack she has lovingly prepared, it is not the snack per se that is the gift. It is her *care* that I experience as a special gift, her support, her refreshment and her rejuvenation of my mission. It is the gift of energy and attention she has given me. She has liberated my energy and attention from the necessity of providing myself with food and water, for example, and now I am free to continue fully aligned with my purpose.

I know this sounds strange to some people with a Feminine sexual essence. It may seem so easy to take a break from your purpose to ex-press appreciation for your partner's care. But if doing so means getting off track, then it is no longer such a gift for the Masculine sexual essence.

We must learn to understand the differences between the Masculine and Feminine if we are to fully appreciate, rather than be disturbed by, their different moods, desires and needs.

For instance, as a person with a Masculine sexual essence, I had to learn to be free, humorous and loving with respect to Ophelia's moods. I had to learn that when she was frustrated and said something like, "Get out of here!" she most often actually preferred that I stayed. I had to learn that when she said, curtly, "I'm fine," it often meant that she wasn't. I also had to learn that Ophelia's Feminine sexual essence was virtually always connected to our relationship, so that if I abruptly popped out of bed in the morning to write down a new idea, she would feel a bit let down unless I came back to bed and shared some intimate time before we got up and started our day. I had to learn that Ophelia's Feminine needs for polarity were quite different from my Masculine needs.

In the same way, Ophelia had to learn that I was not ignoring her when she gifted me with Feminine energy and I didn't take the time to respond then and there. Rather, I was wholly concentrated in my purpose and was indeed receiving her support as a great gift. Later, once I had re-emerged from my mission, I would let her know how much I appreciated her gifts.

In fact, my gratitude would be flowing from my pores. Ophelia's trust and support of my mission, of my purpose, is among the greatest gifts of the Feminine force I receive from her. Her love continually inspires, literally breathes life and love into, my otherwise narrowly focused and goal-oriented life.

MASCULINE AND FEMININE BALANCING EACH OTHER

One morning, Ophelia and I were in bed, making love. We were fully present with one another. I was feeling her, caressing her and loving her. I felt that I was breathing her as I beheld her beautiful form.

Suddenly the phone rang. We let the answering machine get it, but as I listened to the caller leaving a message, I realized that it was a business matter that needed my immediate attention. I jumped out of bed to take the call. Suddenly I was in the "business mode," talking on the phone, examining options and making decisions. After the call was over, I hung up the phone and went over to my desk in the study to jot down some notes and look at a calendar. Ophelia was in bed, still connected to me, waiting for me to return.

Finally, she called to me, "David? What are you doing in there?"

Like the phone ringing, her voice reminded me of her existence; in my business mode, it is as if she does not exist—just as when I am in the "intimacy mode" with Ophelia, it is as if business does not exist.

I am much more naturally able to focus within a mode than Ophelia is. I can, and often do, go for hours, days and even months sometimes, with virtually all of my energy and attention devoted to a specific creative project or a specific spiritual practice. In fact, it is all too easy for me to drive myself to the point of unhealthy physical exhaustion or extreme emotional rigidity.

These are the symptoms of the unbalanced Masculine: His modality becomes so extreme that His life-energy becomes suppressed by the pressure of His purpose, and His emotional range becomes narrowed to a pinhole.

During the period in our lives when the phone rang, I was deeply involved in a large, commercial venture. I was coordinating the start-up of a high-tech, computer software research and development corporation and there were programmers, venture capitalists, lawyers, computer vendors, scientists, real estate agents and more—all of them seeming to need my attention 24 hours a day. I had never done anything like this before, and my attention was narrowed way down while I was involved in this project.

In my current life as a writer and an educator, I have learned to balance myself when Ophelia is not around by taking regular breaks: exercising, swimming in the ocean, wandering on the beach near our house. But when I am with Ophelia, it is extremely pleasurable to also receive her flow of love, as a gift in my otherwise relatively rigid and narrow life. She often places flowers around my computer to remind me of the world outside my office. She entices me away from the keyboard when she feels that I am burning out and notices that my writing is suffering. She opens my narrow focus by massaging me, singing to me, perhaps even taking off her clothes and dancing for me! Ophelia brings such extraordinary and beautiful Feminine gifts into my life, that her presence is far more healing than a radiant summer day on a lush and sparkling tropical beach.

Both of us are quite capable of balancing ourselves when we need to. Without me, Ophelia can certainly focus her own life and reap the financial, creative and spiritual rewards. I can flow in deep love, healing life force and sensual dance, whether I am with Ophelia or not. Both of us can live independent and whole lives, if we so choose. We are each capable, therefore, of contributing equally to a 50/50 Relationship—both of us focusing half the time with our Masculine energy and flowing half the time with our Feminine energy. And for long periods of our relationship we have, in fact, chosen to live in this 50/50 style.

But there are many times when we would each prefer to relax in our native sexual essence and give the gift that springs naturally from our core. In each couple's relationship, these gifts are unique and ever-changing. So it is important to remain open and spontaneous, discovering day by day what these natural gifts are.

Usually, in our case, I prefer to be focused (writing or meditating), in solitude or working intensively with groups of people—that is, "on a mission" for long periods of time—and Ophelia prefers to be flowing in relationship with loving friends or dancing in spiritual devotion (both literally, as an art form, and figuratively, as a happy woman).

I am actually a fine dancer and, in my opinion, Ophelia is a better writer than I am. It is not a matter of who *should* do what or *can* do what, or whether we are contributing equally to relationship. It is just that when we are completely relaxed, happy and doing exactly what we really want to be doing, I am likely to be writing and Ophelia is likely to be dancing. Ophelia enjoys the gifts she receives from my writing and

I enjoy the gifts I receive from her dancing. And in fact, there are also times when I am dancing and Ophelia is writing.

In the practice of Intimate Communion, Ophelia is happy to balance my Masculine "moding" with her Feminine dancing, and I am happy to balance her dancing with my moding. We often prefer offering these gifts to one another, rather than maintaining a daily balance of 50/50 within ourselves. It is often more natural for us to balance each other with our inherently different gifts because we happen to have an extreme Masculine and an extreme Feminine sexual essence, respectively. For other people whose sexual essences are less extreme and more Neutral, they will be just as happy to balance themselves, perhaps in the company of an intimate partner who is also balancing himself or herself.

WHEN THE MASCULINE IS LACKING

Imagine you are a woman with a more Feminine sexual essence. You are getting ready, dressing up to go out on the town with your man. You are excited, happy, looking forward to enjoying the evening with your intimate partner. After dressing you come bouncing out of the bedroom and spin around, smiling, showing off your beautiful new dress to your man, who is sitting on the sofa in the living room.

But he doesn't even notice you. He is watching TV, slouched against the sofa cushions, half awake. You can feel yourself getting angry. Has he forgotten? You were so full of energy, so radiantly Feminine and happy—where is his Masculine energy to match you? He seems as limp as a rag doll.

At this point, the unconscious tendency for most women is to move into their Masculine energy. Since your man is sitting there, direction-less, someone has to take responsibility for navigating the evening! So you attempt to give a little push and ask, "Well, are we going out tonight or not?"

"I don't care. We can go out if you really want," he says, hardly moving his eyes from the TV screen.

So you animate a little more directional energy and say, "I would really like to go out tonight. I spent the last hour getting ready. C'mon. Let's go."

He seems to sink even deeper into apathetic inertia. He very slowly, reluctantly, gets up from the couch and goes through the motions of getting ready. The night is off to a dismal start.

You saw that your man lacked directional energy so you animated your own directional, Masculine energy to get things going. It works. Things do get going. But the situation becomes depolarized. Tense. Just under the surface lies unspoken conflict. It is the conflict between your Masculine and his Masculine.

The Masculine pushes and guides; the Feminine invites and attracts. Both ways are useful in different moments. The key in intimate relationship is to choose the way, Masculine or Feminine, that will enhance or magnify polarity—that is, if you want to enjoy polarity rather than neutrality or repulsion.

In the office and on the street, sexual polarity may not be so important to you. Therefore, it is good to be a whole and balanced person, able to animate either Masculine or Feminine energy, depending on what best suits the situation.

But in intimacy, the number one complaint of men and women, the number one source of conflict, is depolarization. It is depolarizing, for example, when you want caring and directional Masculine love from your man, but instead he gives you wishy-washy, ambiguous, blah-dee-blah. Or, you are a man desiring care and radiant Feminine love from your woman, and instead she gives you sharp, angry pushes and stabs.

When a man with a naturally Masculine sexual essence experiences Masculine energy from his woman, he tends to do one of two things. He either remains in his Masculine and is repulsed by his woman's Masculine, like two magnets are when placed with like poles side by side. Or else he relinquishes his Masculine and allows her to "carry the Masculine energy." Then he is not repulsed, but nor is he attracted. He has given up his directionality and she has taken up the slack—a workable situation, but not sexually polarizing if the partners end up animating the energy that is opposite to their native sexual essences.

Of course, men are allowed to be wishy-washy and women are allowed to be sharp and pushy. Men and women are allowed to be and act however they want; it is good, however, for them to be conscious of and responsible for the energetic effect on their partner.

So what can you do when your man is slouched and undirected on the sofa and you are full of happy energy, raring to go? What is the alternative to gently nudging, and then shoving, your man out the door? One alternative is to animate the extreme Feminine. In fact, you can animate so much Feminine that compared with you, even your man's couch-potato demeanor seems Masculine. Then your extreme Feminine energy may polarize his latent Masculine impulse into full-blown Masculine directionality.

What might this look like?

He is slumped on the couch. You recognize that he is weak in his Masculine for the moment. First, feel in your heart: For his own good, is it better for him to watch TV in this moment, or is it better for him to share in your flow of love and happiness? Let's suppose you decide the latter.

You sit down next to him and relax deeply into your Feminine. You can become more Feminine than he, more Feminine than a 50/50 balance would usually allow. You can reach deep into your Feminine reservoir in order to polarize what remains of his Masculine.

You breathe a deep and sweet breath. You feel your whole body, from head to toe, and allow yourself to incarnate most fully into your body as a woman, whatever that means to you. You feel your Feminine flesh, your Feminine heart, your Feminine desires. You trust the power of your love to enchant and attract your man, and you trust that your love will serve him more than the TV does.

You invite him into his body by making his Masculine body a pleasurable place for him to be, perhaps by touching him as only you know how to do. You invite him into relationship by making it irresistibly more attractive than being distracted by the TV. You empower his Masculine by praising his strength and directionality, which you know lie latent within him. "Whatever you want to do is okay with me," you whisper while snuggling against him and purring. "I trust your decision. I love just being here with you, if that is what you really want to do." (If this is not true of you, then you may want to consider if you are with the right man.)

You consciously relinquish your Masculine directionality and trust his. At the same time, you offer him the gift of your extreme Feminine by lovingly enchanting him with your smile, your touch, your Feminine energy, however you spontaneously manifest your Feminine sexual essence in the present moment.

To the Masculine, there is nothing more attractive than the Feminine. This is a basic law of polarity, one that virtually every woman knows, but for which few are willing to be consciously responsible.

At the first stage, the trusting Feminine body *seduces* the Masculine to yield Himself and enter into physical pleasure, body to body. At the second stage, the trusting Feminine mind *interests* the Masculine to yield Himself and join in meaningful sharing, mind to mind. At the third stage, the trusting Feminine heart *enchants* the Masculine to yield Himself and commune with the power of love, heart to heart.

Our culture is so Feminine-negative, we often look upon the powers of enchantment and attraction as forms of manipulation. As a culture of men and women, we have come to value the directional capacity of a ship more than the gloriously attractive radiance of the deep blue ocean. Somehow, we have come to honor Masculine pushing more than Feminine inviting: We are more likely to nudge our couch-potato partner out the door than we are to enchant him into love.

We have become brainwashed. We have arrived at believing that it is better to tell our partners where we want them to go than to invite them to where we want them to come. We often think the Masculine way of telling someone where we want them to go is "honest" and the Feminine way of inviting someone where we want them to be is "manipulative." These beliefs are artifacts of our culture's pervasive anti-Feminine attitude.

Both the Masculine and Feminine ways are useful in different moments, and every man and woman would be wise to cultivate the ability to use both energies. Equally wise, however, is the man or woman who knows when to use the Masculine power of directionality and when to use the Feminine power of enchantment and invitation.

If you want sexual polarity with your partner in the present moment, then animate the opposite energy that you want to evoke in him or her. Feminine evokes Masculine. Masculine evokes Feminine. Neutral evokes Neutral. Be conscious of this "law of evocation," and then choose what you will do.

THE MASCULINE SERVING THE FEMININE

Suppose you are a man and your woman comes home from her job as a corporate executive. During the day she has little chance to relax into her Feminine, and so when she comes home she is still in the "go" mode. Rather than gracefully flowing through the house as a radiant goddess, she is pacing back and forth and talking non-stop about making a financial killing, like a corporate warrior.

It is all too easy in such a situation to relinquish your Masculine, to give your woman "space" to be as Masculine and warrior-like as she wants. And, at times, this may be the best thing to do. But feel in your heart: In this moment, what would be best for her? She has been in her Masculine all day. Would it be best, for her sake, to continue that way, or would it be best for her to relinquish her Masculine and relax and rejuvenate in her Feminine? Feel into this decision and then act accordingly.

If the latter seems more true, then you must become more Masculine than she, polarizing her naturally Feminine sexual essence, which has become temporarily cloaked by her Masculine energy. There is nothing wrong with her highly developed Masculine energy; it is just that she is not being served by it in the moment. You feel that it would be better for her, in this present moment, to relax in her Feminine energy and to lovingly share, to swoon even, in the force of sexual polarity with you.

So you choose not to give her "space." Why? The only way to give her the space to be Masculine is for you to relinquish your Masculine. Otherwise, if you both remained in your Masculine, you would be like two stubborn rams occupying the same territory, butting heads.

Therefore, you choose neither to relinquish your Masculine and give her space, nor to be as Masculine as she, which will inevitably lead to a competition over who has the Masculine "territory": that is, who carries the directional energy in the moment.

Instead of butting heads or relinquishing ground, you become more Masculine than she and evoke her latent Feminine. You become more Masculine than she by feeling into what would be best for her and then standing your ground with absolute confidence, humor and love. You evoke her latent Feminine by praising her Feminine qualities that you cherish and by touching her as if she were a goddess rather than a warrior.

She is pacing back and forth, barking about this and that, tense and angular. You begin to follow her with a loving smile on your face. She stops and looks at you, angrily. You tell her how beautiful she looks when she wants to kill someone, and ask her if she is in the mood to dance. Before she can answer, you embrace her and dance her around the room, caressing her as your chosen Feminine goddess.

You stand your ground of love by never wavering in your humor or your persistence. You love her, and through one means or another you find a crack in her hard shell and allow your Masculine love to enter deeply into her Feminine heart. The moment this occurs, her body will ease as she relinquishes her own Masculine and receives yours, meeting you with her own infinite reservoir of Feminine energy. The lines on her face will smooth. The squint in her eyes will relax. You continue to love her, to touch her, to praise her Feminine beauty and radiance that have always enchanted you.

Then, if she has something to say, it will be real. It won't merely be excess Masculine tension from the day waving its sword in the air. Your Masculine embrace, your honoring of and reverence for her Feminine, your humor and persistent care will allow her body and mind to relax into her natural Feminine sexual essence. Without arguing about who is right, without butting heads and without watching TV while she spews her warrior slogans, you have served her to relax into her native sexual essence without suppressing whatever she still feels is important to say. You have enhanced polarity and communicated your love.

PRACTICING SEXUAL POLARITY

How do you practice sexual polarity? In a word, Fuck—with a capital "F." This doesn't mean just sexual intercourse. It means opening to the immense flow of universal life force. It means participating with your whole body in the play of polarity between Masculine and Feminine. It is going on all the time, throughout the cosmos, between people, planets and atoms. We are orbiting around one another, held in place by reciprocal forces of attraction and repulsion. To practice polarity, we just relax and allow the universal flow of life to move through us, with or without a human partner. In and out, up and down, round and round, the life force flows strong between every Masculine and Feminine pole.

We can love anything or anyone simply by relaxing into non-separation and opening our hearts without limitation. But we can only enjoy the mystery of Fuck by submitting our minds to the wisdom of our bodies and incarnating the full polarized force of Masculine and Feminine energy.

As we grow in our understanding of sexual polarity, we learn to appreciate our heightened sexual energy, stage by stage. In a Dependence Relationship, we often direct our sexual energy only toward erotic passion, emotional consolation and orgasmic release. Over time, as we grow into a 50/50 Relationship, we learn to use our stimulated sexual energy as healing energy, for ourselves and for our lover. The man is balanced by the woman's energy and the woman is balanced by the man's. In addition to its erotic and healing qualities, 50/50 sexuality can become a deep emotional exchange, a sharing of our real feelings as well as our bodily energies.

But healing and emotional sharing are not the fruition of the mastery of sexual polarity. The practice of Intimate Communion involves the magnification of love carried by the energy of sexual polarity, flowing freely between an awakened Masculine and Feminine sexual essence. It involves loving so freely, so simply, with such unguarded abandon, that our sense of separation dissolves in the single intensity that feels like love, looks like light and is aware as consciousness.

In the practice of Intimate Communion, Masculine and Feminine learn to magnify their love and sexual desire for one another, eventually transforming this energy into a single intensity of life: the intensity that mysteriously lives as both His body-mind as well as Hers.

But this is only the beginning. As the practice of Intimate Communion progresses, both Masculine and Feminine learn to love even more. They learn that love is sufficient. The Masculine lets go beyond every trace of mind, every trace of difference, and He releases into the infinity of love. The Feminine opens and surrenders into the same love, the same unbounded singularity. Their polarity is dissolved into ecstatic oneness—until their bodies re-appear, their energies re-animate and the play of polarity resumes.

By understanding sexual polarity, we open a doorway to a new way of life. With practice, we learn to embrace our daily lives with the same love and openness with which we embrace our lover. We feel our thoughts slide by like skin beneath our fingertips. We feel our emotions move through our bodies like the deep moan of our lover. We notice our recoil in a difficult moment and we bring ourselves fully present, as if suffering with our partner through his or her pain. Our persistence in love is relentless. Our surrender in love is endless. By mastering sexual polarity, we master the forces of repulsion and attraction, of fear and desire. In the practice of Intimate Communion, our love becomes inseparable from the intensity of life itself.

11

Practicing Love

POLARITY AND LOVE

As many of us know, it is often easier to get along with friends we love than with the intimate partner we love. Why? One reason is that with our intimate partner we want to share not only love, but also sexual polarity. We sometimes get frustrated with our intimate partners because few of us have really understood that there is a big difference between sexual polarity and love.

Sexual polarity is a universal and natural force that can be felt not only with people, but also with photos, memories, fantasies, animals and places; in other words, it may occur with anything or anyone, as long as there is a Masculine and a Feminine pole.

Love is non-separation, the willingness to embrace, the openness of a heart that knows no resistance. Love occurs where fear is not. Love is non-avoidance. Love is the realization of no difference, of perfect unity, of coincidence without a "me" and "you."

It is the work of a lifetime to open in love without fear and resistance, to enjoy the ecstasy of perfect unity in relationship. It is actually far easier to learn the basic laws of sexual polarity and enjoy the passionate play between Masculine and Feminine. However, it still requires hard work because we often resist aspects of the Masculine or Feminine, and therefore we resist embracing that which would allow full sexual polarity in our intimate relationship.

If all we want in our intimacy is love, then it is completely irrelevant who animates Masculine or Feminine energy, or when. But if we want love *and* the flow of sexual polarity in our intimate life, then we must accept the fullness of Masculine and Feminine expression.

Especially today, men and women are resisting letting go of their hard-won 50/50 balance. They are afraid of slipping backwards into old sex roles. Instead, they are trying to learn to give and receive love better—but are, for the most part, ignoring the cultivation of full sexual polarity in their relationships. Many partners say, "We love each other, but something is missing in our relationship."

That "something" is usually a clear and uncomplicated enjoyment of sexual polarity. "Something is missing" because one or both partners are weak in the animation of their natural sexual essence. They may try their best to be loving, but the fullness of their sexual gift remains unexpressed, or perhaps even actively avoided.

As we grow through the practice of Intimate Communion, we must practice these two arts simultaneously: the art of opening in love and the art of cultivating sexual polarity by gifting from our unique sexual essence.

We learn to love by accepting each other as we are, letting go of our resistances and learning to relax and truly feel each moment as it arises and disappears. And we learn to gift from our sexual essence by trusting the natural energies of our body, by honoring the ongoing play and pleasurable opposition between Masculine and Feminine forces, and by consciously empowering and understanding—rather than inadvertently negating—the universal force of sexual polarity that we feel every day with our partners, our friends and total strangers.

Of the two, love is far more important to practice than sexual polarity. After all, some of us with more Neutral sexual essences don't even care much about sexual polarity—and most of us will care less and less about sexual polarity as we grow older.

Love is the lesson we are here to learn, from birth to death. In the end, love is all there is—or isn't. We will either die easily in the knowledge of love or we will regret that we have not loved enough. Sexual polarity doesn't make a damn bit of difference in that final moment.

To grow from a Dependence Relationship, to a 50/50 Relationship, into the practice of Intimate Communion, we must learn to love more and resist less. We must learn to accept more and avoid less. We must learn to relax more and contract less. This growth takes constant practice. Over and over again we will discover our unlovingness, and in that moment we will have an opportunity to learn how to relax, breathe, let go of our resistance and love.

We have already examined the practice of sexual polarity in previous chapters. Now let's focus on the practice of love in Intimate Communion.

HOW TO PRACTICE LOVE IN INTIMATE COMMUNION

In the practice of Intimate Communion, the most important thing to remember is to love. When you feel yourself turning away from your partner, turn back toward him or her and, to the best of your ability, open your heart and love. We have many old habits that we learned in childhood: ways of turning away from and even punishing our intimate partners. For instance, when we wanted to hurt our parents we might have gone into our room and hidden, refused to communicate or told them we didn't love them. These old habits of hurting others or hiding from them when we don't feel loved are still active. We perform the same habits with our intimate partners. Intimate Communion provides a counter-practice to these old habits of unlove.

Intimate Communion requires that we practice loving *through* these old patterns. When we want to get away from our partner, we instead practice remaining fully present in the relationship. When we feel our body becoming tense, we instead practice relaxing our muscles and breathing fully. When we feel our emotional shell cutting us off and separating us from our partner in anger, fear or indifference, we instead allow our heart to feel through the separation, into union with our partner. These practices of love in Intimate Communion are a counter-effort to our old habits of separation, withdrawal and punishment. These practices of love involve relaxing the body, opening the emotions and allowing our unguarded heart to feel our partner, directly and fully.

This process of opening is something that we need to practice over and over again. When our partner hurts us, it is often very difficult to remain open to him or her. Yet we gain nothing by closing down, turning away or punishing our partner, even if he or she has intentionally hurt us.

As children, we played this emotional game: If you don't love me, I don't love you. If you hurt me, I'm going to hurt you. If you don't want to be with me, I don't want to be with you. It's a childish game, and the results are that two people who love each other create a situation where they are unable to communicate or break through the tension of separation they have created.

In a Dependence Relationship, this attitude of "If you hurt me, I'm going to hurt you" is prevalent and often acted out in games of with-holding money, sex and attention. "If you don't give me what I want, I'm going to hold back my money (or sex, or attention) from you."

In a 50/50 Relationship, partners think they can "talk it through." They think that if only they could hear each other's needs, they could come to some kind of agreement. In some cases, this is quite true. Clear speaking and good listening can work wonders with conflicts that are based on misunderstandings about each other's needs.

In many cases, however, there *is* a real difference between the part-ners' needs, rather than just a misunderstanding about them. For instance, very often the more Masculine partner wants "space" and "freedom" in a relationship and the more Feminine partner wants more "closeness" and "intimate time" together. What can be done in this kind of situation? Is a 50/50 compromise the only solution?

For the Masculine, the priority in life is the mission, the quest or the desire for increased freedom. For the Feminine, the priority in life is the flow of feeling or the desire for more loving. Throughout an intimate "discussion," the Masculine is always trying to achieve the goal of freedom. The Masculine likes to solve problems, and thus interprets any negative emotional expression that the Feminine makes as a problem to be solved (or something that needs to be "fixed") in order to relax and enjoy relationship. The Feminine, on the other hand, desires to feel contact with the flow of love. Throughout the intimate discussion, the Feminine is not so much trying to fix something or work toward some future goal as hoping to establish intimate contact and real feeling with Her intimate partner.

Thus, the more Masculine partner is always "discussing" in order to solve some problem. The more Feminine partner is always "discussing" in order to create deeper contact, to stay in touch and to allow a greater flow of feeling between partners. That's why discussion can be a good way to work through intimate difficulties, but not a great way. If the two partners are both sexually Neutral, discussion works fine. But if one partner is more Masculine and the other is more Feminine, they are really talking for different reasons and therefore will be fulfilled by different outcomes. The Masculine partner will relax when the "problem" is solved. The Feminine partner will relax when the flow of love is deeply felt.

In Dependence Relationships, you withhold from each other in order to get what you want. In 50/50 Relationships, you talk with one another in the hopes of reaching a compromise so that each of you can get some of what you want. In the practice of Intimate Communion, however, you realize that, regardless of what each of you is saying, you both want the same thing, but in different forms. The Feminine partner wants to feel the flow of love. The Masculine partner wants to feel the freedom of there being no problem. Love and freedom are both expressions of the same, simple, unbounded feeling; by letting down your defenses and resting in the simplicity of open-hearted feeling-consciousness, you are love and you are free.

Therefore, in Intimate Communion you simply relax into loving communion with your partner *first.* You remain fully present with your partner, feeling through any impulse you may have to turn away or close down, and look directly into each other's eyes. You counter any tendency for your heart to contract by consciously feeling through your sense of contraction, so that you are actively feeling and practicing union with your partner, rather than actively contracting and separating yourself from your partner.

Over time, you learn to practice being present, loving and open with your partner even when you disagree strongly with each other. In an active moment of Intimate Communion, something magical happens: The Feminine partner feels the flow of love and the Masculine partner feels that there is no problem. Through the intense unity and openness that Intimate Communion generates, the Feminine partner is already relaxed in the feeling of love and the Masculine partner is already relaxed in the freedom of open consciousness, not driven by any sense of "problem." Practicing partners are simply present with one another, open and feeling.

In any intimate relationship that involves a more Masculine partner and a more Feminine partner, there will *always* be an opposition of desires. The Masculine partner will want to be free to accomplish his or her mission. The Feminine partner will want more quality time in intimacy, more flow of deep feeling. The Masculine partner is likely to desire an opportunity for polygamous sexuality. The Feminine partner is likely to desire a more deeply fulfilling occasion of monogamous sexuality. The Masculine partner will be hurt when his or her direction or purpose is criticized. The Feminine partner will be hurt when his or her radiance or beauty is criticized. There are many, many differences between the needs and desires of the Masculine and Feminine, and all of them can be sources of opposition between partners. The conflicts and disagreements never seem to end.

In a Dependence Relationship, partners usually cycle through phases of abusively painful fighting and passionate making-up. In 50/50 Relationships, partners are constantly trying to achieve better communication so that they can work out their differences and reach a compromise on which they can agree. But in the practice of Intimate Communion, partners realize that as long as one is more Masculine and the other more Feminine, their differences will never come to an end. They realize, in fact, that this is the source of their sexual polarity: their differences.

They accept the fact that as manifestations of sexually polarized universal forces, they will always be in a playful opposition with each other, like two planets kept in orbit with each other by the opposition of gravity and centrifugal force: Gravity works to pull them together while the centrifugal force of their independent motion works to keep them apart, and the result is an ongoing coupling, held together by the tension of opposing forces.

In the midst of their constantly opposing desires and tendencies, Intimate Communion requires that partners practice staying in direct relationship. This is the practice of love. Whatever differences arise, each partner practices relaxing the body, allowing the breath to remain full, feeling through old habits of emotional closure and communing in love with the partner. Each partner is a partner in *practice*. Their relationship is based on a commitment to the practice of Intimate Communion, not a commitment to play the old games of childhood withholding or the new games of adult communication and compromise. Intimate Communion is about relaxing into and as love itself, in the present moment.

When partners are already relaxed in Intimate Communion, then they can work out the details of their lives together. This is a creative matter and is unique for each person and partnership. How you choose to live your lives, independently and together, is entirely a matter of creative investigation and ongoing experimentation. If you are practicing Intimate Communion during this experimentation, then you are already getting what you really want in intimacy, regardless of the details of your lives. The Feminine is already getting the full flow of love. The Masculine is already enjoying the freedom of non-problematic consciousness. On this basis of love and free consciousness, which must be practiced moment to moment, partners engage the creative work of sculpting the style of their lives together.

In Intimate Communion, the Masculine practices the realization of His true nature as free consciousness and the Feminine practices the realization of Her true nature as boundless love. Together, they realize that although their lives may look different, their practice is the same: The moment-to-moment realization of a love that is not threatened by rejection and a freedom that is not limited by fear or loss. Together, they practice this moment-to-moment realization of free love, the open consciousness that *is* love. In the fullness of Intimate Communion, the Masculine and Feminine enjoy the same ultimate realization, although their journey through the stages may appear quite different.

LOVE FLOWS WHEN YOU GIVE IT

Although love is something that we often try to *get* from our intimate partner, we actually feel love most when we are *giving* it.

Is your intimate partner really the source of love in your life? Most likely, if your partner was to die, you would go through a period of grieving and then, eventually, you would find another person whom you loved. Although this person would be different from your previous partner and the texture of the relationship would be different, the love would be the same. Love is love. We are either loving or we are not. We can love anyone with whom we are willing to open, feel, let down our guard and commune.

We don't *get* love from another, as if that person were our precious and only source of heart-fulfillment. We are either open to loving or we are not. We often act as if we need an excuse to love, such as a special person or some certain behavior on the part of our partner, but we could simply choose to open our heart and love right now. We can practice loving in this very moment, even if we are alone, just as we can practice loving in relationship to an intimate partner. We need not wait for a better partner, or a chocolate dessert, in order to relax into the sweetness of love in this moment. We can simply practice loving by relaxing, breathing fully, letting down our guard and feeling throughout our body and into all relations. We can learn to love, whether or not our present experience is painful or pleasurable.

When we are not loving, we close ourselves off from the full flow of life and so we feel empty. We then seek to fill the void at our feeling-center with one source of potential fullness or another. But it doesn't work. This void cannot be filled because it is not really an empty space; rather, it is something that we are doing. This void is actually being created, moment by moment, by our *doing* of unlove, by our acts of closure, tension and separation.

Yet when we cease to divide ourselves from life, when we relax our boundaries and allow ourselves to open in love, we find that we are already full. We are already not separate, but deeply connected, filled with energy and the flow of life. However difficult it may seem, we are always capable of practicing love: relaxing and breathing and feeling.

There is no distance between us and the fullness of love at all. If we are only willing to open and *feel*, right now, then we *are* love. It is this practice of feeling, this practice of loving, that serves to move us from a 50/50 Relationship into the practice of Intimate Communion. We need not wait for anything or anyone, as long as we remember to love in this moment.

HER "COMPLAINTS" ARE ACTUALLY GIFTS

In the beginning of my relationship with Ophelia, like many men, I couldn't understand why Ophelia always seemed to be complaining about our relationship in one way or another. And Ophelia couldn't understand why I seemed to "love my work more than her." It was only after years of observing the same pattern in many other relationships that I began to see that these tendencies of the Masculine and Feminine essences were actually gifts—if understood and used properly.

The Feminine sexual essence is *acutely* sensitive to the flow of love in relationship. In my own life, I witnessed that Ophelia was usually the first one of us aware that something was amiss in our relationship. In fact, as my acceptance of her gift deepened, I saw that the expressions on Ophelia's face were usually direct, moment-to-moment reflections of how distracted or loving I was in relationship with her. So I learned to trust her sensitivity to the flow of love more than my own. After all, she was more attuned to this dimension than I was.

Of course, there were times when Ophelia was just wrapped up in her own emotional weavings. Therefore, along with my trust of her sensitivity, I developed discrimination as to when she was enveloped in her own emotional constructions and when she was accurately reading the flow of our love—usually more accurately and more responsively than I.

If I was in a first-stage moment of dependence, hoping to be fulfilled by Ophelia, then I just wished Ophelia would stop complaining about our relationship. From a first-stage point of view, her complaints seemed to be entirely *her* problem.

If we were in a second-stage moment, assuming independence and equality, then I tried to talk with Ophelia about what she was feeling, and tried to get to the bottom of it. We would spend time sharing our feelings, our thoughts, our desires, so that we could understand why we were dissatisfied with what we were getting from each other.

We also realized our personal responsibility for our own happiness, and therefore we were careful not to become dependent on one another for our happiness. In such second-stage moments, we help each other grow, but we are also careful to maintain our own boundaries in true 50/50 fashion. She has her life to live and I have mine, even though we share a relationship.

But as the years went on, I saw over and over that Ophelia's Feminine sexual essence was uniquely gifted—exquisitely sensitive—in a way that mine was not. So, in my embrace of Ophelia, I learned to honor and receive this gift of hers. I learned to trust her sensitivity to the flow of love. After all, if I was completely honest, I would have to admit that more often than not, I was more concerned with where we were going rather than how we were loving in the moment.

Over time, I learned to trust and learn from her responses in relationship, moment by moment. Ophelia was an especially-suited reminder for me to be fully present in relationship. So, in the practice of Intimate Communion, I receive Ophelia's relational sensitivity as a gift of awakening, as a reminder of my highest purpose and as a reminder to give my highest gift: to give love.

THE MASCULINE COMMITMENT TO LOVE AND MARRIAGE

To the Feminine, marriage or a committed intimate relationship is a fertile ground that provides the basis for love to grow. For the Feminine, true marriage *is* love. And, since love is the main desire for the Feminine, She looks forward to a true and loving committed intimacy or marriage. But this is not true for the Masculine. The main desire for the Masculine is freedom. Therefore, any man or woman who is in a Masculine moment will resist the constraints that marriage seems to pose. Thus, if we are to practice Intimate Communion, it is very important for each of us to understand how the Masculine relates to love in committed intimacy, stage by stage.

The first-stage Masculine simply views marriage as a necessary evil. Something to get over with. Many bachelor parties are filled with phrases like "being shackled to a ball and chain and throwing away the key." This is how the first-stage Masculine views marriage, even if He is deeply in love with His intimate partner. Marriage is viewed as a voluntary loss of freedom, and therefore the best man is supposed to be there to make sure that the groom shows.

The second-stage Masculine is careful to make arrangements so that, indeed, marriage does not become a loss of freedom! The open-marriage, "just living together," 50/50 Relationship with two separate bank accounts and a third to which each partner contributes, are all inventions of the second-stage Masculine, in both men and women. "Why risk constraint when I could have my relationship and my freedom, too?" This is the voice of the second-stage Masculine.

Whereas the first-stage Masculine simply resigns Himself to a ball and chain for the sake of sex, love and family, the second-stage Masculine attempts to arrange an "out," just in case. This out may take the form of a prenuptial contract or simply a verbal understanding that "although we live together and love each other in a 50/50 Relationship, I have my life and you have yours."

Whereas the ante of family and finances is rather high in a Dependence Relationship, the rules of a 50/50 Relationship are agreed to with safety and low risk in mind. The up-front investment is made with great caution and without "rushing into anything that either of us will regret later." The second-stage Masculine is quite skilled at protecting His freedom via uncommitment in the name of equality and healthy independence.

Any man or woman with a highly developed Masculine is especially cautious when it comes to entering a long-term commitment in intimacy. The threat of possible constraint is too great. "Maybe I won't be able to live my life the way I want." So the second-stage Masculine, in man or woman, is always reluctant to commit. He doesn't want to risk His all-important freedom: financial, creative or spiritual. He wants to be able to do what He wants to do when He wants to do it without being tied down.

A great shift occurs for the Masculine as it grows from the second to the third stage. This shift is from wanting to acquire freedom to learning to *be* free, moment by moment, and therefore becoming a gift of freedom in other people's lives. The second-stage Masculine does His best to preserve His own freedom, but the third-stage Masculine is a natural demonstration of freedom in all situations, and therefore a gift of freedom, to others and to the world. Paradoxically, though, this demonstration of freedom is always in the context of limitation.

I remember the day I decided to ask Ophelia to marry me, to enter into formal commitment in the practice of Intimate Communion. We had been living together for several years by that time. I loved her and fully expected to spend the rest of my life with her. Yet, when the time came to actually ask her to marry me, I felt like I was going to die.

We were sitting at a little table in our favorite cafe one evening, and I had ordered a bottle of wine with which to christen the proposal. We were looking into each other's eyes, smiling, and I had a feeling that Ophelia sensed what was about to happen. I poured each of us a glass of wine, and then lifted my glass to propose to her. But when I tried to speak, nothing came out.

I quickly drank my glass of wine and poured myself another as Ophelia watched incredulously. Again I tried. And again I failed. Afterward, when Ophelia was recounting the incident, she said it looked like I was choking to death. The words just would not come out of my mouth. I drank my wine and poured myself another glass. This went on until the bottle was empty.

Finally, I reached across the table and drank what was left of Ophelia's glass! With sufficient lubrication, the words eventually pressed out of my mouth, along with some tears from my eyes. Ophelia was crying, too, although I'm not sure whether from pain or happiness. She accepted my proposal, but what we remember most about the incident was how difficult it was for me to ask her to marry me.

When I tell this story in workshops, most men and an increasing number of women empathize with my difficulty. The biggest desire of the Masculine is freedom, and the biggest fear is constraint. Even though I loved Ophelia without any doubt, my Masculine sexual essence still felt that formal marriage was a possible constraint, a limitation on my freedom, a reduction of possibility, and therefore I was rather, shall we say, reluctant to enter into such an arrangement.

The Masculine always wants to keep as many possibilities open as it can. In fact, many wars have been fought in the name of freedom, in an effort not to be constrained by political ideology. Marriage is certainly as tangible a force in a person's life as political ideology. It is no real wonder then—if the Masculine is willing to sacrifice His life to maintain His ideological freedom—that I had to drink enough wine to soften His grip on the freedom of my bachelorhood.

In the practice of Intimate Communion, the Masculine knows that to be free is to be able to remain open in love through gain and loss. And so he practices this loving, this freedom of heart, even while being crucified upon the limitations of life. His heart remains open to infinity, even though his life is wrought with necessary constraint. This practice of fearless freedom, or love, is the mission of a third-stage man.

Also in the practice of Intimate Communion, a third-stage man is willing to practice loving even as he knows the inevitable loss of all that he loves. Ultimately, therefore, he realizes that love is the only practice that transcends the appearance and disappearance of all things and people. When his practice of love becomes sufficient, when he no longer fears constraint in relationship or in the world, then the Masculine is absolutely free: Fearless.

In the practice of Intimate Communion, the Masculine commits to marriage knowing that ultimate freedom is in perfect and fearless love, and that marriage is an ideal form in which to practice such love. Paradoxically, by committing to the practice of love in the form of limitation, the Masculine realizes freedom.

This is the practice of Intimate Communion, moment by moment: You practice giving love, even when you fear unlove, even when you fear loss and even when you fear hurt. By doing so, you eventually realize that you are always able to love and you are always able to be free, as the force of love. But this realization requires great practice. The marriage commitment in Intimate Communion is a commitment to the moment-to-moment practice of love, and therefore to the realization of freedom.

Since the Masculine is inherently committed to freedom, He is also paradoxically committed to marriage—if and when He realizes that freedom lies in the moment-to-moment practice of love. Intimate Communion is about committing to the practice of love. It is not a commitment to family, sex, financial support or creating a beautiful life together—although a marriage founded in Intimate Communion may certainly involve any or all of these things. A commitment to a relationship of Intimate Communion is nothing more and nothing less than a commitment to the practice of love, and therefore to the realization of perfect freedom—which is the ultimate Masculine desire.

12

Embracing the Taboo

LOVING HER TO SMITHEREENS

For many years, I was afraid to make love with Ophelia the way I wanted to. Yet, I had fantasies about subduing a woman with my love, ravishing her passionately, wildly, with no holding back. I wanted to Fuck Ophelia to smithereens, but, because I was so afraid of expressing my true desires, I ended up being a consistently gentle and sensitive lover. Ophelia never complained about this; she seemed to like the way we made love. But secretly, in my fantasy life, I imagined loving a woman wildly, passionately and aggressively while she enjoyed my loving her this way.

I never really talked about these inner fantasies of mine. I figured most men shared my fantasy, since it was such a common theme in popular movies and novels. And I also figured women must have a similar fantasy, since TV soap operas and romance novels are filled with scenes of a man passionately expressing his love and desire to a woman who, perhaps after initial resistance, is overwhelmed by his love and swoons in his embrace. Still, I was conflicted inside.

One night, Ophelia and I were in bed making love. It was good. We were both very affectionate and happy, but I suddenly became aware of a part of me that wanted to love her in a much more passionate and aggressive way. I realized, without really thinking about it, that it was ridiculous to be holding myself back from loving my intimate partner the way I really wanted to. So I let go of my inhibitions.

I began loving her forcefully, passionately, aggressively even, and a part of me was waiting for Ophelia to complain that I was being too rough and insensitive. But she didn't complain; in fact, Ophelia opened herself even further and writhed and embraced me and pulled me closer to her. She moaned for more and loved receiving my strong Masculine passion—and I loved being received. Both of us relaxed into a deeper, wider, more spontaneous and wild part of our sexual essence. Our lovemaking, as well as our overall relationship, has never been the same since.

Masculine energy is neither good nor bad—what matters is how it is used. My desire to make love with Ophelia forcefully and passionately was an expression of my Masculine love. If I inflicted passion and force on Ophelia without love, if I attempted to control and suppress her according to my own needs without taking her into account, then my Masculine energy would be felt as a violation.

However, if I embrace her fully in my loving, if my love for Ophelia opens my heart to her, and my passion for her moves me to love her in a forceful and powerful way, then she experiences my real love in the fierceness of my passion. She trusts me, opening herself to be ravished, enjoying it fully, rather than feeling like she was being violated.

OUR BASIC IMPULSE IS TO RELAX INTO HAPPINESS

To understand the fullest expression of our sexual essence, we must first understand our basic impulse. We must understand that the basic impulse of our life is to relax into happiness. The Masculine in each of us searches for more freedom in the hope of gaining happiness. "If I had more money, I would be more free to relax and enjoy life." The Feminine in each of us searches for more love in the hope of gaining happiness. "If my intimate life were more alive, I would be happier." This search for love and freedom continues to shape our daily lives, as we grow through the three stages of intimacy: Dependence, 50/50 and Intimate Communion.

Men and women in Dependence Relationships often fight and argue about issues of power and control, especially in the arenas of money and sex. In a first-stage moment of dependence, our need is to acquire more money, sex or affection. In such a moment, we believe these things will make us happy. Typically in a Dependence Relationship, women depend on men for money, men depend on women for sex and they both depend on each other for affection, security and care, including care for their children.

Very naturally, as we learn to stand up for ourselves and create healthy boundaries in our lives, we grow from first-stage Dependence needs to second-stage 50/50 needs. In a 50/50 Relationship, men and women seek relatively independent lives rather than relationships based on dependence; they participate in a 50/50 Relationship, based on the notion of shared responsibility, divided right down the middle, like a business arrangement.

Although a 50/50 Relationship emphasizes communication and fairness, it often lacks sexual passion and deep emotional fulfillment.

244 Embracing the Taboo

Why? Because in an effort to achieve a strict 50/50 Relationship, men and women often deny the full expression of their true sexual essence. For instance, they are afraid of their desire to passionately ravish their partner in love and they are afraid of their desire to be passionately ravished, overwhelmed by love. They are afraid that if they let down their guard and give themselves uninhibitedly in love with their partner, they might lose their boundaries, their independence and the 50/50 equality they have worked so hard to gain.

But the basic impulse of life continues to move them. If they are honest, they eventually admit to themselves that in the deepest part of their heart, they are not yet satisfied. No matter how much money they have, it isn't quite enough to release their need to seek more. No matter how good their relationship seems to be compared with that of their friends, they still feel incomplete and yearn for a deeper sharing— sexually, emotionally, spiritually.

And so this basic impulse to grow in happiness, this basic dissatisfaction with what they have, moves men and women toward the fullest expression of their sexual essence. The Masculine isn't satisfied with relative financial freedom; He wants something more, but He isn't quite sure what that is. The Feminine isn't satisfied with relative emotional fulfillment; She yearns for a deeper fulfillment, but She isn't quite sure how to get it. At this point, both the Masculine and the Feminine are ready to grow from a 50/50 Relationship to the practice of Intimate Communion.

Men and women grow into the third-stage practice of Intimate Communion by sacrificing all their desires into the basic impulse of their life—the desire to relax into happiness, into love and freedom. When we are willing to sacrifice our false sense of security, when we are willing to surrender our lesser motives into the basic impulse that has always moved us, then our energy and attention become aligned with the deepest desire of our hearts.

When you cease looking backward or forward in time for more freedom or more love, you can begin to relax into who you are, right now—into your very "Being." This ability to directly relax into the heart of Being, rather than trying to acquire love and freedom or improve one's self, is the principle practice that is cultivated in Intimate Communion.

DEVIATIONS OF THE MASCULINE HEART

Like it or not, you are obliged by the inherent force of your very Being to grow from darkness to light, from contraction to openness. You are obliged to love, to be free and to be happy—not because of some moral dictate, but because simply Being in itself is loving, free and happy. This is its nature, as everyone discovers when they allow themselves to relax into who they really are.

Since you are of the nature of Divine Being, and since you *are* yourself Divine Being, you are also inherently loving, free and happy. However, we tend to deviate from our true nature, and so we suffer the temporary loss of our inherent disposition.

When we no longer feel happy, free and loving, we begin to search. The direction in which we search—whether through greater power or creativity, more money or better sex—is always a deviation from the direct realization of our true Being.

Whereas the Feminine tends to deviate by searching for more love, the Masculine tends to deviate by searching for more freedom, release or even death-like states of tension-free stillness.

Many men, for example, experience orgasm as an approximation of this feeling of freedom, release and tension-free stillness. Their feeling after orgasm is like a little death.

A very common deviation for men, therefore, is to become addicted to seeking orgasm. That is, rather than following their basic impulse all the way to the point of true freedom—which is called ego-death in many spiritual traditions—many men settle for the repeated little death of orgasm. Orgasm (or TV or beer) is their chosen method for being released from their constricted sense of self. They are not yet awakened to the absolute freedom of their true nature, relaxing deeply into the vast openness of their true Being. Instead, they repeat their habitual method for attaining temporary and relatively superficial release.

All men (and women) with a Masculine sexual essence contemplate various forms of release into freedom. They may not know its full expression as the realization of true Being, however. They may deviate into forms of release such as engaging in real or fantasized forms of war and murder, beating their wife, having an orgasm, drinking beer, watching TV, skydiving, making money or studying philosophy. These may be the only ways they know to approximate their Masculine impulse toward authentic self-dissolution in the freedom of Being. They are all forms of seeking release from feeling constrained by others, their life or themselves.

The first-stage Masculine tends to deviate into ritualized forms of war such as gang violence, football and boxing, spouse abuse or actual life-threatening situations, either for real or on TV or the movie screen. The second-stage Masculine tends to deviate from true freedom and happiness by seeking ever more satisfying sexual play, ever more profound philosophical explanations, ever more communicative relationships. The second-stage Masculine loves losing Himself—dying to His awareness of Himself—in a good conversation, in good music or in a good book.

We must realize that there is nothing wrong with the Masculine desire for "death" and release, in and of itself. It is our obligation, however, to couple this desire with the true motive of our heart, the deepest desire for freedom, love or happiness, inherent to our being. It is certainly more loving, free and happy to experience the release from an orgasm than the release from striking someone in anger. But it is even more loving, free and happy to "die" directly into your true nature, to let go of your essential tension as you relax directly into who you are in truth. To do so, however, you must let go of your old habits of searching, your past deviations.

How do we grow out of our habits of deviation? How do we grow beyond our obsession with violence, orgasm and philosophy? (Philosophy is, after all, a desire to be released by knowledge, rather than by sex or violence.) We grow out of our present deviance by reconnecting with our fundamental Masculine impulse for release, for freedom.

The third-stage Masculine has recognized that His craven desires for violence, orgasm, creativity and knowledge are, in themselves, dead ends. The death-like peace they provide does not last very long. They are deviations from His original impulse toward perfect release, perfect peace.

We must admit, finally, that orgasm does not satisfy this desire for very long. True, we experience a blissful peace after orgasm—and such temporary bliss is also reported by soldiers, athletes and philosophers. There are many ways to approximate the ultimate realization of ego-death, but none of them are the real thing.

And this is what we must come to admit: However satisfying our deviation is, we are not perfectly released into the happiness of our very being. Rather, our craving soon begins again, and we are locked into a life-long cycle of repeating our deviation, our approximation of death-like release, through sex, through inebriation, through losing ourselves in TV or at the movies, and even through the release we experience from artistic creation or from understanding an elegant philosophical theory. None of these things bring an end to our search for release.

But true ego-death does. We know we have truly fulfilled the primary impulse of the Masculine sexual essence when we cease our search for release—and not just temporarily. When we have touched upon our true nature as conscious Being, our core resonates with such certainty that all of our seeking for release (through violence, drugs, sex, art and knowledge) comes to an end.

Whether through a graceful incident, a visionary experience or the blessings of a teacher, the Masculine can become baptized by the peace that lies in His heart, the infinite openness into which every moment arises, lasts for a while, and then disappears.

The third-stage Masculine practices resting into this continual sacrifice of experience, always occurring in the present moment. He relaxes His effort, His search for the peace of release, and finds it by easing or "dying" into His very nature, which is already effort-free, already open, already blissful.

In any moment that this realization is active and true, the Masculine is free. Unlike the experiences of drugs, violence, orgasm, creativity and knowledge, this realization is not dependent on re-creating a state of mind or body. But it *is* dependent on active realization, moment to moment. That is, it must be practiced. And this is the work of the third-stage Masculine.

We may, again and again, lose touch with our true nature and begin again to seek for release in some future state of body, mind or environment. We may slip back into one of our old deviant patterns of Masculine expression. But now, in the third stage, we know this search is a dead end. We know that what we must do is directly reconnect, in this present moment, with our primary heart-impulse.

When you reconnect with your primary impulse, your energy and attention are gathered from the deviant pattern and you can relax into the true contemplation of your very Being, which is inherently free, loving and happy. In any moment of this third-stage practice, you have ceased pouring your energy and attention into a deviation, into an approximation of death-like release, and you have instead gathered yourself into the singular realization of true Being. This is your daily practice in Intimate Communion.

The way the Masculine grows in His practice of Intimate Communion is by learning to relax into who He really is, yielding His tension of self into the very heart of this conscious moment. The more He relaxes into the nature of His Being, the more He sacrifices His tension, His searching. Finally, He yields so thoroughly into His true nature that He feels transparent to its native qualities. In His fullest realization, the Masculine *is* Consciousness, the nature of which is freedom. The freedom felt after winning a football game or an argument pales in comparison with the infinite freedom of unbounded Consciousness. "Dying" into the peace after orgasm or intellectual achievement is nothing like dying into the realization of eternal Being.

Rather than searching elsewhere, the third-stage Masculine has relaxed into the love, freedom and happiness that are alive as His true nature. He has died to the deviations of His search. He has yielded into His true self, His very Being, and He rests deeply in that for which He has always been seeking and approximating, through violence, orgasm, money, creativity, philosophy and other forms of release. Now, He can use sex, work, art and philosophy to express His true Being, rather than create a temporary and shallow imitation of it.

DEVIATIONS OF THE FEMININE HEART

Just as the Masculine in each of us seeks perfect freedom through progressively more enlightened ways of dying to Himself, or of releasing Himself, the Feminine in each of us seeks perfect love through progressively more enlightened ways of "surrendering" Herself. The Feminine wants to open Herself and be filled with love. Thus, stage by stage, the Feminine may find Herself surrendering to and hoping to be filled by intimate partners, family, food, sensual expenditures and social causes.

When the Masculine has truly released His self-focus and the Feminine has truly surrendered Her self-protection, then true Intimate Communion is possible. Communion is surrender to the point of oneness; it is "unguarding" your heart and welcoming a free flow of love, until all sense of difference has melted and your sense of separate self has disappeared in the fullness of love. Like true Masculine ego-death, true Feminine surrender is also a form of liberation, a form of dying to resistance, a form of yielding into love, so that all refusal has been rested in the deep surrender to love itself. Intimate Communion for both men and women is oneness with, in and as love.

The Feminine first seeks love by surrendering Herself to various people or activities. She surrenders to Her family, to Her lover, to Her friends, to Her teacher, to Her own desires, to Her career or perhaps to a form of therapy. Because She doesn't understand Her heart's primary impulse, the Feminine tends to deviate from true and ultimate fulfillment—whole bodily surrender in inherently fulfilling love-communion—by surrendering to people and activities that are far less than fulfilling.

In a first-stage moment, the Feminine might even hope to fill Herself with love by surrendering to abuse. Charlene, a client of mine, would come for a session every week. And every week Charlene would tell me how her lover would yell at her for hours, criticizing and belittling her, even beating her, slapping her face and sometimes throwing her across the room. Within a few hours or a few days, he would apologize and they would make passionate love. Everything would be okay for a while, and then the cycle of abuse, violence and making up would begin again.

I have counseled as many women who remain in abusive relationships as I have men who continue to be angry and violent. Aside from the co-dependent fears of losing their partner, these women and men experience a deviated form of satisfaction throughout the cycles of abuse and passionate sex. He continues to release himself through his fits of violence and orgasm, and she continues to surrender herself to the strong presence of his physical dominance and sexual aggression. Although they may feel guilty, hurt and confused, a part of them enjoys this drama. Part of him feels emptied of tension via release, and part of her feels open to and filled by love via surrender.

When understood from the point of view of the Feminine's primary heart-impulse, this form of deviance can be seen as an unhealthy approximation of loving self-sacrifice. For the Feminine, any form of giving Herself up to the Masculine force is an approximation of surrender. Although it is a far cry from being sweetly ravished and overwhelmed by love in the ultimate embrace of perfect Intimate Communion with a partner, it is still a form of surrendering to another in the hope of fulfillment, just as is raising a family, opening sexually with Her lover, or giving Her time and energy to a social cause. In each case, She hopes to be filled with love by surrendering Her sense of self to something else. In the case of a woman in a Dependence Relationship like Charlene, this "something else" is often the control or aggression of her man—receiving his angry attention fills her more than receiving no attention at all.

If Charlene was able to reconnect with her primal impulse—the impulse to be deeply surrendered to and overwhelmed by love itself— then she would be able to pull herself out of the deviance she has entered. She would be able to cease surrendering to the aggressive force of her angry man, regather her energy, and follow her primal impulse to give and receive true love more and more deeply.

As Charlene becomes less dependent on her abusive relationship, she will grow naturally toward a 50/50 Relationship. When she is finally able to stand independent and free of her abusive relationship, however, Charlene will probably notice a strange sense of loss. Intellectually, she knows that she is better off letting go of the abusive relationship. But emotionally, she feels something is missing. In a strange way, in a way she may be reluctant to admit even to herself, she misses the feeling of fulfillment that her old relationship did provide—she misses the sense of surrender and love that was at least an approximation of her heart's true desire. It was the deepest love her heart knew.

Of course, she shouldn't go back to her abusive Dependence Relationship. That would be taking a step backward. Nor should she remain forever on guard against surrender, since the only way to fulfill her core desire is to lose her fearful resistance and allow herself to be overwhelmed in the knowledge of love. Rather, she should become integrated by balancing her internal Masculine and Feminine and strengthening herself, growing out of her Dependence Relationship and toward a 50/50 Relationship, should she choose to be in any relationship at all.

In a second-stage moment of internal balance and integration, the Feminine is more independent, strong and self-assured than in a first-stage moment. However, the second-stage Feminine has Her own way of deviating from the primary impulse at Her sexual core, the impulse to be surrendered whole-bodily in the blissful, ravishing, overwhelming force of real love.

Many second-stage women deviate from the primary impulse of their heart into an apparently safer course of surrendering to a career or to a social or spiritual ideal. They know better than to surrender to a man— they have already suffered this form of surrender in a Dependence

Relationship and they have been hurt.

So a second-stage woman may refuse to surrender in intimacy at all, holding herself separate and well-guarded for the rest of her life. Or she may surrender half way, into a 50/50 Relationship, and continue to seek the pleasures of greater surrender through other less risky means. She may seek fulfillment by surrendering herself into her career, her therapy, her social cause or her creative art.

For example, it would be very natural for Charlene, after leaving her abusive Dependence Relationship, to seek fulfillment by losing herself in her career, going to a therapist or joining a weekly support group of some kind. She would then surrender not to a man's anger, but to her daily professional schedule and her work of self-integration. As a second-stage woman, she would tend to deviate from her basic impulse by attempting to achieve fulfillment through devoting herself to herself: to her work, her creativity and her personal growth.

The modern world is filled with men and women like this: men and women who are driving around and around in the cul-de-sac they originally discovered in the hope of achieving fulfillment. The second-stage Masculine in each of us drives around and around searching for His approximation of a death-like sense of release through Epicurean sexing, through knowledge or through creative accomplishment. The second-stage Feminine in each of us circles through Her friendships, Her career, Her artistic creations and Her intimacies, as if Her heart would be truly fulfilled, someday, through these means. Throughout this search for fulfillment, She is careful to remain independent, to stand Her own ground, and especially to not surrender too much to an intimate partner.

If the second-stage Feminine clings to Her position of independence too long, however, She will suffer the loss of deep emotional and sexual loving. Why? Because the pleasure of being ravished in love is precisely negated by holding too tightly to one's own ground. Eventually, the second-stage Feminine realizes that, try as She might, whether dependent or independent, She can't seem to get enough love. However satisfied She is with Her career and Her friendships, She still feels an emptiness in Her heart that yearns to be filled—a sense of loneliness that yearns to be touched.

By recognizing our second-stage obsession with career, creativity or therapy as a deviance, we can regather our energy and align our life with our basic impulse: the impulse for limitless freedom, ecstatic love and boundless happiness. If you have a Feminine sexual essence, then the texture of your impulse will probably feel like a desire to be overwhelmed by love, to be surrendered into love. Therefore, rather than surrendering yourself so much into your career, for instance, you must learn to take a portion of your energy and devote it to surrendering directly into love—not to a lover, not to a therapist, not to your creativity, but to the force of love itself, which lies latent in your heart.

By making this shift in how you devote your energy, you grow from a second-stage orientation and a 50/50 Relationship into the third-stage practice of Intimate Communion. You begin to truly embody your heart's desire, directly in each moment. You understand that you have been deviating from your primary impulse by making the mistake of assuming that you would be fulfilled by giving your energy to your family, to a lover, to a career or to a creative endeavor. In the practice of Intimate Communion, you begin to give your energy to the expansion of your heart, directly. More and more, you rest in the real knowledge of love.

SEX AND DEATH

For the Masculine, death and sex are inextricably interwoven; that is, good sex is mind-blowing, self-obliterating, so ecstatic and loving that no shred of self-containment remains intact. Instead, the boundaries of self are melted in the heat and light of desire expanded into love beyond limits. It is this ecstatic loss of self I am referring to when I say that sex involves the desire for death: the death of self into ecstasy and love. This form of whole-bodied self-yielding into the force of radiant love is far more blissful than the spasmodic release of physiological tension that an orgasm affords.

In the practice of Intimate Communion, the Masculine learns that sex can be a way to yield His self into love. His sexual passion becomes converted by His heart into penetrating and pervasive love, shining through His sense of self and other—that is, melting the difference between lover and the beloved, obliterating them in unity, dissolving them in the bliss of overwhelming love.

His partner is dissolved in surrender to loving, just as He is dissolved in the yielding of His mind and body in the bright fire of their loving. Love outshines His human self, and thus He is obliterated in the force of love. Both partners are opened beyond themselves, into communion with all-pervading love and the flow of life-energy, which is magnified through their passion. Such is the sweetest and most delicate death, in which lovers smile beyond their skin and love beyond their minds.

In a 50/50 moment, a man is not ready to die so deeply. His sexual deviation from the realization of his free being is toward shared sensual release. He wants to die within the folds of his lover's fragrance. He wants to lose himself in the rhythm of their loins, rather than in communion with the naked force of love. His death is a romantic death, sighed over an erect nipple and moistened lips, a death into his senses, rather than a death beyond all sensation. The 50/50 man wants to die into a pleasurable sharing with his partner.

In a moment of Dependence, a man is unaware of the possibility for true communion or even the sharing of pleasure. His release involves the building up of genital tension until he spasms in ejaculation—whereupon he savors the deathlike peace that remains. First-stage men frequently need some form of violence or anger to precede their sexual release. They only know death as a cessation of life, as the emptiness after a spastic release. They are uncomfortable with the vulnerability of sharing pleasure; they are uninitiated into the mind-blowing, body-blissing, heart-expanding, selfless love of communion.

A first-stage man only knows release via struggle: release via control and submission. So his sexuality expresses this knowledge. It is wrought with struggle, power and the need to be in control, as well as the need to experience submission to control.

In a first-stage moment, a man contemplates sexual death via struggle, fear, power and submission. In a second-stage moment, a man contemplates sexual death via sharing and sensual pleasure. In a third-stage moment, a man contemplates sexual death via the yielding of his self and his lover into communion with love itself, so that no separateness remains—only the single intensity of love-light native to the feeling of Being itself.

The Masculine always seeks death via sex. The difference is whether first-stage fear and tension, second-stage sensuality and sharing or third-stage selfless love informs His desire for dissolution. And it is the Masculine's primary responsibility to grow more and more free in the motive of boundary-less love, the motive of His true Being. Eventually, He learns to relax into His true nature and rest as the free expression of love that He is. Then, His sexual expression may

be calm or wild, receptive or forceful, but He is always rested in openness only, expressing the love, freedom and happiness natural to the
easeful confidence of true Being.

SURRENDERING INTO LOVE

Love is native to our being. When you are in love with a man or a
woman, the love you feel does not come from him or her; it is the love
flowing from your own heart that you feel. Your partner is simply
giving you an excuse to love. Love is always found flowing in your
heart, not in your family, lover, career or art.

You may open your heart and feel love flowing in response to any
person, animal, object or activity; but unless your heart remains open,
you will inevitably lose the feeling of love again and yearn for more.
You will suffer the illusion that love is coming to you from someone
else, unless you learn how to open your heart and *be* love, relaxing any
resistance and surrendering into the flow of love. This is one power of
the Feminine in each of us: to surrender the whole body into the radiant
flow of love, so the whole body becomes radiant with love.

We know love in this moment by opening our heart, relaxing our
body and breathing love, now. When we are not closing or adding
stress to our heart (when we are not adding defense or resistance), our
heart is naturally open. And from our open and unguarded heart, love
naturally radiates.

By relaxing into the pleasure of our radiant heart, we no longer
need to deviate, seeking to approximate the deep fulfillment of true
love-surrender. We are radiant *as* this surrender, this love, in every
moment of real practice. We are no longer deviating from our heart,
seeking fulfillment elsewhere. We are simply relaxing into our deepest
impulse: the impulse of love. Here, the Feminine is liberated from

isolation, emptiness, dependence and independence, since she is rested in love itself.

The Feminine is a genius of love, of surrender, of deep emotional and sexual communion.

Sexually, the basic desire of most women with a Feminine sexual essence is to be overwhelmed by love, but few men can match their power, their sexual capacity, their emotional force. A woman whose intimate partner can match her is a happy woman. It is not simply that a woman wants to be totally loved, entered by love and ravished in love. Rather, it is when she is loved this way that the fullness of her native capacity to *be* love can be given full expression.

A woman with a Feminine sexual essence may be gifted at many things, including professional achievement, raising a family and creative accomplishment of all kinds. But the giving of these gifts will still leave a subtle emptiness, a subtle need, in the Feminine heart. The only gift that leaves no need is the gift of total and uninhibited loving, expressed from the heart and through the body. In the moment of giving love totally, of surrendering Herself in the gifting of love, of being overwhelmed by love and dying into the force of love, the Feminine genius is given full bodily expression.

The Masculine can talk all He wants with the Feminine; what She wants is to dance. She wants to surrender Herself totally in the dance of love, in the bodily, emotional and sometimes sexual communication of love, with a partner who is likewise surrendering. And when She knows love absolutely, when Her body is filled with love, when She is moved and breathed by love, then Her search is over.

FEMININE SEXUAL SUPERIORITY

Outside the bedroom, men and women may argue about which is the stronger sex. But inside the bedroom, there is no competition: The

Feminine form and force is sexually far superior to the Masculine.

I'm not merely referring to the obvious Feminine superiorities: deeper and more numerous orgasms, a greater proportion of sexually excitable flesh, and emotional responsiveness that far exceeds most Masculine involvement with sex. I'm talking about something more subtle and more demanding. I'm talking about the native ability of the Feminine to communicate love through the body. Most men can't match it.

The Feminine is the master of the bodily communication of love, of complete and ecstatic surrender in love. Whereas sex for the Masculine is often used for purposes of tension release, sex for the Feminine is almost always a dance of emotionally felt sharing and surrender in love. Whereas sex for the Masculine is often over-wrought with concern about performance, sex for the Feminine is more often motivated by the desire for a deep flow of love.

In the ancient, traditional cultures of the East, such as in Asia and India, people understood the native sexual superiority of the Feminine. When a boy reached the age of sexual maturity, he was brought to an older woman, an experienced woman, a woman who could initiate him into the art of truly ecstatic sexual loving.

A boy's sexual education was not left to locker-room talk and groping around with a girl in the back seat of a car. Rather, his sexual education was entrusted to a skilled initiator, an experienced third-stage woman, whose natural expertise in such matters was acknowledged and honored.

After being thus initiated, the young man was prepared to make love with his chosen intimate partner. He was well-instructed in the true potential of sex: not merely to release tension through orgasm and not to gain self-esteem through his sexual prowess, but to magnify and communicate love to the point of ecstatic self-surrender in love. After learning this exquisite art of sexual surrender from an initiatress, a young man was truly prepared to embrace his chosen partner and fully commune in the force of love.

Today, however, most men are lucky if they can get it up, keep it up, continue for 15 or 20 minutes, and then have an orgasm—hopefully while their partner is also having an orgasm. Most men of today were initiated into sex not by a gifted third-stage woman, but by their own hand. As teenagers, they learned how to masturbate to the point of orgasm, and now they have sex with their partner in much the same way. It may involve some foreplay, some affectionate talk, but for many men today the sexual act itself is basically a form of masturbation— shared masturbation, gloriously synchronized masturbation, but masturbation all the same.

Most women, however, are dissatisfied by such superficial sexing. Their Feminine essence is naturally wise with love. At their core, they know how deeply love can be communicated through sexual embrace, and even though they may never have experienced it with a man, most women are intuitively quite capable of the most profound sexual union. When they don't experience it, they miss it. They may not be able to say specifically what it is they miss, but they feel like their intimate relationship is missing something. In body and heart they know that true sexual and emotional communion is missing, even though their mind may not find just the right words to express it.

Sexually, most men just can't match a woman's depth of surrender. Her need to be overwhelmed by love is so great and her capacity to gift love is so infinite that most men are reduced to anxiety in the intimate presence of the Feminine who knows Her true need, Her primary impulse.

Therefore, most women are left unsatisfied. Their energy is suppressed, since most men are unwilling to receive their fully expressed gift. Few men seem to have the energy to dance with a woman, or to match her depth of loving. Most men are quite willing to surrender themselves to the little death of orgasm, but very few are willing to surrender so deeply that they become the immense force of love that moves the Feminine to tears.

Most men are willing to be aroused by the Feminine, by Her smell and Her smooth form, but few men are willing to overwhelm the Feminine with love. Most men are willing to give themselves up to a seductress, but few men will dance with a true enchantress, a wild goddess of love, a woman who will tolerate nothing less than complete surrender in love.

Such a woman is willing to give of herself totally. She knows therein lies her happiness. But she is only willing to give herself to love. Not to abuse, and not even to mere pleasure. But only to love. If a man is unwilling to love, she has no lover with whom to dance and her gift remains ungiven. Over time, this ungiven gift creates a sense of depression and she may seek a lesser form of self-surrender as a deviation—as an approximation of the gift she really wants to give.

Most men don't have anywhere near the sexual capacity that most women enjoy. Orgasmically, anatomically, emotionally and psychologically, most women are simply superior to most men when it comes to sexual intimacy. Therefore, it is a mistake for a man to try to satisfy a woman's true sexual desire through mere sex. He won't be able to do it. No matter what he gives her, she will want more.

There is only one way for a man to give a woman what she truly wants, and that is through his strength of loving when he is not compromised by fear. A man who lives in fear—of losing his woman, of failing in his career—is weakened in his expression of love. His core is compromised. He is unable to ravish his woman because he is unable to let go of the clench in his gut. His woman lies waiting, heart-ravenous, desiring to be overwhelmed by love, ready to give every ounce of her loving and surrender all resistance, but he is shriveled by his own fear.

Furthermore, a man's energy is drained into every deviation to which he devotes himself. His energy is drained by his work, by his thinking, by his drinking, by TV. By the time he comes to his woman, her Feminine energy is too much for him.

If her Feminine energy has nowhere to express itself, it may take the form of a deviance: she overeats and attacks her man's weaknesses, through silence or through fury. This causes the drained Masculine to retreat even further. The Feminine's energy, whether Her radiant energy of love or Her deviated emotional neediness, is just too much for most men. Most men have not grounded themselves in the freedom of Being. If they had, the howling winds of the Feminine might swirl around them, but they would simply stand strong, already full, unafraid of loss or gain, and therefore free of the Feminine's push and pull.

When a man is rested in his true Being, he may be deeply involved in an intimate relationship, but it is not essential to his happiness. He knows he is happy alone. He knows he is happy in relationship. He knows he loves this woman. He knows he could love that woman. If his chosen partner wants to love him, his love flows freely. If she wants to bitch, his love flows freely. He will make his choices based on freedom. He will offer his love without flinching. He will dance unencumbered and without compromise. And he will discover daily who (if anyone) wants to share in the dance of love with him.

Faced with this immovable third-stage Masculine presence, the Feminine has few choices. Her pushes and pulls no longer hook into Her man's fear. He simply stands free, loving, with no holding back. His presence is inherently demanding, because he is unattracted to anything less than love. His demand serves her longing. Her basic impulse has found an absolutely trustable partner. Finally, She has found a man whose commitment to love is fierce enough to overwhelm her heart. As practitioners in Intimate Communion, the Masculine continually releases His fear, the Feminine continually surrenders Her resistance, and together they die into love, submitting themselves to the force of love, freeing themselves from unfulfilling deviations. Nothing less feels right to the third-stage Masculine and Feminine in Intimate Communion.

THE FINAL SEARCH

No man can be fulfilled unless he has ceased searching for release and is founded in the present relaxation of true Being. No woman can be fulfilled unless she has ceased searching for a way to fill herself and is founded in the present relaxation of radiant love.

When a man is founded in true Being, he is no longer afraid to lose his woman, nor is he afraid of losing himself in relationship with a woman. Rather, he welcomes her radiant enchantment and freely surrenders himself in her loving. He ravishes her, pervades her with his presence, loves her with no inhibitions, and she opens to love, surrenders to love and is fulfilled. She is not fulfilled by him. Rather, she is fulfilled by resting in her own fullness as love. She is fulfilled by her own expression of the powerful love overflowing in her heart.

Uninhibited loving is the fulfillment of her heart. It is just that few men are ready to dance with such dynamic love and deep surrender. Likewise, for a man, relaxation into the native freedom of his true Being is the fulfillment of his quest. It is just that few women are ready to receive a man who is already free, who neither needs her nor fears her.

We receive very little support to rest in our inherent freedom or to express the radiant power of our natural loving. Instead, we are supposed to be searching. The search is supposed to be the basis for our lives. Daily, we are supposed to go out on our quest for freedom, whether it is financial freedom, creative freedom or psychological freedom. Daily, we are supposed to involve ourselves in relationships that promise love: family relationships, marriage relationships and friendship relationships. Our quests and relationships are supposed to eventually fulfill us, but do they?

When do we realize that no matter how much money, sex, knowledge or affection we have experienced, we are always seeking more? When do we realize that our feeling of insufficiency results from the tension of the search itself, and if we only relaxed into our heart right now, we would be rested in sufficiency?

As long as we doubt the sufficiency of our true Being and heart, we will continue deviating into cul-de-sacs of hope. And most of us deviate into the same ones: food, family, money, work, sex or philosophical knowledge. Most of us also know that, no matter how good our lives seem on the surface, underneath we feel somewhat unfulfilled. We do not feel totally free or ecstatic in love. Even in our intimacies, our deepest desires are often denied.

EMBRACING THE TABOO

In order to fulfill the deepest desires of our heart, we must embrace the taboo. We must admit, for instance, that we desire some form of ultimate and final release or ego-death, even as we are afraid of *really* dying. We must admit that we desire to surrender to an other in love, even as we are unwilling to give up our independence. We must see that we are afraid of the thing we most desire, and so we live a mediocre life, never bringing to consummation the primary impulse of our heart.

A man must feel the Masculine force inside of him, as well as his desire to feel a woman open to him, and couple his force and desire with love. When given from the heart, his energy of force and desire becomes converted into passionate, ravishing love, given by a man willing to yield himself in Intimate Communion with his woman.

A woman must feel her desire to be loved and her impulse to surrender herself in relationship. She must realize that there is nothing wrong with her desiring. It is not necessarily true that she "loves too much." It is just that in the past, she has sought love from a man who could not match her and so she surrendered herself to a relationship that denied her gifts, rather than blooming her into fullness.

Embracing the truth of her primary impulse, she can cease surrendering to the personality of a man, which will always fall short of her need. Instead, she surrenders to the love that naturally flows in her heart. She learns to relax her body in the present knowledge of love. Then, she no longer doubts love. She no longer asks, "Do you still love me? Do you really love me?" She understands that love is true for her when she is loving, not when she is in doubt, hoping to be loved.

To be fulfilled, emotionally, sexually and even spiritually, man and woman must embrace their passion, their aggression, their desire and their need to surrender themselves in love. They must embrace the fullness of the Masculine and Feminine. To ravish and be ravished in love, the Masculine and Feminine must reconnect with their primary impulse to be finally released and fully surrendered in love.

Then, man and woman alike can yield into love, releasing and surrendering themselves into the fullest expression of their hearts. Rather than standing separate, they each submit themselves to their primary motive. Rather than trying to satisfy their hearts through a deviance, they cease all searches and relax into their very Being, their feeling-core, and give the gift they always wanted to give, without inhibition.

During sex, for instance, man and woman must be willing to

surrender and release their fearful hold on themselves. They must be willing to overwhelm each other in love, to sacrifice and be sacrificed in love. The pleasure of sacrifice, of release, of being overwhelmed by love, of dying into the love that we truly are, is our deepest fulfillment. We may deviate into hope, giving ourselves to our family, surrendering our time to a corporation, devoting our energy to a social cause and dying into the waves of an orgasm, but our search is not thereby ended. We are not quite fulfilled. We are not finally rested in the bliss of our true Being, our inherent love and freedom. Our style of sexing reflects this unrested tension, our unrelaxed search, our unwillingness to sacrifice our selves entirely in the giving of uninhibited, passionate love.

I want to surrender.

I want to feel you surrender.

We must confess this to our lover and to ourselves. This is the beginning. Every desire, every taboo must be embraced and then converted, by love. In this way we become free, even in our bodily confession of sexual love with one another. Our full Masculine and Feminine forces are free to ravish and enchant and overwhelm our lover with love. Our sexual essence is deeply fulfilled because it is able to give its deepest gift—the gift that is often difficult and even taboo to discuss in public.

By embracing the taboos of ecstatic release and blissful surrender, by admitting our deep and secret heart-desires, we are able to actually live on the basis of our primary impulse. We may certainly enjoy our family, our career and our intimate relationship, but we are no longer craving to be ultimately fulfilled by them. Rather, we are fulfilled already. Releasing or surrendering our search in this present moment, we allow ourselves to feel who we are when we are not adding the stress of seeking.

Moreover, by embracing the taboo, we allow ourselves to be moved by our primary impulse, beyond Dependence and 50/50 Relation-ships, and even beyond all our ideas of what an intimate relationship should look like. Our loving is no longer determined by presumed roles in any kind of fixed or fearful relationship. We are free in our loving.

We are willing to sacrifice our need to know "where we stand," and thus we are free to let go of old roles and discover, day by day, the style of intimate relationship that best serves our expression of love. We are willing to discover, moment by moment, how to cultivate an intimate relationship that empowers us to give our greatest gifts. We are free to do this when we have observed our deviations, grown out of our Dependence and 50/50 needs, and are ready to follow our most primary impulse to release ourselves and be overwhelmed by love. Understanding the futility of our *search* for release and fulfillment, we relax into our true nature, into the heart of this moment, which is inherently open, loving and unboundedly alive. In the practice of Intimate Communion, the dance between man and woman continues, but the need for it to fulfill us has come to rest in the present fullness of our heart.

ABOUT THE AUTHOR

David Deida is internationally known for his transformative work in personal growth and intimate relationships. He completed advanced graduate work in psychobiology, sexual evolution and theoretical neuroscience, and has more than 20 years of training in such traditional spiritual disciplines as hatha yoga, tai chi, meditation and tantra. He has taught and conducted research at the University of California Medical School, San Diego; University of California, Santa Cruz; San Jose State University; Lexington Institute, Boston; and Ecole Polytechnique in Paris, France. David is an extraordinary teacher. He has appeared on radio and television, and his work has been published in scientific as well as popular journals, books, audiotapes and videotapes. David travels frequently, offering residential intensives and retreats, professional trainings for doctors and counselors, and a series of seminars and workshops for single men and women, as well as couples.

For information about David Deida's other books, audiotapes and videotapes, or for a schedule of upcoming seminars, workshops and intensives, send your name and address to:

David Deida Seminars
6822 22nd Ave. North #142B
St. Petersburg, FL 33710
or call (813) 824-7972